THE SYMBOLIC LANGUAGE
OF VINCENT VAN GOGH

H. R. GRAETZ

THE SYMBOLIC LANGUAGE OF
VINCENT VAN GOGH

McGRAW-HILL BOOK COMPANY, INC.

NEW YORK — TORONTO — LONDON

© 1963 by H.R. Graetz

Library of Congress Catalog Card Number 62-18006
23862

Printed in Belgium

CONTENTS

PUBLISHERS' NOTE

The publishers wish to express their gratitude to Mr. Vincent W. Van Gogh, nephew of the painter and Chairman of the Van Gogh Foundation. Impressed by Mr. Graetz's new approach to Van Gogh's art, he wholeheartedly cooperated by opening to him all available sources, including the artist's original letters and sketches. We quote with his kind permission from a letter he wished to be published, written by him to Mr. Graetz on the completion of his work: *"My most hearty congratulations that your book on Vincent's paintings will be published shortly. It is a fine result of many years of hard work. For the reader this new approach of looking at paintings opens a lot of possibilities for thought, reflection and application. I am convinced the book will find its way to a large and modern-minded public."*

The translation of the painter's letters into English was done by the author; it differs frequently from earlier translations. French words used by Van Gogh in his Dutch letters were usually maintained, with the English translation following within square brackets. In some cases where exact translation from letters written in French was impossible, the original term is equally quoted within square brackets. All quotations are printed in italics. Direct quotations carry quotation marks, e.g.: *"Religions pass but God remains"*; indirect ones do not, e.g.: Now the *hard subject* that Vincent *wants to conquer* is his house. Words underlined were likewise underlined by Van Gogh.

The numbers in the margin of the pages correspond to the numbers given to the letters in the editions of *The Collected Letters of Vincent Van Gogh*, Wereldbibliotheek, Amsterdam, 1953/4, and New York Graphic Society, 1958. Most of Van Gogh's letters are undated, and the dates assumed later by the editors were sometimes found to be erroneous. A revision was made a few years ago by Mr. Jan Hulsker of The Hague. Therefore, the numbers of the letters do not always indicate the sequence in which they were written.

PREFACE

When at the end of his life Vincent Van Gogh wrote "we must make our paintings speak", he made it clear that he wanted his work to be understood as an appeal. He explained in his letters that he saw in his vocation as a painter the demand to render his works comprehensible so that they should bear witness to the truth in whose service he lived and for which he fought an inexorable battle.

This book has been written by a man who stands in a spiritual succession to Van Gogh. Not as a painter, or an art historian, or a writer, but as a man who has been deeply struck by a new and powerful language that summoned him to a task, namely that of acquiring this language himself; for he would understand the appeal only if he devoted himself so thoroughly to the master as to become his recorder. Once conscious of this task, he discontinued his regular occupation and resolutely applied all his means to this extraordinary study. Now, after ten years of relentless labour, he presents an interpretation of Van Gogh's work that enables us to conceive the great painter's language in a more profound and essential manner than would be possible if we were without this revealing medium.

Graetz's work shows the road of Van Gogh's life on which he was led out of the obscurity of his origin — through the darkness of his questing youth — finally to burn in the glow of the glaring light for which he was striving all his life. Was this a self-immolation? We cannot tell. This road is now made clear in the sequence of his works. Step by step we are led from one painting to another, and each of these paintings is shown in its inner connection with the necessary course of this artist's life. Here the particular achievement of the author comes to light. For each of the paintings which he describes — no, which he lets speak — he has gathered a wealth of material. Not only is its abundance without precedent, but the intention is also new: he lets Van Gogh, as it were, "freely associate" with his works, and only

9

intervenes occasionally, and with the restraint and devotion that would do honour to a psychoanalyst, in order to make manifest a coherent significance that would otherwise escape us. The paintings, with details that are often overlooked, the sketches and items in his letters, some of them little known, are the "material of association".

As we read this book we forget its author. This is what he wants, for his aim is not to teach us about Van Gogh, but to leave to the artist's language the immediacy by which he was spell-bound on his own first encounter with these works. At the same time he wants this language to communicate to others that stirring spirit which was the mainspring of his book. In this way, through Graetz, Van Gogh himself speaks to us.

Under his guidance we go with Van Gogh through all stations of his road of suffering and creating, until this life stands before us in the compelling directness of his fate, and we understand that Van Gogh has lived for us and our time.

For us and our time: throughout his life imbued with the hidden fervour that is to be found even in the most common existence, his burning need of love expressed this in his paintings with the power of a voice that calls us today. The real meaning of his *œuvre*, however, is brought near to us by Graetz's unique interpretation which thus becomes not only an essential stage on the way to the understanding of Van Gogh's art but of painting in general.

If I take the liberty to express these thoughts here it is because of my gratitude to the author for allowing the reader to accompany him on the laborious way of clarifying and unfolding the basic impulse in which he had to put his faith. I thereby learned that one must follow the same course which the author himself took, if one wishes to obtain the benefit that Van Gogh's work is able to confer. Only after reading this book in its entirety and experiencing it as a complete whole will its deeper meaning become evident, for although Graetz proceeds chronologically, the dark beginning will be conceivable only at the end, namely in the blazing light of this self-consuming life.

Gustav Bally.

Zurich, April, 1963.

10

INTRODUCTION

In 1949, during a great Van Gogh exhibition at the Metropolitan Museum of Art in New York, I had occasion to talk about the painter's work with his nephew and namesake, Mr. Vincent W. Van Gogh, to whose father the famous letters had been addressed. When we met again after some years and resumed our discussions, Mr. Van Gogh suggested that I should publish certain views which I had privately expressed. This led me to investigate more thoroughly the effect which the drawings and paintings had on me. There was something in the impact of these works which I increasingly felt was in the nature of a symbolic content, and it is the purpose of this book to give an interpretation of that content.

It will be obvious that in a task of this kind I am making use of subjective observation. In my youth I already had received from Van Gogh's work strong though merely intuitive impressions. This had been before I discovered from a published version of his letters that some of his thoughts were also mine. Thirty years later my studies had of necessity to extend to psychological research, although in this connection I have tried to keep to a minimum all technical terms in psychology pertaining to the different schools of thought.

The chapters that follow, showing as they do my personal way of seeing works of art, make no claim to completeness or finality. If my approach to the understanding of Van Gogh's symbolism should stimulate further interest in the subject, the aim of the book will have been achieved.

In this approach I have relied to the greatest possible extent on what the painter himself had to say in and about his work. When translating the passages from his letters quoted in this volume, I have been faced with the problem of the unusual language often used by Van Gogh, whether writing in Dutch or in French. I have sought to translate his original text without

11

modification, including his frequent oddness of expression, and not to render his idioms more smooth or conventional, just as one would not want to correct or improve his drawings or paintings. Moreover, mistakes have their meaning, and may point to undercurrents in works of art as well as in the artist. Van Gogh once quoted an opinion expressed about a great painter's

149   masterpiece that *"the only fault of this painting is that it has none."*

The quantity of the material—a recent edition of his letters runs to 1700 printed pages—presents in itself many difficulties, one of which relates to the choice of quotations. Van Gogh was a man of unusually strong contrasts, as is evident from frequent contradictions in his letters. It was, therefore, incumbent on me, whatever my own views, to see that in quoting certain passages I did not omit to take into account, and sometimes to quote, contradictory ones. Only by trying to understand these contrasts can his distinctive personality and the consistent unity between his life and work be perceived.

One example of his contrasting attitudes may be given here. He con-
317   tinually stressed *the personal character* of his work, which was for him a
297, 335 means of expressing *his personal feeling;* he pointed out that *his heart was*
450   *in it.* He fought against *mechanization,* against *mediocrity,* against the *total*
339a   *wrongness of public opinion.* He was a solitary man, a lonely fighter, an "individualist". Yet at the same time he started to create a community of
194   painters on a cooperative basis. He considered himself a worker, *feeling at home*
469   *in the working class,* and he was *always hoping not to work for himself alone.*

The fact that along with his work we can study his letters, which are often direct and passionate enough to be comparable to his paintings, enables us to gauge the effect of his art against the background of his own words. I have sometimes been asked whether Van Gogh was aware of the symbolic meaning which, in my eyes, exists in his works. The many quotations from his letters may contain the answer. He dealt repeatedly with the problem of realism and symbolism, in his own as well as in other painters' work. While, of course, he knew that there was symbolism in his art, it seems to be in the very nature of this symbolism to preclude rational knowledge of the whole of the subtle content which it communicates. He himself characterized this
R 43   content by saying: *"...art wells up from a deeper source out of our soul."* He obviously referred to an unconscious level, and this may contribute to the extraordinary—one may almost call it universal—appeal that his paintings and drawings have. (An exhibition in Tokyo and Kyoto in 1959 drew 800,000 visitors, a remarkable record.)

12

Whether attracted or repelled by Van Gogh's paintings, hardly anyone remains indifferent to the powerful colors by which, as he said, *he expressed*   533 *human passions,* and to the other compelling symbols in his art. They portray an inner situation, with its impulses, urges and yearnings, its impediments and frustrations. If one seeks to understand why his works have such a strong effect, one may find a guide in the stars, suns, moons, lights, candles, houses, fields, trees, flowers, and many other forms and objects which by virtue of their particular composition, become striking symbols in his portraits or figure studies, landscapes or still lifes. These symbols substantiate the unity between his art and his life. They give an insight into the nature of his work, drawn from sources deep within him, unspoiled by any purpose of expediency.

Van Gogh drew and painted exactly as he lived, in the face of great physical and mental hardships, and never compromising in his convictions. He told his brother Theo: *"My having a definite belief about art also makes me know*   423 *what I want to get in my own work — and I shall seek to get it even if I myself perish by it."* He wrote this while he was still working in Holland, and later from the south of France he exclaimed: *"Oh, my dear brother,*   531 *sometimes I know so well what I want. In life and in painting too, I can well do without a good Lord, but I cannot, suffering as I am, do without something which is greater than myself, which is my life, the power to create."* The source of that power — of all creativeness — is unknown, and yet Vincent's art seems to have become a medium between this unknown force and the latent receptiveness in ourselves.

We are the more receptive because his life and work personified, in an outstanding way, the basic contrast between light and dark forces within man that threatens the balance of the individual and thus mankind as a whole. Symptoms of this conflict — confusion, fear and loneliness, and a consequent inability to love — prevail today to an even greater degree than in the past. Against this background, Van Gogh's work conveys to us, as if it were inspired by a leitmotiv, his passionate cause: the struggle for love.

Many people stress the human character of his art. They may not know that when he started to draw he had written to his brother that *he hoped to*   136 *have something human in his scribblings.* In other letters of his early Dutch period he wrote: *"I feel my work lies in the heart of the people... I must grasp*   197 *life in its depths".* *"One must work long and hard to come to the truth...*   218 *I want to make drawings which strike some people... so that one will say of my work: 'This man feels deeply... in spite of his so-called roughness, perhaps*

13

PART I

THE DARK BEGINNING

Belgium and Holland

1. EN ROUTE (ON THE ROAD)

EN ROUTE

The theme of the lonely fighter, the man struggling for love, appears in Van Gogh's work from his first drawings in 1880-81, and persists throughout his creative years until his last paintings in 1890. In one of his early sketches (plate 1), we see a man walking along a road carrying a miner's lamp. Behind him the branches of a knotty tree strike out forcefully in all directions against the sky. In the background is the horizon and a house; in front, down below, are the words "En Route."

This clumsy little drawing already portrays all the important elements of his life. It is, like every drawing or painting, a self-portrayal; this does not require the artist's own features, and, in fact, the subject need not even be a human figure. Landscapes, still lifes, compositions — like handwriting — can convey the inner condition of a human being.

In one of the many letters to his brother and friends about his art, Van Gogh wrote: *"I do not wish to express in figures and landscapes something sentimental or melancholy, but severe suffering."* And a little later, when he had just begun to work with color: *"There is something infinite in painting — I cannot explain it to you so well — but it is so delightful just for expressing one's feeling. There are hidden things of harmonies or contrasts in colors which cooperate by themselves and which cannot be used in another way."* In a following letter to Theo, he sees in everyday scenes a symbolic meaning: *"I see in the whole of nature, for instance in the trees, expression, and, so to speak, soul. A row of pollard willows sometimes has something of a procession of orphaned men about it. The young wheat can have something indescribably pure and tender, which rouses a similar feeling, as for instance the expression of a sleeping child. The trodden-down grass at the side of the road has something tired and dusty about it, like the people of the slums. When it snowed recently, I saw a small group of savoy cabbages*

218

226

242

17

standing as if benumbed, and it reminded me of a group of women I had seen early in the morning standing in their thin skirts and old shawls by the water-and-fire cellars." (These were little shops where hot water and glowing peat were sold in the winter.)

Vincent had realized his vocation as an artist in the summer of 1880, shortly before he left the Borinage, a mining district in Belgium. He had gone there two years earlier, at the age of twenty-five, and was commissioned as a lay preacher by the Belgian Evangelical Church Committee. The people in the Borinage lived in extreme poverty and misery, *"...in huts around the mines, with a few dead trees, black from smoke, thorn hedges, dunghills, ash dumps, heaps of useless coal, etc.,"* as Vincent described his field of activity. He mentions a visit to the primitive and dangerous mines: *"Going down a mine is a dreadful thing; in a kind of basket or cage, like a bucket into a well, but a deep well of 1500 to 2000 feet, so that if one looks up from the bottom, the daylight is about the size of a star in the sky."* In great depths and darkness the miners — men, women and children — were working under conditions which nowadays would be considered unbearable and incredible.

He sought to bring his love into the gloomy huts of the miners. He was not a man to talk only; in fact, speaking was his weak point. Rather by deeds than by words, he tried to help and take part in the miners' struggle to better their existence, devoting himself especially to the care of the sick and wounded. He writes of *the many sick and bedridden people, emaciated on their beds, weak and miserable,* citing an example: *"In one house they are sick with fever and have little or no help... 'Here it is the sick who care for the sick,' said the woman* [of one family], *'and the poor man is the friend of the poor'."* After a bad mining accident, he gave his warm clothes and his bed to the injured miners. He slept on the floor and wore the same kind of clothing as they did: rough, used jute sacks. When the church authorities found him in this condition, they considered him unfit to represent them and ended his employment. However, he did not give up and carried on with his mission on his own. In addition to giving Bible lessons to the miners and teaching the children, he continued to attend to the sick and disabled. It was a difficult and arduous task to get the *underdeveloped, ignorant and suspicious miners* to accept him as one of their own.

He had once before tried to enter the ministry, long before he thought of becoming an artist. At school, and also later, he had drawn only occasionally. His employment in an art dealers' firm [1] during the years 1869-75 in

18

The Hague, London, and Paris had brought him into close contact with art, for which he showed great interest. Yet he seemed to have rejected the idea of becoming a painter, which Theo apparently had suggested. What he then wanted was to be like his father, whom he deeply admired, and to follow him in his profession of a minister. In 1877 he went to Amsterdam to prepare himself for the theological college, but although he was keenly devoted to his studies, he did not complete them. A letter written to Theo at that time is particularly noteworthy. He mentioned some etchings by Rembrandt which he had just seen, and went on to talk about their father, who *"...equipped* **110** *with a lamp, many a time walks long distances at night to visit a sick or dying man, to talk to him about Him whose word is still a light in the night of suffering and fear of death."* The self-portraying nature of the little drawing "En Route" becomes evident. Vincent draws himself in the figure of the man with a miner's lamp in his hand.

The lamp symbolizes the light of love burning in him which he longed to bring to man. He once wrote to Theo: *"Love is something* **276** *eternal. It may change in aspect but not in essence. And there is the same difference between one who loves and the same person before he loves as between a lighted lamp and one that does not burn. The lamp was there all right, and it was a good lamp, but now it also gives light and exercises its real function."* Earlier, when he was still in Amsterdam, he had written: *"This* **112** *love is the light of the world in which we live, that is the light of man."* The light, symbol of Vincent's love, becomes tremendously powerful in his development as a painter — from the burning light of the small lamp to the ever-lightening colors of the sun, the sunflowers, the glaring stars, the bright yellow wheatfields. In his prolific period at Arles, years later, he wrote: *"There is a sun, a light, which for want of better words, I can only call* **522** *yellow, pale sulphur yellow, pale lemon gold. How beautiful yellow is!"* The magnetic quality of light in his paintings — particularly his yellow as the color of love — was to become an outstanding mark of Van Gogh's work.

The words "En Route" at the bottom of the early drawing are of importance. *"And now I am on the road...,"* he had written to Theo in his last **136** letter from the Borinage before leaving for Brussels, where he did the drawing. He had taken the decisive turn on the road of his life, to follow his calling as an artist. The trials of his earlier occupations as a shop assistant, art dealer, teacher, seminarian, and lay preacher were over. They had been diversions, all ending in failure. He would now proceed on his final road,

19

2. WILLOWS

3. WILLOW

with the light in his hands, and express through his art the substance of his being. The inscription "En Route" underlines the road that runs parallel both to the field and to the line of the horizon. This line will appear later in his work as a symbol of the road of man's life along the horizon, the separating line where earth and heaven meet, and of the movement which that road implies.

Movement is a principal element in Van Gogh's art. His paintings are never static, and there is a close relationship between movement and space in his landscapes. It is as if the stretches of land, the mountains and clouds, the little figures or objects—a cart, a train, the rays of the sun, the stars—were in motion, enhancing the impression of space. The depth of his landscapes is increased by an airy, rough foreground while the composition becomes more detailed the further it moves towards a clearly defined distant skyline.

He explained these ways of working: *"Theo, I am decidedly not a*   182
landscape painter; when I make landscapes there will always be something
of a figure in them." He refers to his sketch book, which *proved that he*   190
tried to catch things in the very act, and continues in another letter that he
wanted to learn to express the bustle of laborers in the streets or in the fields.   229
Later he resumes the subject: *"It is always very tempting to draw a figure*   251
in repose, while to express action is very difficult. The effect of repose is
more pleasant to many people than anything else, but we must not therefore
lose sight of the truth, which is that in life there is more toil and sweat than
rest." He sees *"splendid figures ... for instance, the heaving movement of a*   324
woman's breast," and again later, in Nuenen, he writes: *"And what I try to*   408
acquire is not to be able to draw a hand but the gesture, not a mathematically
correct head but the great expression, the sniffing of the wind by a digging
man as he just looks up, for instance, or the [man] *speaking, enfin, life."*
He concluded with the thought that *action should be painted for its own sake.*   418
There should be life, and he would despair if his figures were good in the
sense of being academically correct.

Another characteristic subject in Vincent's art is the tree. His early "Willows" drawn in 1881 and 1882 (plates 2 and 3), were already typical of his feeling for trees. When he was engaged in the first studies, he had written to Theo: *"If one draws a willow as if it were a living being, and it is really like*   152
one, the surroundings follow automatically if one has only concentrated all
one's attention on the tree in question, and if one has not rested until one has

4. TREE ROOTS

brought into it something of life." The trees he drew and painted in the progress of his work, from the willows of the Dutch plains to the fruit trees, the olive trees, and the cypresses in the south of France, are striking proof that he achieved his aim *to bring life into them.* About some tree roots (plate 4), done in 1882 at The Hague, he had this to say: *"Now I tried to put the same sentiment into the landscape as I put into the figure: the convulsive, passionate clinging to the earth, and yet being half torn up by the storm. I wanted to express something of the struggle for life in that pale, thin woman's figure* ["Sorrow", plate 7] *as well as in the black, gnarled and knotty roots."*

195

In one letter he wrote: *"The trees were superb, there was a drama — in each figure, I was going to say, but I mean in every tree."* The knotty tree, as seen in the drawing "En Route", with its branches outstretched against the sky like the gesticulating or struggling arms of a man, often becomes a poor, broken tree; sometimes it is bare among other flourishing trees, or

319

22

further reduced to a stump or broken branch. The tree is one of the predominant symbols in his art. While the light of the lamp, the sun, the stars, symbolize his love, the gnarled, knotty tree expresses his struggle, and the broken branch or stump is symbolic of defeat and frustration. Of similar meaning is the contrast of the withering or dying plants in his thriving flower pieces, or when one object lies low among other erect ones in his still lifes.

In the drawing "En Route," there is a large house in the distance and light shines from its windows into the cold night, adding a note of warmth and security to the scene, in contrast to the dark single tree and the solitary man on the road.

The man, the light, the road, the tree, the house are ever-recurrent symbols in Vincent's art, from this early little drawing until his last canvases in the summer of 1890, when he ended his life in the fields at Auvers.[2]

5. GIRL IN THE WOOD

6. GIRL IN THE WOOD (SKETCH)

Vincent started to paint in August 1882; until then he had made only drawings. When in December 1881, he had ventured for the first time to use colors, he interrupted these attempts, feeling that he had not sufficiently advanced with drawing. Thus, in the first two years of his work, he concentrated on drawing, which he did with extraordinary fervor and intensity. This fact contributed to his mastery of form when he started to paint. Indeed, according to his own words, *drawing was the backbone of painting,* and he *was drawing in color.* He was so imbued with this conception that for a while he almost had to fight it in order to give color its due. He tried this by looking at the subject *more through the eyelashes, instead of analyzing the structure of things, seeing them more like patches of color, one against the other.*

224
226

309

25

A significant theme appears in one of his earliest paintings in 1882, "Girl in the Wood," of which he also made a rough sketch in a letter to Theo (plates 5 and 6). He often described his work in his letters, sometimes adding quick little sketches of the canvas upon which he was engaged. One sees here a young girl in a large sunny forest, her arm leaning against one of the huge trees. In front of her lies a dark broken branch. He did the sketch and the painting while he was living at The Hague with Christine, a woman who had been a prostitute, pregnant and ill, when he picked her up in the street after another woman had rejected him.

Once before he had been refused by a woman he loved. This had been eight years earlier, in London, when he was just twenty. He had then stayed in a small boardinghouse and been very fond of the landlady there, a widow. He fell in love with her daughter, Ursula, without knowing that she was already engaged. His disappointment had been very great. He had felt well in London and worked satisfactorily in the art dealer's firm until the girl's unexpected rejection brought about a complete change in his behavior. He did not want to accept her decision and tried repeatedly to approach her without success. A transfer in the following year to his employers' staff in Paris brought no improvement in his state of mind, and his work was so affected that he finally had to leave his job.

The second woman Vincent loved was his cousin Kornelia (of whom he writes as "K"), a young widow who had a little boy. She was staying in his parents' house in Etten after his return there from Belgium in the spring of 1881. It was only shortly before that he had decided to become a painter and he worked with enthusiasm and joy. Kornelia's determined rejection of him caused a reaction similar to that in Ursula's case, but greatly intensified. He stubbornly would not believe that he had no hope and could not understand why she, her parents, and his own parents were so strongly opposed to his love for her. When she avoided him and returned home to Amsterdam, he followed her in the vain hope of meeting her. In a letter to Theo, he relates a scene in which he asked her parents *to let him see her only as long as he could keep his hand in the flame of a lamp*. When he actually put his hand into the flame, they blew out the lamp and insisted that he should not see her. He writes: *"My love ... had literally been slain."*

This second disillusionment again had a serious effect; his wound was as deep as his love had been intense. It brought him into grave conflict with his parents who had not helped him, although in his opinion they could and

26

should have done so. In December 1881, he left the house and went to The Hague, where he met Christine. The fact that he, the son of a respected minister, could defy the conventional strictness of Holland by daring to live openly with an outcast, determined to marry her, was symptomatic of his character. It shows his uncompromising attitude and his predisposition to go to extremes. He had been so hurt and *as a man of nearly thirty — was so in* *need of a woman's love* that he just took the first he found, notwithstanding her despicable state, or perhaps because of it. The apparent paradox of the attraction of a man of Vincent's high qualities to a sordid creature like Christine can be understood from his letters to his brother. Some of them directly reveal his self-punishment for his failure to win the woman he loved and his identification with Christine's misery.

164

In the painting "Girl in the Wood", the broken wood, lying in front of the young girl who stands among the strong erect trees, portrays his humiliation. The same piece of broken wood is in an analogous position in the small sketch. This repetition seems to emphasize its importance as a symbol of frustration which is found frequently in his work in varying forms of broken or cut wood. Yet there is also hope in this painting, symbolized by the young shoot on the right which again is shown in the sketch. It goes across a heavy black stroke, whose downward movement is repeated by similar dark lines between the trees.

For nearly two years he and Christine lived together as husband and wife and he was like a father to her two small children. Feeling a profound moral urge to lift her from the mud in which he had found her, he gave her what had remained of his bruised love and made it his task to educate her and the children. He did this with a tenacious zeal and an exhausting devotion to which his letters to Theo bear eloquent witness. He opposed the clergy for *condemning and damning these women,* and wrote about his own attitude towards them : *"Often when I walked the streets, quite lonely and forlorn, half ill and in misery, without money in my pocket, I looked at them and envied the people who could go with them, and I felt as if those poor girls were my sisters as regards circumstances and experiences in life. And you see this is an old feeling in me and sits very deeply. Even as a boy I often looked up with infinite sympathy and even respect to a half-faded woman's face on which was written, as it were: life in reality has left its mark here."*

164

Christine often sat for him as a model. The pathetic drawing of her which he called "Sorrow" (plate 7) conveys his deep feeling for human

7. SORROW

misery. He portrays the cruel truth in the bent profile of her emaciated naked body, the head lowered in exhaustion on her arms. When he compared this drawing to the "Tree Roots" (plate 4), he added: *"...involuntarily something of that great struggle is shown in both cases."* That struggle is once more brought out by the conspicuous stabbing twigs surrounding the woman. He

195

28

8. OLD MAN

underlines the sorrow expressed in the portrait by writing below it a sentence
of Michelet: *"How can it be that there is a lonely desperate woman upon*   186
earth?" He draws Christine squatting on one of two tree stumps, identifying
her fate with the *physical frustration* by which he once characterized his own   531
life.

29

Another portrait, done half a year later, shows an old man sitting on a chair in a position similar to Christine's in "Sorrow." About this drawing, 248 "Old Man" (plate 8), he wrote: *"It seems to me the duty of a painter to try to put a thought into his work. In this sheet here I have tried to say this (but I cannot say it so beautifully and so strikingly as the reality, of which this is only like a weak reflection in a dark mirror) that it seems to me one of the strongest proofs for the existence of quelque-chose là-haut [something above] in which Millet believed, namely the existence of a God and an eternity. And that the expression of such a little old man — perhaps without he himself being conscious of it — is unspeakably touching when he sits so quietly in his chimney corner. It reveals something precious, something noble, something which cannot be destined for the worms... This is, far from all theology, simply the fact that the poorest little woodcutter, heath-peasant, or miner can have moments of emotion and a frame of mind which give him a feeling of an eternal home to which he is near."* When Vincent had 204 drawn "Sorrow," he described to Theo his own appearance: *"I am a man of thirty years with wrinkles on my forehead and lines on my face as if I were forty, and my hands are all furrowed..."* In the "Old Man," the symbol of frustration is seen in the small broken wood in the fireplace, Vincent's signature lying below parallel to it.

He finally had to recognize the futility of his attempt to rescue Christine and, heartbroken, he left her in September, 1883. He withdrew to the desolate Drenthe region in the north of Holland to work in complete solitude, concentrating on subjects of peasant life. His only contact with the world outside of his work was an intensified exchange of letters with Theo.

30

FOUR TREES / POTATO EATERS / WEAVER'S LOOM
BIRDS' NESTS / OPEN BIBLE

About three months later Vincent returned to his father's home, the minister's house at Nuenen. It was another home-coming after a failure, not unlike the first, two and a half years earlier, after his bitter experience in the Borinage. Although he was again cordially received by his parents, he had inwardly broken away from them since the conflict over Kornelia. The atmosphere in the house soon became tense. He threw himself completely into his work, restricted his dealings with the other members of the household to a minimum and barely spoke to them. However, when his mother had an accident (she broke her leg and was laid up for some months), he showed extraordinary patience in the care he took of her. His family and acquaintances were surprised as they had not thought him capable of so much devotion.

He had been in Nuenen only a few days when he wrote to Theo: *"I feel* 346 *how father and mother instinctively (I do not say comprehendingly) think about me. It is a similar dread of taking me into the house as it would be to have a big rough dog in the house. Good — but this beast has a human story, and although a dog, has a human soul, and even a sensitive one, itself to feel how people think about it, which an ordinary dog cannot do. And I, admitting that I am a kind of dog, leave them in their dignity."* The landscapes which he painted at that time conspicuously convey these feelings. In "A Walk Near Nuenen" (plate 9), one small and bent tree stands, as if crippled, among many straight tall trees. "Sunset" (plate 10), of the same

31

9. A WALK NEAR NUENEN

10. SUNSET

11. FOUR TREES

period, shows one broken tree beside four others in full foliage. A painting
(plate 11) known for many years as "Three Trees" has the same theme.
It was recently renamed "Four Trees" [3]; the former name was inappropriate,
for it is the fourth, the bare tree, portraying the *rough dog* at the side of the   346
three luxuriant trees, which makes the painting a Van Gogh. In all these
works the small, bare or broken tree symbolizes his isolation, frustration
and struggle.

Vincent was greatly attracted by the somber colors of the soil, and the
rough austere life in the country fitted his own mood. He drew and painted
for days and nights, going into the fields and entering the poor huts, just as

33

he had done when he was with the miners in the Borinage. He wanted to render the life of the peasants and workers, their hard, earthy labor as it was in reality. He painted them *"with the earth in which they were sown"* repeating what had been said about Millet, and *"in the color of a very dirty potato,"* telling Theo: *"You will receive a large still life with potatoes where I tried to bring corps [body] into it, I mean, to express the material in such a way that it becomes lumps which have weight and are solid, and which one would feel if they were thrown at one, for instance."* He preferred the company of the simple laborers to that of his parents and family, from whom he felt ever more apart.

His famous painting the "Potato Eaters" (plate 12), done in 1885, warrants close attention. At first the canvas seems very dark, but the longer one looks at it, the lighter it becomes. In a greenish-gray, stable-like room five people are sitting round a table, eating their supper of steaming potatoes. The evening meal has gathered the family together after a day of hard work, but if we observe the faces and bodies of these men and women we see that each one seems lonely and isolated and that there is no response, no relieving communication between them. They are not looking at one another. The two men are turned towards the elder woman on the right, but the approach of the old man and the mute appeal of the younger man on the left are alike disregarded. She looks down while pouring coffee into the cups. Her own isolation is underlined by a wall between her and the old man next to her. There is also no contact between any one of the adults and the young girl in front. Particularly sad and forlorn is the expression of the younger man. Inside the upper slat of his chair the name "Vincent" is painted in such dark color that it can hardly be detected.[4] The young woman at his side looks at him, but he does not seem to notice her attention. His absent-minded look is directed towards the old woman on the other side of the table and goes beyond her into infinity.

But there is one uniting feature in this somber atmosphere of isolation: the lamp. It throws equal light on everyone in the room and brings out the warming effect of the steam from the hot potatoes and coffee. The same light which Vincent had once taken into the huts of the miners, he now brings into the hovels of the peasants and weavers. The *burning lamp,* his symbol of love, is the light to console them in the loneliness from which he himself suffered so much in his own life.

In the dark tone of this painting, he portrays the feelings he had

34

expressed to Theo about the lack of understanding in his parents' house and
347 his yearning for *a ray of light, or kindness.* In one of these letters he pointed
351 to isolation as *a kind of prison* and added that he felt more at ease in being
"*...with peasants and weavers who do not even know the word* [isolation]
than with educated people." Nevertheless, he described the weavers as *"very*
355 *miserable people in miserable little rooms.*" The frequent portrayal of their
cage-like huts suggests a projection of his own isolation and imprisonment in
371 his work. Vincent himself hinted at it by saying that he *wanted to be more*
himself in his studies. He wrote this just before he did the "Weaver's Loom"
(plate 13), a subject he drew and painted many times at that period.

The "Potato Eaters" was the result of long searching work, the cul-
mination of his strenuous effort to paint the life of the peasants. He had made
hundreds of studies for it, heads and details of figures of peasants, and he
did several versions before the final painting. This work brought about a sharp
controversy with his painter friend and teacher, Van Rappard. Vincent was
so upset about a letter in which Van Rappard had strongly criticized a litho-
graph of the "Potato Eaters" that he returned the letter to him. From then
on their relations became strained until they finally ceased altogether. Van
R 51a Rappard had written: "You will agree with me that such work is not meant
seriously. You can do better than this, fortunately; but why then did you
look at and treat everything so superficially? Why did you not study the
movements? At present they are posing. That coquettish little hand of the
woman in the background, how far from true! And what relation is there
between the coffeepot, the table and the hand resting on the handle? Whatever
is that kettle doing? It isn't standing, it isn't being held — so what then?
And why can the man on the right not have a knee, no belly and no lungs?
Or are they in his back? And why must his arm be a meter short? And why
must one half of his nose be lacking? And why must the woman on the left
have such a little pipe-stem with a die at the end for a nose? And dare you,
working in such a manner, invoke the names of Millet and Breton? Come!
Art stands in my opinion too high to be treated so carelessly."

Vincent replied in several letters which bear out the basic difference
between his own approach to art and that of other painters who were
recognized at the time. Van Rappard's artistic qualities were above the
average, and Vincent had certainly benefited from the contact with him, but
he had not the spirited fire that distinguished Vincent from other artists,
whether they were technically superior to him or not. When returning

36

expressed to Theo about the lack of understanding in his parents' house and
his yearning for *a ray of light, or kindness*. In one of these letters he pointed
to isolation as *a kind of prison* and added that he felt more at ease in being
"*...with peasants and weavers who do not even know the word* [isolation]
than with educated people." Nevertheless, he described the weavers as "*very
miserable people in miserable little rooms.*" The frequent portrayal of their
cage-like huts suggests a projection of his own isolation and imprisonment in
his work. Vincent himself hinted at it by saying that he *wanted to be more
himself in his studies*. He wrote this just before he did the "Weaver's Loom"
(plate 13), a subject he drew and painted many times at that period.

347

351

355

371

The "Potato Eaters" was the result of long searching work, the cul-
mination of his strenuous effort to paint the life of the peasants. He had made
hundreds of studies for it, heads and details of figures of peasants, and he
did several versions before the final painting. This work brought about a sharp
controversy with his painter friend and teacher, Van Rappard. Vincent was
so upset about a letter in which Van Rappard had strongly criticized a litho-
graph of the "Potato Eaters" that he returned the letter to him. From then
on their relations became strained until they finally ceased altogether. Van
Rappard had written: "You will agree with me that such work is not meant
seriously. You can do better than this, fortunately; but why then did you
look at and treat everything so superficially? Why did you not study the
movements? At present they are posing. That coquettish little hand of the
woman in the background, how far from true! And what relation is there
between the coffeepot, the table and the hand resting on the handle? Whatever
is that kettle doing? It isn't standing, it isn't being held — so what then?
And why can the man on the right not have a knee, no belly and no lungs?
Or are they in his back? And why must his arm be a meter short? And why
must one half of his nose be lacking? And why must the woman on the left
have such a little pipe-stem with a die at the end for a nose? And dare you,
working in such a manner, invoke the names of Millet and Breton? Come!
Art stands in my opinion too high to be treated so carelessly."

R 51a

Vincent replied in several letters which bear out the basic difference
between his own approach to art and that of other painters who were
recognized at the time. Van Rappard's artistic qualities were above the
average, and Vincent had certainly benefited from the contact with him, but
he had not the spirited fire that distinguished Vincent from other artists,
whether they were technically superior to him or not. When returning

36

13. WEAVER'S LOOM

R 52 Van Rappard's letter he said: *"I answer you that I suggest to you simply not to fight with me. I myself go my own way, you see, but I seek a quarrel with no one—nor with you. I would just let you talk whatever you liked, if you had more such expressions—and it would leave me completely cold and nothing more. So much however for the moment—that I don't care for the form of the figure—what you have said already more than once—it is beneath me to attend to this and, my dear fellow, it is beneath you to say something so unwarranted. You have known me for years now... Have you ever seen me other than working from the model and allowing myself the sometimes so heavy costs though I am poor enough. What you wrote about technique, not in your last but repeatedly in previous letters, to my annoyance, was the reason for the letter which you did not answer. What I reply to you and reply again is—the conventional meaning which one gives more and more to the word technique and the real meaning—science."*

R 55 The following parts of Vincent's letters are particularly significant: *"All that comes up in a person does not just come straight out of his conscience"*.

R 57 *"The "Potato Eaters" is a subject that I tried to paint, being carried away by the singular light of the grimy hut... Now you call the ensemble [whole] of my work utterly weak and show at great length that the faults exceed the qualities. As with my work, so with myself. Well, I do not accept that, certainly not. The work in question, painting peasants, is such a hard job that the utterly weak left to themselves would not even start it... And yet I believe that even if I keep on producing work in which one can, if one so desires, especially looking at it just from that side and with that purpose, point out mistakes, it will have a certain life and a raison d'être [justification] of its own which will outdo those faults—in the eye of those who appreciate character and the passings of things through the mind. And with all my faults I cannot be so easily outdone as one would think. I know too well which purpose I am aiming for. I am too firmly convinced that after all I am on the right road—when I want to paint what I feel and feel what I paint—rather than that I bother much about what people say of me. Still it makes life very difficult for me at times, and I think it quite possible that some people will later be sorry, either of the things they said of me, or of the opposition or indifference with which they have pestered me. What I do against it is to withdraw so far that I literally don't see people any more other than the little peasants with whom I am directly concerned in order to paint them. And this will remain my system and it is quite possible that before*

38

long I shall give up my studio and go to live in a hut so that I don't hear or see any more of those who call themselves civilized people."

This withdrawal had more than one reason. It was at this time that Margot Begeman, a woman whose family were neighbors and friends of Vincent's parents, had been attracted by him. She was somewhat older than he and not pretty, yet cultured and intelligent. She showed a lively interest in Vincent while his attitude towards her was more passive. They used to visit the poor of the village together, and she sometimes accompanied him when he painted out-of-doors. Their companionship developed into the idea of marriage, but her family would not permit it because they did not consider him acceptable. There were painful scenes between her and her mother and sisters which finally drove the sensitive woman to attempt suicide. She was taken to a hospital in another town and her life was saved, but the relations between Vincent and herself were broken off.

He was depressed by this episode, not because of passionate love on his side, but out of sympathy for her ordeal. His feelings are shown in a letter to Theo condemning the existing society *"...which in my opinion will dis-* 381 *appear through its own fault."* He continued his reflections: *"For me per-* 388 *sonally there is a cardinal difference between before and after the revolution* [of 1848], *the change of the social position of women, and the collaboration that one wants between man and woman with equal rights and equal freedom... Conventional morality is in my eyes very wrong, and in time I would like it to be reformed and renewed."*

Later, in 1885, Vincent painted various still lifes with birds' nests. Collecting them had been a hobby since his childhood, and from his lonely excursions he brought many home to keep in his room. In one of them (plate 14) we see some eggs in the nest's almost black cavity. He did five different versions, one after the other, and when he wrote to Theo about them he added some thoughts on *"reality and at the same time symbolism in art."* 425 His keen interest in such nests, with their deep, dark holes, is another intimation of his somber mood at the time he chose them as a subject. Indeed, deep in his heart, he always looked for a nest — a home, and never really found one. His expressions, both in words and in his work, of loneliness at home, were reaffirmed in a later letter to a friend: *"...and feeling nowhere* 459a *so much myself a stranger as in my family and country."*

One of his last paintings before he left the parental home at Nuenen, at the end of the year, was the "Open Bible" (plate 15). The severely painted

39

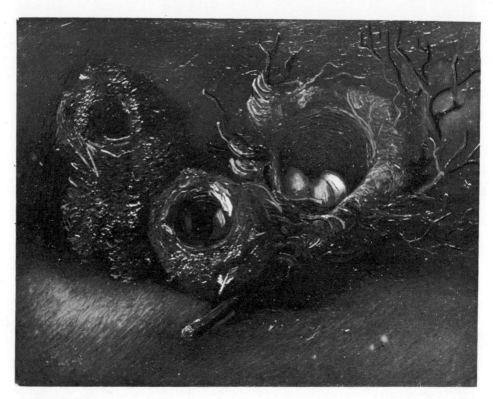

14. BIRDS' NESTS

solid Bible is open at Isaiah and in the foreground lies a small yellow book, slightly torn at one corner. Its title is clearly legible, *La Joie de Vivre,* the novel by Emile Zola, which had been published the year before. The significance of this still life is its portrayal of a major problem, the emancipation from his father. The contrast between the young and the older generation becomes more pronounced and personal in the emphasis on the son-father relationship — by two pointed erect objects, a candle and a hasp, one strong and the other weak. The little novel lying in front of the weighty Bible symbolizes the opposition between the modern way of life and the strong religious tradition with the condemnation in Isaiah of joy in living — of *joie de vivre.*

40

15. OPEN BIBLE

From many of Vincent's letters to Theo, it is evident that he had been an enthusiastic adherent of the church until disillusioned by his experiences in the Borinage. He also had an unusually deep admiration for his father, the parson, who was the idol of his childhood and youth. His break away from these strong ties of his earlier life — father and church — did not take place without pain; it is reflected in the contrast between the powerful Bible with its reinforced edges and the tiny frayed *Joie de Vivre* with its visible marks of injury. Vincent's inner condition as portrayed in this painting is less one of achievement than of conflict, aggravated by his father's death which had occurred suddenly in the preceding spring.

41

This is the first still life with books. They appear later repeatedly, both in still lifes and in portraits, and we shall see more of the little yellow book in the years to come. Vincent had expressed his thoughts about books shortly

351 after his arrival in Nuenen: *"The book... is not only all books or literature, it is at the same time conscience, reason, and it is art."*

15a. OPEN BIBLE (DETAIL: LA JOIE DE VIVRE)

PART II

LIGHT BREAKS THROUGH

Paris

After a stay of three months in Antwerp, Vincent arrived in Paris in February 1886, and there a new life began for him. Most important of all, he was no longer alone. He now lived with his brother Theo, to whom he had been very close since his early youth. Of all his relatives, acquaintances, and friends, it was Theo and Theo alone who always stood by him, steadfast and indefatigable, and who tried seriously to understand him. On Vincent's side the attachment to Theo was quite extraordinary. His love, at first directed mainly to his father, then to Ursula and Kornelia who had rejected him, and at last to Christine, became in time completely centered on his brother. From him he had also accepted regular financial support ever since he had left the Borinage. This did not mean that they were always in agreement. Sometimes they criticized each other severely, as in the case of Vincent's liaison with Christine to which Theo naturally objected. Their correspondence on this subject was not without mutual reproaches and bitter reactions from Vincent. But even at that trying time Theo remained as close to him as ever and continued his unflagging moral and material support.

Very significant of his relationship with Theo are the letters from his solitude in the autumn of 1883 after the separation from Christine. He had then suggested that Theo, who worked in Paris for the art dealers by whom Vincent had formerly been employed, should leave his job and become a painter like himself. He was sure that Theo, because of his great love and understanding of art, would make a good painter. He imagined how they would live together in the country, painting nature and the peasants, as *two painter brothers*. His profound need for a companion made him repeat his

338

45

proposal in one letter after another. The persistence to have Theo near him showed the intensity of this desire. He saw his brother as he saw himself and also attributed his own creative ability to him. He thus seemed in a way to identify Theo with himself. This irrational attitude was due to a deep underlying urge which outweighed his sense of everyday reality. Even the fact that they would both lose their source of subsistence if Theo gave up his employment did not deter Vincent.

Theo had not followed that suggestion and when, two years later, Vincent proposed they should live together in Paris, he evidently again showed reluctance. As fond as Theo was of his brother, he must have been apprehensive of difficulties that might arise if they lived together. This is not surprising as many of Vincent's letters, especially those written in a very depressed mood from Nuenen, were so provoking that it required the exceptional greatness of Theo's character not to break with him. When Vincent finally arrived in Paris, Theo received him with open arms.

The unusually close tie between the two brothers was bound to have both positive and negative sides. It had developed progressively into a mutual dependence, which has been termed by some authorities a symbiosis.[5] This condition was more evident on Vincent's part, although Theo's attachment eventually proved to be of the same kind. Vincent's letters also show signs of ambivalence[6] towards his brother which point to ups and downs in their always intense contact. On the whole Theo had assumed the rôle of the father on whom Vincent was virtually dependent, though Vincent as the elder brother sometimes gave Theo advice in a fatherly way. One reason for Vincent's feeling of inferiority was the fact that he did not earn his living. Theo was not a rich man and had to work hard for his own livelihood, but he supported his brother with unfailing loyalty throughout his painting years until his death.

The positive part of their relationship yet appeared to outweigh by far the negative. The appreciation and devotion they felt for each other overrode many countercurrents in their relations. With Theo, Vincent could exchange unrestrictedly the most intimate thoughts; he knew there was one human being who was deeply concerned with him and on whom he could always rely. The bond with Theo had become a central point in his life and inseparable from his feeling and thinking. Only in the light of this symbiotic tie can the tragic development of the brothers' lives and its correlation with Vincent's art be understood.

46

16. TWO SHOES

It was when Vincent lived with Theo in Paris that he first chose shoes
as a subject and painted the "Two Shoes" (plate 16). One shoe is a little
slimmer and stands erect; its lace, ending in the form of a sickle, is conspicuous in the foreground. The upper part of the other shoe is bent down
and touches the upright one. A light stroke goes from the interior of the
taller shoe towards the other. Inside the shoe on the left a piece of light lace
shoots upwards; the other end moves to the fore. The darkness within both
shoes is deepened by the contrast of the light ground behind.

47

Shoes are coverings for man's feet, carrying his weight as he walks on this earth. They bear the imprint of his movements and thus attest to his travelling along the road. In the common expression "to be in someone's shoes," the shoe stands for the wearer and, as in other still lifes, we have a portrait here, this time in the form of shoes. They seem to be a pair, though their shape could also suggest two left shoes. Time, wear, and weather have left their marks equally on them as on twin brothers, worn in *toil and sweat*. The lace on the left-hand shoe changes direction and suddenly turns to the upright shoe, again almost touching it — as if Vincent's thoughts were going from him to his brother. In such close touch with each other, the two shoes are like a symbolic expression of the two brothers together on their road.

17. SIX SHOES

At the same time he did another still life of six shoes, most of them untorn, but all showing signs of a rough road and hard times (plate 17). The first two on the left in this larger group seem to be the same as in "Two Shoes." The row of shoes guides our thoughts to Theo's painter friends in Paris. As an art dealer Theo was in the center of the art world and brought Vincent into contact with other painters of the period, particularly the Impressionists such as Bernard, Degas, Gauguin, Monet, Pissarro, Signac and Toulouse-Lautrec. In this circle Vincent's idea of an artists' community, which had been on his mind for some years, became more concrete. He had many discussions with Theo and the artists about their common problems and about his own plan that they should work together and sell their paintings for the common gain. Although this project was never realized, it did not cease to preoccupy him.

The exchanges with the young active painters were very welcome; Vincent was wide open to all the new impressions, which he gathered hungrily. His productive capacity was greatly stimulated, and the varying style and color of his work in Paris reflect the influence of the other painters. A most sensitive person, he was susceptible to these influences, but he did not merely submit to them; his strong personality made him criticize his fellow artists and their meetings often turned into heated disputes.

Most of the time Vincent had worked on his own. From The Hague he had written to Theo in 1882: *"I had no guidance nor teaching from others, so to speak, but taught myself, and it is no wonder that my way of doing, when looked at superficially, is different from others."* Not that he disregarded professional training for he had worked with Mauve and Van Rappard, both well-known painters of the Dutch school. He also studied at the Academy in Antwerp, and at Cormon's studio in Paris, but he remained only a few months in them. All these associations were sooner or later marred by conflicts with his teachers. 195

He realized that the more he wanted to achieve, the more he would have to learn, but instead of choosing the academic way, he considered himself an ordinary workman, and drew and painted with assiduous zeal and a phenomenal capacity. He used to rise before daybreak and work practically without ceasing until late at night, hastily taking frugal meals, often only dark bread, cheese, and black coffee. His artistic output was unprecedented; from 1882 until his death in 1890, he did more than eight hundred oil paintings and a still greater number of drawings and water colors. The volume of his correspondence is also astounding; he wrote over eight hundred letters, frequently many pages long and dealing with intricate problems of human relations, of art and religion, from their social, ethical, and psychological aspects.

Shortly after he had started working with colors he had written to Theo: 228 *"In a certain way I am glad that I have not learned painting... How I paint I don't know myself. I sit down with a white board before the spot that strikes me, I look at what I have before my eyes, I say to myself that white board must become something — I come back dissatisfied. I put it away, and when I have rested a little I look at it with a kind of fear. I still remain dissatisfied, because I have magnificent nature too well in my mind to be satisfied with it — and yet I see in my work an echo of what struck me; I see that nature has told me something, has spoken to me, and that I have written it down in shorthand. In my shorthand may be words that cannot be deciphered, mistakes and deficiencies, but there is something in it of what the forest, beach, or figure told me, and it is not a tame and conventional language, that does not come from nature itself but from a studied manner of a system."*

228 His words suggest his quick grasp of a subject when *nature spoke to him.* But then he touches the essential in creative art from another angle. He tried 255 to explain to Theo that his work developed so slowly because: *"... I am searching for a great thing... I am not yet that far — but perhaps it takes a long time just because I look for the root or origin of so many things at the same time."* Later from Nuenen, he expressed his belief in the existence of profound laws underlying the phenomena with which the artist has to cope: 371 *"I intend to learn the theory very thoroughly. I do not at all consider it useless, and I believe that often what one feels, by instinct or by intuition, becomes certain and clear, if one is guided in one's search by some really practical words."* In the same letter he wrote: *"The laws of color are unspeakably wonderful, just because they are not accidental. Just as nowadays one no longer believes in arbitrary miracles, in a God who moodily and despotically jumps from one thing to another, but as one begins to acquire more respect and admiration for and faith in nature, in the same way, and for the same reason, I find that in art the old-fashioned ideas of innate genius, inspiration, and so on — I don't say should be set aside, but should be thoroughly looked at, verified, and quite considerably modified. However, I do not deny the existence of genius, and even not of the inborn, but I definitely deny the inference that theory and instruction should, as a matter of course, always be useless."* By studying the laws of color, he reiterated on 429 another occasion, *"one can from an instinctive belief in the great masters come to account to oneself why one finds beautiful what one finds beautiful..."*

50

18. OUTSKIRTS OF PARIS

At the beginning of his stay in Paris, he still worked in the dark tones that had characterized his canvases in Holland, but soon lighter colors took the upper hand. One of the early works was "Outskirts of Paris" (plate 18) in which, as in the paintings of the shoes, the darker colors predominate. A man stands by himself. Behind him is the black silhouette of a single street lamp as if to emphasize the solitude of the man in front of it. At some distance groups of people are walking together, a couple, a woman with children — a distinct contrast to the single man with the lamp. In front of him on the road, some sharp black strokes seem to repeat the movement of a few dark birds flying high up in the sky over the road behind the man. Vincent's varying reaction to the life in Paris is evident in this clouded painting which again conveys his feeling of loneliness.

51

The still lifes and landscapes which followed clearly illustrate the lightening of his palette. It does not seem accidental that as he got used to the company of other painters — whom he soon called his *copains*[7] — his light, symbol of love, changed from the lamp of the somber Dutch period to the brightness of day. This transformation of his color is symptomatic of the emancipating process within Vincent himself, as increasing light intimates growing consciousness.

A notable example is his painting "Paris Novels" (plate 19). It symbolizes in a striking way his contact and spiritual exchanges with Theo and 351 the artists in Paris. The books, meaning to him *conscience, reason and art,* as he had said in Nuenen, look thrown pell-mell together. They are like a disorderly heap of blocks, as if poured out at random from a box. Most of the books are painted in yellow, recalling the little *Joie de Vivre* in the "Open Bible" (plate 15). But now the yellow novels and the all-yellow background prevail over the subdued greyish color of the Nuenen painting. Supported by the light white-pink of the table, they spread a joyous, cordial atmosphere. Strong orange and red, near a green book, complete the lively color range.

All the books are closed with the exception of one in the foreground. It lies alone, unlike the rest which are grouped together. Wide open, it just touches some of the piles. Painted in a darker grey, this book suggests Vincent's own position: on the one hand alone, a newcomer to the Paris crowd, but, on the other, open to the life of the artists there with whom he has established contact. Among the yellow books in the center lies another grey book with bordering lines in a darker color similar to that of the strongly drawn contours of the open book in front. This dark-bordered grey, in contrast to the surrounding pink and yellow, relates the two books to each other, as though they were portraying Vincent himself and Theo, who is more in the center of the "Paris Novels." Years later, in St. Rémy, Vincent wrote to **W 14** his sister about the books they were then reading: *"But I who read books to seek in them the artist who made it, should I be wrong to love so much the French novelists?"*

Quite different from this still-life, which almost looks like an "abstract" painting, are his numerous realistic scenes in and around Paris, some of which in their design are in a sense counterparts of the "Paris Novels." There is again an open foreground in such scenes as "Boulevard de Clichy" (plate 20), and in "View from Montmartre" (plate 21) where the realistically rendered roofs of the houses in the bustling city of artists and writers are densely

20. BOULEVARD DE CLICHY

21. VIEW FROM MONTMARTRE

54

22. POT OF HERBS

crowded together. On the left the sharply silhouetted wings of a windmill reach to the sky; the signature below is painted in a dark brown similar to the contours of the books in the still life.

While the sharp dark lines against the sky indicate Vincent's struggle, his frustration is symbolized by the falling flowers and wilting plants, seldom missing in his flourishing flower pieces, most of which he did in Paris. In the small canvas "Pot of Herbs" (plate 22), the young blades push healthily upward. It appears to be simplicity itself in its lively fresh green. But quite a contrast in the center is the one withering spear which falls abruptly down toward the dead tuft below. The seemingly naïve little painting thus becomes a symbol of simultaneous growth and decay.

55

23. FISHING IN SPRING

Whenever the weather allowed, Vincent worked in the open. "Fishing in Spring" (plate 23) shows the river Seine with a bridge and vivid new green and flowers bordering the banks. Two boats are moored in the river between long poles stuck in the water. A man sits fishing in the boat in the center. In front, on the left side, are some trees and stumps; on the right young leaves quiver over the water. The spring sunshine, the delicate light green, and the quietly flowing river create an encouraging atmosphere of tranquility. The sun warms the back of the man who calmly waits in the boat for his fish.

But is he waiting only for fish? There are two boats; the second one is empty as if ready for someone. Not only the boats form a pair. There are two mooring poles for each boat, also the conspicuous stumps are in pairs as are the flourishing trees behind them and the two young shoots to their left.

56

24. WHEATFIELD

All these pairs surround the single man — gathered like Vincent's thoughts of a companion, as if he felt Theo to be near and the second boat were waiting for him. The two stumps seem freshly cut and point in the direction of the man in the boat, while tender foliage spreads over him. As symbols of frustration, the stumps, so imposing in the foreground, correspond to the loneliness of the man on the river. But the flourishing trees have their roots in common with the stumps and symbolize new life growing from old. Also the solitary man waiting patiently amidst the many pairs and the young sprouting green may hope to find his companion.

In the "Wheatfield" (plate 24) Vincent's colors continue their lightening trend. The new fresh green wheat, moved by a mild wind, grows lustily towards a light blue sky full of white summer cloudlets. Some red and blue

57

flowers are scattered about. The foreground is a greenish-yellow which from now on will continually brighten until it becomes the powerful yellow of his landscapes in Provence.

This is a gay painting and reminds us of a letter to Theo, written not long after Vincent had set out to work with colors: *"It seems to me that a painter is happy for the reason that he is in harmony with nature as soon as he can to some extent reproduce what he sees."* But such a joyous canvas would not be his if some stalks were not bent down by the wind and falling to the ground to wilt. In the center of the painting a single little bird flutters in gentle movement over the field, symbolizing Vincent's thoughts as it flies in a marked silhouette against the wide open sky.

248

SELF-PORTRAIT WITH EASEL

During his stay in Paris, Vincent did most of his self-portraits — over twenty in less than two years — more than in all the other years together. This is characteristic of his continuous search within himself, in reaction to the life in the great city with his brother and the other artists. *"To know oneself is difficult — but painting oneself is not easier,"* he once wrote to Theo.   **604**

In the "Self-Portrait with Easel" (plate 25), which he did just before leaving Paris for Arles in February 1888, his inner condition is transparent. The bare head and sturdy figure stand solidly against a light background. His searching eyes look straight and calmly over the easel, but there is grief in them as in the drawn line of the mouth. The expression of his face is tense and stern. It is in contrast to the composed bearing of his body, the lively colors on the palette and the brushes pointing firmly upward. These contrasts, stressed by the light and shade of his head, express both disillusion and longing, as well as struggle for strength and self-control.

Vincent's name, prominently signed in red within the frame of the canvas, underlines his identification with his work and his determination as a painter. There should be no mistake: this was Vincent as he portrayed himself in his own personal art. He added the year "88" on the canvas, which marked the end of his Paris period.

Most of his paintings are not signed; only about one hundred and fifty out of the over eight hundred bear his name. It is often assumed that when he signed a painting he considered it completed, although he himself said *he would really never find his own work finished or completed.* Whether or   **405**
not he added his signature to a canvas has, of course, no bearing on quality or value; its significance is of a different nature.

The fact that if he signed his paintings at all he signed his first name only has been repeatedly commented upon. According to some of his contemporaries, he used the signature "Vincent" because French people found it hard to pronounce the name Van Gogh. This seems to be a somewhat rationalized explanation, as his earliest drawings in Holland had already been signed "Vincent" when there was no question of pronunciation. It is more likely that in signing his first name he expressed his intimate bond with his art.

312 *"As my work is, so am I myself,"* he had declared to Theo, and in his letter to Van Rappard he had identified himself with his work in no less definite

R 57 terms: *"As with my work, so with myself."* When Vincent mentioned later to Theo the difficulty the French people had in pronouncing the name Van Gogh, he was referring to the art catalogues printed in France, but was not discussing his long-established practice of signing his work "Vincent." It is also possible that he had been influenced by Rembrandt van Rijn, whom he tremendously admired and even copied, and who had signed only "Rembrandt." Indeed, the signing of his work "Vincent" is probably responsible for the fact that he is now often called Vincent instead of Van Gogh.

More than once he was concerned with the problem of signing his work. When he did one of his most important canvases, the "Potato Eaters," he

399 wrote to Theo: *"I will rather not sign yet because I would not like to have paintings in circulation which later when one will have made some name, one may have to buy back."* Such a statement made at the time of his determined letters to Van Rappard shows Vincent's changing evaluation of his own work. It is interesting that he nevertheless signed the "Potato Eaters," though in the most inconspicuous manner. He once told Theo that he found

524 it *too stupid to sign his canvases.* In the last letter of his fruitful Arles period
590 he said: *"As a painter I shall never signify anything of importance, I feel it absolutely."* And in the autumn of 1889 he wrote from St. Rémy: *"With*

604 *another year of work perhaps I shall arrive at a certainty of myself as regards art."* This was after he had completed his famous landscape "The Reaper" (plate 82), about ten months before his death.

On the one hand, Vincent was very sure of himself. Convinced of the inner value of his art, he repeatedly voiced the belief that one day it would be appreciated. On the other hand, he was very modest and uncertain about the artistic achievement and the tangible worth of his work in his time. In any case, whenever he signed, the word "Vincent" becomes an integral part of the painting. And as his name denotes his own person, it can assume par-

60

ticular importance. Usually he signed in one of the lower corners of the canvas, but a few times also in one of the upper. There are notable exceptions such as when he signed his name within the contours of a certain object in the painting, e.g., the "Potato Eaters" and the "Self-Portrait with the Easel." But what a difference between his obscure name in the chair of the Dutch painting and the prominence of his signature now in the Paris self-portrait. In both cases the word "Vincent" is enclosed in a frame, yet its changed position and color hint at the development which his life and work were taking.

The life of the two brothers in Theo's apartment was not easy. Vincent was a difficult man to live with, and a letter from Theo to their sister in the winter of 1886-87 gives evidence of considerable friction.[8] The letter reads: "It is almost unbearable at home; nobody wants to visit me any more as it always comes to quarrelling. He is also untidy, so our household is anything but attractive. I only hope that he will go and live for himself. He has talked about it too, but if I were to tell him that he must go, it would just be a reason for him to stay... It is as if two men were in him — one wonderfully gifted, fine and tender, and the other egoistic and hard-hearted. They show themselves in turn, so that one hears him reasoning once in one way and then in another, and this always with arguments that plead as much for as against. It is a pity that he is his own enemy, because he makes life difficult not only for others but for himself too."

Such a complaint coming from the tolerant and patient Theo shows the brothers' dilemma. When the sister suggested to Theo that he should "in heaven's name leave Vincent to himself," he refused to do so. Insisting that Vincent was an artist, Theo replied to her that he had to continue to do what he did so far and could not act differently in this case.

Despite these difficulties they remained together, and in the spring Theo could tell her that he felt better now than in the winter and hoped to render their relations more pleasant. After all he was glad that Vincent had stayed on because: "We are already sufficiently apart from each other so that it will be no use to let it come to a still greater rupture." The summer would make things easier again as Vincent worked out-of-doors whenever possible. At the end of the preceding summer he had written to an English painter
459a friend: *"In one word, with much energy, with a sincere personal feeling of color in nature, I would say an artist can get on here notwithstanding the many obstructions. And I intend remaining here still longer."* But he also

ticular importance. Usually he signed in one of the lower corners of the canvas, but a few times also in one of the upper. There are notable exceptions such as when he signed his name within the contours of a certain object in the painting, e.g., the "Potato Eaters" and the "Self-Portrait with the Easel." But what a difference between his obscure name in the chair of the Dutch painting and the prominence of his signature now in the Paris self-portrait. In both cases the word "Vincent" is enclosed in a frame, yet its changed position and color hint at the development which his life and work were taking.

The life of the two brothers in Theo's apartment was not easy. Vincent was a difficult man to live with, and a letter from Theo to their sister in the winter of 1886-87 gives evidence of considerable friction.[8] The letter reads: "It is almost unbearable at home; nobody wants to visit me any more as it always comes to quarrelling. He is also untidy, so our household is anything but attractive. I only hope that he will go and live for himself. He has talked about it too, but if I were to tell him that he must go, it would just be a reason for him to stay... It is as if two men were in him — one wonderfully gifted, fine and tender, and the other egoistic and hard-hearted. They show themselves in turn, so that one hears him reasoning once in one way and then in another, and this always with arguments that plead as much for as against. It is a pity that he is his own enemy, because he makes life difficult not only for others but for himself too."

Such a complaint coming from the tolerant and patient Theo shows the brothers' dilemma. When the sister suggested to Theo that he should "in heaven's name leave Vincent to himself," he refused to do so. Insisting that Vincent was an artist, Theo replied to her that he had to continue to do what he did so far and could not act differently in this case.

Despite these difficulties they remained together, and in the spring Theo could tell her that he felt better now than in the winter and hoped to render their relations more pleasant. After all he was glad that Vincent had stayed on because: "We are already sufficiently apart from each other so that it will be no use to let it come to a still greater rupture." The summer would make things easier again as Vincent worked out-of-doors whenever possible. At the end of the preceding summer he had written to an English painter 459a friend: *"In one word, with much energy, with a sincere personal feeling of color in nature, I would say an artist can get on here notwithstanding the many obstructions. And I intend remaining here still longer."* But he also

26. CUT SUNFLOWERS

said in that letter: *"In spring — say February or even sooner — I may be going to the south of France, the land of the blue tones and gay colors."* He concluded: *"What is to be gained is progress and what the deuce that is, it is to be found here. I dare say as certain anyone who has a solid position elsewhere let him stay where he is. But for adventurers like myself, I think they lose nothing in risking more. Especially as in my case I am not an adventurer by choice but by fate, and feeling nowhere so much myself a stranger as in my family and country."*

In the late summer of 1887, the last that Vincent was to spend in Paris, he repeatedly did still lifes of sunflowers. A large composition, "Cut Sunflowers" (plate 26), shows four huge cut sunflowers[9]. They are painted with tremendous power, almost giving the impression of slaughtered and dismembered bodies, with the stems lying like bones in front of them. On the left are many small red strokes like flecks of blood. One of the four flowers lies face down, reminding us of the Nuenen landscapes (plates 10 and 11), in which one tree was singled out among the others, and of the "Six Shoes," (plate 17) with one shoe turned upside down.

Another similar work "Two Sunflowers," dated "87" (plate 27) is one of three canvases, all showing two heads lying cut off and left to wilt. If one compares the "Two Shoes," done at the beginning of his stay in Paris,

27. TWO SUNFLOWERS

with the "Two Sunflowers" one sees in them a reflection of Vincent's positive and negative feelings towards Theo. The two shoes were standing side by side like comrades who face the same fate, thus conveying the positive link between the brothers. The two sunflowers, cut and dying, their faces turned away from each other, intimate the negative side of their relationship. They could no longer live together and this awareness was foremost in Vincent's

64

mind. Much against his will, it became clear to him that his stay with Theo was coming to an end. He had again to live alone, and the disappointment of his failure to share life with Theo must have greatly aggravated his tense inner condition.

These feelings are portrayed in the strained expression of Vincent's face in the "Self-Portrait with the Easel." Soon afterwards, in his first letter from Arles, he writes to Theo: *"During the voyage I have thought of you at least* 463 *as much as about the new country I saw."* His state of mind at the time he left Theo was later described by him to Gauguin: *"When I left Paris quite* 553a *heartbroken and ill, nearly an alcoholic and hardly able to keep my head up, and my strenght gone — then I withdrew into myself and no longer dared to hope. Now, however, from an indistinct horizon comes hope, that hope in eclipse which has sometimes consoled me in my solitary life."* In this last of the many self-portraits done in Paris, Vincent shows himself with the canvas on the easel as his only companion — in the painting as it was in life. The vivid experiences and contrasts of the two years behind him, culminating in this portrait, made him leave the big city for a more natural and secluded country life in the south of France.

PART III

THE SUN SHINES AND BURNS

Provence

PART III

THE SUN SHINES AND BURNS

Provence

BLOSSOMING ALMOND TWIG / ORCHARD IN BLOSSOM (Souvenir de Mauve) / BLOSSOMING PEAR TREE

The "Blossoming Almond Twig" (plate 28) was one of the first works Vincent did shortly after his arrival in Arles, in February 1888. In the little painting there is a twig of young white almond blossoms in a glass of water standing on a light ground with large strokes, yellow in front and green in back. The glass of water and its shadow are light white and blue. A thick red line extends across an airy grey background; Vincent's name in the upper left-hand corner is also painted in red.

Although there was still snow when he arrived, the spring blossoms were already breaking through in the little twig. Soon afterwards the real spring of southern France started, with all its charm and warming sunshine. This spring in Arles was Vincent's happiest and lightest period during his creative years. To it belong the bright flowering trees, the orchards, the drawbridges, the fishing boats and the jubilant landscapes.

The delicate white and pink buds of the almond twig are like a first greeting of springtime, with its reviving force and renewal of creative strength. The flowering twig in the glass of water is a heartening picture, simple, natural and familiar. Yet the broken branch, the recurrent symbol of frustration, also brings to mind the meaning of the glass in which it stands. A vessel containing water and containers in general, such as a glass, a vase or a box, are interpreted as female symbols both in mythology and in modern psychology[10]. Vincent's own concern with symbolism had been evident in his perceptions of light, trees, wheat, etc. (pages 17, 19). Adding to these earlier thoughts, he wrote to Theo from Arles: *"To express the love of two lovers* 531 *by the marriage of two complementaries, their blending and their oppo-*

28. BLOSSOMING ALMOND TWIG

sitions, the mysterious vibrations of kindred tones. To express the thought of a brow by the radiance of a light tone on a somber background. To express hope by some star, the ardor of a being by the radiance of a setting sun. Certainly there is nothing in that of delusive optical realism, but is it not something that really exists?"

Very prominent in this small canvas is the line, as of the horizon, which he painted in an exceptionally heavy red. "It seems to me now and then that my blood will more or less start again to circulate; this was not the case in Paris lately, I really could not have stood it longer." These words in a letter to Theo, shortly before he did the painting, seem to give additional import to the red line.

Many times he referred in his letters to the horizon, and in one of them from Drenthe he had called it *the line separating earth from sky*. He believed that man knew only a part of the whole life; the other though hidden from us, nevertheless existed. From Arles he wrote to his friend, the painter Bernard: "Once people believed that the world was flat; however, science has proved that the world is round... Now in spite of that, one still believes that life is flat and goes from birth to death. However, life is probably round and much superior in extension and capacity to the hemisphere known to us at present. Future generations will probably enlighten us on this so interesting subject; and then science itself might arrive — willy-nilly — at conclusions more or less parallel to the sayings of Christ relating to the other half of existence." A little later, when in a letter to Theo he dealt with the material misfortunes of artists, he added: "It unearths the eternal question: is the whole of life entirely visible to us, or rather do we know only one hemisphere of it before death?" On another occasion he said: "If life had yet a second hemisphere, invisible it is true, but where one would arrive when one dies." At St. Rémy, he again speaks of "... the other side of life where one might perhaps understand the existence of pain which looked at from here occupies so much of the horizon."

The horizon symbolizes Vincent's thoughts about the whole life of which we see here *only one hemisphere*. While it is the line which separates the sky from our world, at the same time earth and heaven also meet at the horizon. This infinite line delineates the eternal motion of the universe. Running parallel to the level of our eyes, it is like a life line, conveying the ancient concept of man's road of life as a circular movement of simultaneous advance and return to an indefinable origin upon life's completion[11]. However, we see this circle only in one dimension — like the line of the horizon.

71

In those first days at Arles, Vincent must have felt his journey to the South as a decisive step on his road of life. This road stays open to him for renewing himself by an increasing creativeness, just as the little blossoming almond twig announces the renewal of life. The expression of these feelings seems to be reiterated by a second red line below his signature. It does not run under the whole name but leaves the last part open: the remaining part of his creative life is still ahead of him for the completion of the road, the closing of life's circle. The circular movement, symbolized by the red lines, is repeated in a more obvious form by the rim of the glass and again by the level of the water from which the little twig receives its reviving strength. Vincent apparently was so impressed by the blossoming twig that he immediately painted another version. After the dark winter in Paris, those first blossoms meant to him a message of hope and revival at the time of his move to the south of France, the land of the sun.

The springtime in Arles, announced by the small twig, had a wonderful effect on him. The warmth and light of the South inspired his activity to such an extent that even he, so used to relentless work, was surprised. He 473 writes to Theo: *"I am in a rage of work since the trees are in blossom and I wanted to make an orchard of Provence of monstrous gaiety."* All the beauty of spring is in "Orchard in Blossom," of which he made two studies (plate 29). They were followed by a large number of blossoming trees and orchards, all done during the few weeks of their bloom.

The painting vibrates in a bright air of sunshine, sparkling light and fresh, flowering growth; it breathes of the *monstrous gaiety* which Vincent wanted to convey. He was just working on this canvas when he received the news of the sudden death of his former friend and teacher Mauve. He instantly dedicated it to the widow as a *"Souvenir de Mauve,"* a choice characteristic of his feeling for contrast. While he usually adds wilting and decay to his flourishing flower pieces, he shows his reaction to sorrow by this joyous painting. Against the darkness of death and mourning he places the 472 young blossoming tree in brilliant sunlight and writes to Theo: *"...a painting in memory of Mauve should be something tender and very gay, nothing more serious than that."* He adds a verse:

"Do not think the dead are dead.
As long as man will be alive,
The dead will live, the dead will live."

72

29. ORCHARD IN BLOSSOM (SOUVENIR DE MAUVE)

In one of his next letters to Theo he said: *"Mauve's death has been a hard*   474
blow for me. You will see quite well that the pink peach trees have been
painted with a certain passion."

30. BLOSSOMING PEAR TREE

31. BLOSSOMING PEAR TREE (SKETCH)

That in this light gay atmosphere of the fruit trees the symbol of frustration is not missing, can be seen in the "Blossoming Pear Tree" (plate 30), which shows a young pear tree in its charming first bloom. Vincent described it accurately to Theo: *"The earth violet — in the background a wall with straight poplars and a very blue sky. The little pear tree has a violet stem and white blossoms, a large yellow butterfly on one of the tufts. In the corner on the left a small garden bordered by yellow canes, with green bushes and a bed of flowers. A pink cottage."* 477

In this detailed description he omitted an outstanding feature in the right foreground — the yellow stump which is cut straight off. The little stump is also clearly shown in a rough sketch (plate 31) added to the letter in which he wrote about the painting. It is the same symbol of frustration that appeared frequently in his paintings since the early "Girl in the Wood" (plates 5 and 6). The repetition of this symbol both in the rough sketches and in the finished works proves its underlying persistence. An analytical

75

approach might help us to understand the meaning of the stump which despite its prominence is ignored in Vincent's precise account of this canvas — as it is in all the many similar cases.

His letters show how unceasingly he was thinking about his work; since his beginnings as a painter there is hardly one in which he did not deliberate 237 on what he was doing. In 1882 he wrote to Theo: *"We both have a liking in common to look behind the curtains; in other words we have a tendency to analyze things. I believe this is just the quality one must have in order to paint — in painting and drawing one must exert that power."* His interest in analyzing comes out strongly in many more long letters of that time, as also 381 later at Nuenen: *"But it is not enough to know ever so much by instinct; in my opinion just then one must do one's best threefold in order to come* B 22 *from instinct to reason."* On the other hand, he wrote from Arles: *"I often* 543 *do not know what I am doing"* and *"...the painting comes to me as in a dream."* His ideas about the symbolic expression of love, hope, thought, ardor, etc., were quite explicit in his creative mind. Not less important, however, are those symbolic factors to which he did not refer in any, even the most detailed, letter. He was probably not conscious of them, which may have 237 been one of the causes for his *tendency to analyze.*

Since Van Gogh's time that tendency to analyze has developed to a more 237 extended *looking behind the curtains.* In the psychological terminology of today it is called a search into the unconscious. While containers such as a vase, a kettle, or a house are, as already mentioned, seen as female symbols, erect objects like a candle or a tree are taken for male symbols, as are long articles such as a stick or a knife. In this interpretation the bent and cut trees, broken branches and stumps in his art, frequently among other trees standing erect and high, impart his feeling of masculine inferiority[12] and frustrated love. In fact, much as Vincent was yearning for love in his life, his longing remained unfulfilled.

In the "Blossoming Pear Tree" the stump represents the other side, the side which Vincent does not mention. The painting is a typical example of the existence of inner contrasts in his work: beauty and love, expressed by the graceful, thriving pear tree in its maidenly bloom, and defeat and frustration, conveyed by the stump. These opposing positive and negative elements were active in him as they are latent in us, and their symbolic portrayal gives his art its particular capacity to communicate between his life and ours.

76

He signed the canvas in the left hand corner near the trunk of the tree where it grows out of the earth, although there would have been much more space on the other side. As if to signify a trend in his own condition, he places himself close to the growing and blossoming tree, away from the stump. In this flourishing, reviving springtime, the positive elements in him seem to gain the upper hand over the negative feeling of inferiority. Nevertheless, it is clearly expressed by the conspicuous stump and even stressed by a branch of the tree pointing sharply down to it.

The stump is painted in yellow, Vincent's color of love. The light yellow again causes another, though different, contrast to the violet trunk of the delicate tree which stands lonely in the bare yard: the violet and the yellow not only contrast but also complement each other in a greater harmony of color. The large butterfly symbolizes Vincent's thoughts as did the bird over the wheatfield (page 58). But here the butterfly is yellow and alights on the blossoms of the young tree as if to tender its love.

32. THE DRAWBRIDGE

78

THE DRAWBRIDGE

After his first two months of work in Arles, Vincent wrote to Theo that the fruit trees together with a drawbridge *formed a first series*. The drawbridges in southern France very much resembled the characteristic Dutch drawbridges. He painted them several times, always showing people nearby; in some versions a horse-drawn cart rolls over the bridge, in another a woman is walking over it. In lively colors the drawbridges stand as clear, straight silhouettes against the sky. The accurate drawing of their construction is striking, and in their natural simplicity these bridges seem to give a feeling of security to the people as they pass over the river.

478

The "Drawbridge" shown in plate 32 is the first version of this subject. The bright yellow beams of the bridge and the yellow hood of the cart are in a vivid contrast to the pure blue of a cloudless sky and the water. A group of women is seen on the grass-grown bank washing laundry in the river. In front of them lies a wrecked boat. In the second painting (plate 33), a green bordered path runs along the river, both sweeping to the fore, diagonally across the light canvas. Vincent's name in dark blue is prominent in the left foreground. Above it, in the distance at the end of the road and opposite a twin bridge, is a single tree, his symbol of struggle.

The drawbridges recall another structure which he had once rendered with similar precision. It was the "Weaver's Loom" (plate 13), done years earlier in his home town Nuenen. He had often portrayed the weavers in their looms as in cages, depicting in his dark colors their small, gloomy hovels. His letters to Theo at that time had been full of sympathy for those *very miserable people,* whose plight had been as near to him as that of the poor peasants and miners with whom he had lived.

351

A closer examination of the looms and drawbridges shows a remarkable resemblance between their principal parts — the strong understructure, the heavy beams above and at the sides, and the ropes by which they are operated. Yet despite this similarity, how different they are: in Nuenen the weavers appeared to be caged inside their looms, but at Arles people move freely over the bridge. Vincents's own condition seems to be reflected in this development of his work. In April 1888, when he was preoccupied with the drawbridges, he mentioned in a letter to Theo "... *a prison which one sometimes misses after leaving it because one feels confused in the so-called freedom...*"

478

Since his youth Vincent had felt the problem of freedom as a vital challenge. The letters he wrote from the age of twenty until his death at thirty-seven, and his drawings and paintings in the last ten years of his life, are a stirring record of his unflinching fight for *liberation from prison;* aimed at his isolation and loneliness, it was, in fact, identical with his struggle for love. One might be struck with awe on realizing the magnitude of this battle, in which the intense impact of the light and dark forces within him showed itself in violent outbreaks. It was this overwhelming power of his inner life which, while causing these shattering attacks, also gave him the strength for his tenacious fight for self-control and survival. The following is but a part of one of his many long letters to Theo which touch upon the underlying nature of his suffering. Vincent wrote this letter in the summer of 1880 from the Borinage. He was then twenty-seven and in greatest misery, without a job and with no prospects for the future. It was just before he found his vocation as a painter.

133

133

"I am writing you a little at random what comes into my pen: I would be well pleased if somehow you could see in me something other than a kind of idler. Because there are idlers and idlers who are a contrast. There is the one who is an idler out of laziness and cowardice of character because of the meanness of his nature; if you think it right, you can take me for one like this. Then there is the other idler, the idler quite in spite of himself who is inwardly gnawed by a great desire for action, who does nothing because of the impossibility for him to do anything, since he is as if imprisoned in something, because he has not got what he needs to be productive, because the fatality of circumstances reduces him to this point; one like this does not always know himself what he could do, but he feels by instinct: Yet, I am good for something, I feel my right to exist! I know I could be a completely different man! What then could I be useful for, what could I

80

33. THE DRAWBRIDGE

serve! there is something inside me, what is it then! This is a completely different idler; you can if you think it right take me for such.

"A bird in a cage in spring knows very well that there is something for which it would be good; it feels very strongly that there is something to do, but it cannot do it, what is it? it does not remember well, then it has vague ideas, and it says to itself, 'the others make their nests and make their young and rear the brood,' and then it hits its skull against the bars of the cage. And then the cage remains there and the bird is mad with pain. 'Look at the idler,' says another bird which passes by, 'that one is a kind of rentier[13].' Still, the prisoner lives and does not die, nothing is visible externally of what goes on inside; it is in good health, it is more or less gay when the sun shines. But come the time for migration. Attacks of melancholy—but, say

81

the children who look after it in its cage, it has everything it needs—but for it to see outside the sky laden with storm and to feel a rebellion against the fatality within itself. I am in a cage, I am in a cage, and so I need nothing, imbeciles! I have everything I need, I! Oh mercy, freedom, to be a bird like the other birds! That idle man is like that idle bird. And men are often faced by the impossibility of doing anything, prisoner in I don't know what horrible cage, horrible, very horrible.

"There is also, I know it, the liberation, the late liberation. A ruined reputation, rightly or wrongly, constraint, the fatality of circumstances, unhappiness—this makes prisoners. One cannot always say what it is that encloses, that walls in, that seems to bury, but one feels just the same, I don't know what bars, what grills, walls.

"All this, it is imaginary, fantasy? I do not think so; and then one asks oneself: My God, is this for long, is this for always, is this for eternity? Do you know what makes the prison disappear, it is every profound, serious affection. To be friends, to be brothers, to love, that opens the prison with a sovereign power, with a very powerful spell. But he who has not this remains in death. But where sympathy is reborn, life is reborn. Sometimes the prison calls itself: prejudice, misunderstanding, fatal ignorance of this or that, suspicion, false shame."

478   It is noteworthy that Vincent spoke of *missing a prison in the so-called freedom* at the time he painted the drawbridges which were so typical of his native country. His words reveal that the old predicament had remained latent in him. They in fact sustain the self-portraying meaning of the motif he chose: the bridge which enables man "to cross the river," a common expression for an important step in life. Since ancient times the bridge has been thought of as a symbolic link between two sides, a means to overcome, to bridge a gap. Arising from this conception, one of the interpretations of the bridge symbol in modern psychology is that of a passage from one stage to another on the way of man's life, from the sheltered condition of infancy towards maturity. Fear of crossing a bridge is frequently found to be caused by inner difficulties connected with the release from certain maternal ties; anxiety, frustration and depression may be symptoms accompanying this condition[14].

133   Here in Arles the *something in him* and the *great desire for action* were making a good battle in Vincent's fight against frustration, against his *impossibility of doing anything*. His signature in the first version of the "Draw-

82

bridge," below the group of washerwomen, is tiny and almost hidden in the reeds compared with the large letters of his name in the other painting. As if he himself, like his name, or the wrecked boat, were smaller or subdued when he was near women, these variations suggest his vacillating inner condition: on the one hand still held in infantile bondage to the mother, but on the other walking determinedly beside the water on the road towards maturity. He is going a step forward in the liberating movement on his road of life. In Holland he had depicted his state of mind inside the dark cage, portraying himself as *a prisoner* like the weavers who looked for the light   133 outside. Now, although the roots of confinement are still within him, he chooses his subjects in the open in bright sunshine.

In this spring of Arles, the jaunty drawbridges with their gay colors and solid construction convey an atmosphere of relief. In all versions they are drawn down, ready to carry men over them. But the bridge does more than link the two sides of the earth horizontally; it also has a vertical aspect towards depth and height. As man stands or moves over it, he can breathe freely in the open air between the deep water and the infinite sky, symbolic of Mother Earth below and Eternity above.

34. THE BREAKFAST TABLE

84

35. THE BREAKFAST TABLE (SKETCH)

In May 1888 Vincent painted a large still life, the "Breakfast Table" (plate 34). He wrote about it to Theo: "*A coffeepot in blue enamel, a cup (on the left) royal blue and gold, a milk jug checkered light blue and white, a cup (on the right) white with blue and orange patterns on a plate of earthenware yellow-grey, a pot of barbotine or majolica blue with red, green, brown patterns, finally two oranges and three lemons; the table is covered with a blue cloth, the background yellow-green, thus six different blues and four or five yellows and oranges.*" He added a small sketch of the painting (plate 35) and described it similarly to his friend Bernard. In a later letter to Theo he took up the subject again: "*The last canvas absolutely kills all the others—there is only one still life with the coffeepot, the cups and plates in blue and yellow, which holds its own. This must be because of the design.*"   489   497

85

497   *Because of the design* means the form and composition of the objects; they suggest the interior of a house. Since his arrival in Arles, Vincent had frequently written to Theo about his great desire to have a little house. When he looked for a place to store his paintings, he found an empty building which he rented for the purpose and he also worked there sometimes. He entertained the hope that in time he might be able to furnish it so that he and other painters could work and live there.

     In the following months, he became more and more possessed with the idea of the house. When he described the "Breakfast Table" to Theo, he
489 wrote: *"Because solitude, worries, contrarieties, the unsatisfied need for friendship and sympathy, you see, that is the worst, the moral emotions of sadness undermine us more than a gay life — us, I say, who find ourselves to be the happy possessors of disturbed hearts... In the midst of the artistic life there is and there remains and always comes back at times the homesickness*
476,600 *for the true life, ideal and not realizable."* By the *true life* he meant, as expressed in many letters, life with a wife and children.

     In his repeated and very detailed descriptions, Vincent did not say that this was one of the rare works with a border or frame painted directly on the canvas itself. He did this in the same color as the two oranges and his name. The frame around the breakfast table is like an enclosing wall or the walls of a room or a house. All the dishes and the fruit are grouped round the coffee-pot and touch one another, except one orange at the extreme left which is only partly inside the painting. It is notable that almost all the objects are in pairs, as if the table were set for two people. The coffee-pot has of course the conventional two parts fitted into each other, but there are also two jugs, two cups, two plates and the two oranges on the left. Only the three lemons lying at the base of the coffee-pot do not form a pair.

     This large dark blue coffee-pot with the three bright yellow lemons in front is of particular significance. In the center of the painting it takes the most important position amidst the other domestic objects on the table. The little yellow lemons nestling under the large round coffee-pot could give the idea of chicks with a hen. One may recall the many birds' nests that Vincent had painted in Nuenen (plate 14). All but one of these studies showed three eggs whenever there were eggs in the dark nest. Once he had compared
290 Christine and her children with *a mother hen and her chicks*. A year after painting the "Breakfast Table," when Vincent had to leave the house of
587 which he was now only dreaming, he wrote to Theo: *"Sometimes, just as*

the waves break against sullen, hopeless cliffs, [I feel] *a storm of desire to embrace something, a woman, a kind of domestic hen; well, one must take it for what it is, the effect of hysterical over-excitement rather than the vision of actual reality."*

However, as an inner reality Vincent's *homesickness* for a family life and his longing for a *woman, a kind of domestic hen,* are portrayed in this still life. He enhances the female character of the interior of the house by the dominating central figure of the coffee-pot which stands for the woman, the nourishing mother. It might be remembered that in the "Potato Eaters," he had chosen to show the old mother while she was pouring coffee into the cups. The homelike atmosphere in the still life is sustained by such familiar objects as the jugs, cups and dishes around the coffee-pot. They all assist in dispensing nourishment, the foremost domestic function of the woman in the house. [489] [587]

Because of the extraordinary value this still life held for Vincent, a more specific observation may be warranted. Both in mythological and psychological terms the coffee-pot is of a dual symbolism: the lower part, the pot, has a female meaning like the jugs and cups. But when the upper part, the filter, is fitted into it, the coffee-pot becomes the tallest object in the group and thus acquires also a male character. An additional intimation to that effect is the shape of the spout pointing at the rim of the milk jug. This movement recalls the position of the almond twig in the glass of water (plate 28); it is repeated in many other paintings. Male and female appear here as one in the coffee-pot which, together with the fruit, is a symbol of fertility. But despite the male parts, its female nature is predominant.

By his assertion that the still life in blue and yellow *holds its own,* Vincent lays emphasis on these two opposing colors; they are most striking in the dark coffee-pot and the light lemons. Two so strongly contrasting colors heighten the effect of his underlying theme, which in the "Breakfast Table" is womanhood and family life. [497]

Another detail of the painting is, as it were, an expression of his feeling that *the true life could not be realized.* By their position on the left the two oranges, painted in the same color as his name above them, appear like symbols of the two brothers. While the one orange is grouped with the other objects on the table, the second is isolated and only partly inside the frame. Also in the rough sketch it is cut in half by the frame, which implies that this distinctive position is not accidental. It conveys the ambiguity of Vincent's [489]

87

own situation, his being partly inside and partly outside the frame — the walls of the house. He does not seem sure whether he will be in the house at all. As the house stands symbolically for woman, Vincent portrays his attitude towards the woman as divided, like the orange isolated from the rest and cut by the frame.

497
496   The canvas that *killed all the others,* except the "Breakfast Table," was the "Harvest" (plate 36), of which he wrote to Theo: *"I have a new subject in hand; fields as far as one can see, green and yellow, which I have already drawn twice and which I am starting again as a painting, absolutely like a Solomon Koninck, you know, the pupil of Rembrandt who did the immense flat countrysides."*

The "Harvest" is one of Van Gogh's most accomplished landscapes. It shows the wide fields near Arles in the early summer, a complete harmony of warm colors, natural movement and serenity, the gratifying time of the first crop. Like the "Drawbridges," it diffuses a cheerful atmosphere, a feeling of heartening assuredness in its rural simplicity of harvesting men and women in the fields, with the small carts and horses and the farmhouses; with the rustic objects and the vegetable gardens in the foreground against the wide open plain extending far away to distant mountains under a cloudless sky.

A woman in Arlésienne dress walks in an enclosed plot in the foreground. On the right in front of a house, another woman stands on a laden cart and helps to unload the hay. On the left is a large haystack with two ladders leaning against it, and behind a red-headed man is reaping. The movement of the reaper, who will be seen again in several later landscapes,
251 may remind us of the *toil and sweat* (page 21), *the action which was so difficult to express.* Below the haystack, in the left hand corner, Vincent signed his name.

He later wrote to Theo about himself in connection with the "Harvest"
507 and another landscape, the "Haystacks": *"But when I come from such a session I assure you my brain is so tired that if that kind of work renews itself often as it did during this harvest, I become absolutely absent-minded and incapable of a lot of ordinary things."* Yet, although he continued his strenuous work without interruption, he never failed in one other respect: in his correspondence with Theo. As had been the case after his break with Christine, it again became very intensive on his leaving Paris. In the first three months alone, some fifty letters were exchanged between them, which shows the persistence of their close contact.

88

36. HARVEST

37. HAYSTACKS

Vincent's letters leave no doubt that the separation was only external and all through them runs his longing to be with Theo again. He took a keen part in every aspect of Theo's life, his health and state of mind, his relations with women and his situation in business. He related to himself Theo's position with Goupil's, the art dealers' firm in which Theo was employed, and for whom he himself had once worked. Shortly before he painted the "Harvest," he suggested that he should accompany Theo on his business trips. He was even prepared to give up his painting and be re-employed by the art dealers, if he could thus travel with Theo. He was worried that Theo was wearing himself out to earn money for them and asserted: *"People matter more than things ... rather let us remain together in any case."*

It was a proposal in reverse to the suggestion he had made when leaving The Hague, namely that Theo should give up his job and become a painter.

492

90

Repeatedly he stated that Theo had a part in his work and that it was *done* 473
by them together. About his "Orchard in Blossom" he had told him: *"And* 472
I wrote on my painting: 'Souvenir de Mauve, Vincent and Theo,'" though
in fact the canvas was only signed "Vincent" (plate 28). All these contradictions had one and the same cause: his unbreakable tie with Theo.

In the "Haystacks" (plate 37) two mighty stacks dominate the painting.
The haystack on the right has two ladders leaning against it, as did the
stack in the "Harvest." There is also a farmhouse with a woman in front,
this time on the left side. The fact that Vincent again took the haystack with
the two ladders as a subject and even painted two stacks, including the
repetition of the woman and the house, suggests a connection between the two
paintings. He himself called the "Haystacks" a *companion piece* to the 497
"Harvest."

Both works are signed below the stack with the two ladders, the "Harvest" on the left and the companion piece on the right; the signature moved,
so to speak, with the subject. His name near a certain thing sometimes
underlines his particular closeness to its symbolic content and stresses the
self-portraying meaning. With Theo constantly on Vincent's mind, the two
haystacks and the two ladders — both male symbols, accentuated by the
ladders' upward striving — could thus indicate a pair like Theo and himself.

In the background between the two stacks, the silhouette of a tree
stands out against the sky. The single tree, symbol of the lonely fighter, is
personified in the companion piece, the "Harvest," by the reaper. The man
and the tree appear separately in these canvases, while in later landscapes such
as the "Sower" (plates 39, 55) and the "Reaper" (plate 82) they will be
together in one painting, and then even more cogently convey Vincent's
struggle.

38. FISHING BOATS AT SAINTES-MARIES

FISHING BOATS AT SAINTES-MARIES

In the early summer Vincent made a trip to the Mediterranean seashore. He was impressed by the small fishing village of Les Saintes-Maries-de-la-Mer and it did not take him long to find his subjects. He wrote to Theo: *"One night I strolled by the sea on the deserted beach. It was not gay, but neither was it sad — it was beautiful."* In this letter he also speaks of *"... a peculiar thing, the family — quite involuntarily and in spite of myself I have often thought here of our uncle, the sailor, who certainly has many times seen the shores of this sea."* 499

On the beach there, in June 1888, he painted one of his most popular works, the "Fishing Boats at Saintes-Maries" (plate 38). Like the looms and the drawbridges, the boats are painted with a notable exactness, extending to minute details, as if in a token of respect to other men's craftsmanship. The boldly colored masts are clearly silhouetted over the horizon, like trees in a vigorous young forest. Some white birds are playing in the light air. One group of boats is moored on the beach while on the sea another group rides gaily under a bright sky, the sails moving in a fresh breeze.

The inner meaning of the painting unfolds as we notice that all the boats are arranged in pairs. In three pure colors, yellow, red, and blue, with green as a combination of yellow and blue in the middle, the boats are a complete unity of color, a harmonious team. In the center, on the bow of one of them, Vincent painted in big letters "Amitié" — Friendship — as though by this word to bring into focus the underlying pairing motif.

While the word "Amitié" points to the harmony in the boats and thus between their owners, the fishermen, Vincent does not join them. In the foreground lies a lemon-yellow box, and within its contours is his signature.

93

There is another similar box on the left. The two boxes lie aground like stones. Both painted yellow, his color of love, they form a pair as if symbolizing the two brothers who remain ashore. Of a still brighter yellow is the mast of the first boat. As the highest of the masts it is like a symbolic flagpole — carrying the color of love. Contrary to the usually dark birds seen in Vincent's works, in this painting the birds are white — Vincent's thoughts are not somber or sad. Circling gracefully around the masts, they glide between the two men who stay behind and the fishing boats ready to put to sea. Yet the bright, joyful colors of the boats and masts, the gentle movement of the sea, and the gay sails, make man on land long to join the fishermen.

This is one of the canvases where Vincent signed his name within the contours of an object. The large "Amitié" on the bow of the boat that reaches out towards the open sea is in striking contrast with the small "Vincent" enclosed in the box. But his signature has shifted from the side to the middle of the painting, a singular instance among his landscapes, reminding us of its earlier move from the obscure corner in the "Potato Eaters" to its conspicuous place in the "Self-Portrait with the Easel" (plates 12, 25). His name now comes to lie straight below "Amitié," as though the two words were linked by an invisible line.

The painting is a remarkable portrayal of Vincent's inner condition: within the confines of the box, a female symbol, he longs for the friendship and freedom which the boats convey. Only a few weeks earlier, in the first version of the drawbridges, he had shown a wrecked boat in front of the washerwomen. Lying disabled in the foreground, it was in a central position, like the yellow box marked "Vincent" in front of the Saintes-Maries boats. The bird in the sky has left *the cage* of the Borinage, but the box remains grounded on the shore — Vincent is still *enclosed,* still *walled in,* he has not yet been freed from his cage.

133
133

94

THE SOWER (June 1888)

39. THE SOWER (JUNE 1888)

When Vincent returned from Les Saintes-Maries he *had a week of intense* 501
and stiff work in the wheatfields in full sun, as he wrote to Theo. He went
on: *"The result is studies of wheatfields, landscapes and — a sketch of a sower."*
The "Sower" (plate 39), the first of two paintings of the same name
reproduced in this book, shows a large field, mainly in violet, covering about
three quarters of the canvas. On the rough field a sower is walking with
great strides, followed by some dark birds. His figure reaches above a yellow
strip of wheat into the sky; the head is just at the level of the horizon.
A large solar disc in bright yellow spreads its rays in all directions from the
center of an all-yellow sky. In the background are some houses and trees. One
tree is again singled out and silhouetted against the sky. Below the sun, a

95

large furrow extends to the foreground. In the lower left hand corner, below the tree, is Vincent's name, slanted and directed towards the sower's arm which strews the seed.

In several letters to Theo and his friends he described the painting: 501 *"On a plowed field, a large field of violet clods of earth — rising towards the horizon a sower in blue and white. At the horizon a field of short wheat. Over all that a yellow sky with a yellow sun. You feel by the simple nomenclature of tonalities that the color plays a very important rôle in this composition. Also the sketch as it is — canvas of 25 [15] — it torments me very much in this sense that I ask myself whether one ought not take it seriously and make a terrible painting of it: my God, how I would want to! But I keep asking myself if I shall have the necessary strength to carry it out. I put the sketch aside as it is, hardly daring to think of it. It has already for such a long time been my desire to do a sower, but the desires I have had for a long time are not always realized. I am thus almost afraid of it. And yet, after Millet and Lhermitte, what remains to be done is ... the sower with color and in a large size."*

503 In a second letter to Theo he wrote: *"I worked yesterday and today at the sower who is completely done over again. The sky is yellow and green, the ground violet and orange. Certainly there is a painting to be done like that of this magnificent subject and I hope that one day one will do it, either someone else, or myself. The question remains this — the "Boat of Christ" by Eugène Delacroix and the "Sower" by Millet are of an absolutely different making. The "Boat of Christ" — I speak of the blue and green sketch with violet and red spots and a little lemon yellow for the nimbus, the halo — speaks a symbolic language by the color itself. Millet's "Sower" is colorless grey as are also the paintings of Israels. Now, can one paint the Sower with color, with a simultaneous contrast of yellow and violet for instance (like the ceiling of Apollo, which is just that yellow and violet, by Delacroix), yes or no? Certainly yes. But do it then! ... But go ahead and one falls into full metaphysics of colors à la Monticelli, a mess from which to get out with honor is devilishly troublesome. And this makes you absent-minded like a sleepwalker. Still, if one did something good."*

501a In a letter to a painter friend he said: *"Am working at a sower: the great field all violet, the sky and sun very yellow. It is a hard subject to treat."* He added a small sketch in which the sower and the single trees behind are in the center between the sun and the house (plate 40).

96

40. SOWER (SKETCH)

At the same time he wrote about the painting to Bernard and sent him another sketch (plate 41). Once more there is the sower and the sun. As in the other versions, the single trees in the background are in a movement like that of the sower himself, thus identifying him with the recurrent symbol of the lonely fighter. Vincent writes to Bernard: *"I don't hide from you* **B 7** *that I do not detest the country, having been brought up there—gusts of memories of former times, aspirations towards that infinite of which the sower, the sheaf are the symbols still enchanting me, as formerly. But when then shall I do the starry sky, that painting which always preoccupies me. Alas! alas! it is like the excellent friend Cyprien says, in En Ménage by J.K. Huysmans: the most beautiful paintings are those one dreams about*

97

when smoking a pipe in bed, but which one does not do. The matter is, nevertheless, to attack them, as incompetent as one may feel in face of the ineffable perfections of the glorious splendours of nature." Very significant

B 7 are his concluding words: *"Here is what I wanted to say about the black and white. Let us take the Sower. The painting is cut in two, one half is yellow, the upper; the lower is violet. Well, the white trousers rest the eye and distract it at the moment when the simultaneous excessive contrast of yellow and violet would irritate it. That's what I wanted to say."*

41. SOWER (SKETCH)

There are some obvious mistakes in this description. The upper part in yellow is not half but only one quarter of the painting. Also the trousers of the sower are not white but blue. How could Vincent with his piercing eyes and keen observation make such errors, especially as it concerned his own

B 7 work? His assertion that *the painting is cut in two* may contain the answer. He thereby stresses the dividing nature of the *excessive contrast* between violet and yellow which he connects with black and white.

The problem of black and white was a constant challenge to him, particularly from the time he started working with colors and their light and

306 darkness. In 1883 he had written to Theo from The Hague: *"There will always remain something unfathomable, worries and melancholy will remain. But*

98

*against the everlasting negative stands the positive of the work one still gets
done in this way. If life were so simple, if things were as in the story of decent
Hendrik or in an ordinary sermon, then it would not be so difficult to find
a way. But it is not so, it is rather much more complicated, and good and bad
by themselves exist no more than black and white in nature."* This was an
attitude different from the one he still had in the Borinage that *what was* 133
good came from God and what was bad did not come from God. Later in
the year he wrote again: *"...in all matters of life there is always something* 336
*I do not know of almighty good and also an element of bad of which one
feels that it is infinitely above us and infinitely greater and more powerful
than we are."* Vincent thus expressed the view that black and white, dark and
light in nature, stood for bad and good in life. He says it in the same passage
in which he mentions the everlasting negative and positive. The one never
existed by itself but only together with its opposite, in a contrast.

The unique Van Gogh colors, the outstanding characteristic of his work,
substantiate a statement he had made at Nuenen: *"Color by itself expresses* 429
something." His colors were based on the uncompromising application of
the great truths in which Delacroix also believed, as he then wrote to Theo, 401
namely the three primary colors: yellow, blue and red. The combination of
any two of these primaries give secondary (also called binary) colors: green
(yellow + blue), orange (yellow + red) and violet (blue + red). A leading
trait in his coloring, Vincent's personal mark, so to speak, were his complementaries — namely any primary color in contrast to a secondary which
does not contain that primary — i.e. yellow contrasting violet, or blue against
orange, or red against green. These complementaries, blended in many variations of strength balancing the three basic primaries, were a formidable and
absorbing task on which he repeatedly elaborated in his letters. He once
compared them to *pairs enhancing and completing each other like man and* W 4
woman.

It was after he had painted the "Sower" that he had written to Theo
about his exhaustion when *returning from a session like the "Harvest"* and 507
stressed *the mental work to balance the six essential colors, red, blue, yellow,
orange, lilac, green.* He continued : *"Work and dry calculation and where
one's mind is extremely strained, like an actor on the stage in a difficult part,
where one has to think of a thousand things at one time in a single half
hour... Don't think that I would artificially keep up a feverish condition,
but understand that I am in the midst of complicated calculation, from which*

result quickly, one after the other, canvases done quickly but calculated a long time in advance. Now then, when one will say that this is done too quickly, you can reply that they have looked at it too quickly." He excelled in contrasts, from brutal to the most refined, between primaries, secondaries, complementaries, pure and broken, and the tremendous impact of these opposing colors is symbolic of the contrast of dark and light within him.

503   This is Vincent's *symbolic language by the color itself.*

     If the three primary colors or the complementaries are placed next to one another, their effect is greatly enhanced. However, as Vincent once

401   quoted from Delacroix, by a singular phenomenon when all the three primaries are mixed in equal quantities, the law of colors causes their mutual

503   destruction. The result is the *colorless grey* which was typical of Vincent's early Dutch period when his works had been very dark. Shortly after his

347   arrival in Nuenen he had written to Theo: *"My youth was somber and cold and sterile under the influence of the rayon noir [black ray]. And, brother, your youth really too... Enfin, I don't want to reproach anybody but myself, but the black ray is unspeakably cruel, unspeakably... And now I say as brother to brother, as friend to friend: Let us from now on, even though our youth was somber and against the grain, look for the gentle light for which I do not know any other name than the rayon blanc [white ray] or kindness."* This letter will help us to understand what he later expressed to

459a   a friend: *"...in color seeking life."* The destruction of color, as of light, had meant darkness and chaos, *the cruel black ray.* Yet if the colors prevailed together, side by side, they might bring *the white ray,* the gentle light — consciousness and kindness.

503   When Vincent now asks whether one can *paint the sower with colors,* it is no longer a general breaking away from Millet's *colorless grey.* Since his stay with Theo in Paris, his colors had begun their ever-increasing lightening. In the spring and early summer at Arles, he had attained the brilliancy of his orchards and landscapes. Why then was he so frightened of the sower?

501   His doubt *whether he would have the strength to carry it out* and his fear

503   of *falling into full metaphysics of colors* must have had a particular reason.

     Since his earliest beginnings as an artist, Vincent had been occupied with the motif of the sower. In fact, one of his very first attempts at drawing

134   was to copy a "Sower" of Millet. He reported this to Theo in August 1880, while still in the Borinage, only a few weeks after he had spoken of himself

as the *imprisoned bird*, and of *the impossibility of doing anything*. In 1890, the   133
year of his death, he again took up the copying of the same "Sower," but as
he then explained: *"... it is not purely and simply copying... It is rather*   623
translating into another language — that of color — the impressions of light
and shade in white and black."

The sower had become one of his most important subjects; there are
about thirty paintings and drawings in various versions. Vincent himself
attached great symbolic significance to it. From Nuenen he once wrote:
"Painting is sometimes sowing, though the painter may not reap." Now in   427
Arles he calls the sower and the sheaf *enchanting symbols of the infinite.*   B 7
When in the following year in St. Rémy he painted the "Reaper" (plate 82),
he reverted to the subject. He saw in the wheat an *image of ... humanity* and   604
added: *"So it is — if you like — the opposite of that sower I tried to do before."*
The sower strewing seed thus sows the wheat — the image of humanity. This
makes him a potent symbol of creation in the work of Vincent, who *plowed*   612
on his canvases like the peasants on their fields. The *real life* with a wife and   476
children has been denied him. *"And if one is frustrated physically in this*   531
power, one tries to create thoughts instead of children, thus one is nevertheless
part of humanity," he wrote in early September, 1888, and a few days later:
"The idea of the sower still haunts me all the time."   535

Indeed, the "Sower" is one of Vincent's most outstanding self-portrayals,
symbolic of the core of his life, his spiritual struggle against what he called
physical frustration. No wonder he was doubtful and afraid whether he would
have the necessary strength to accomplish the idea of the sower which always
haunted him. His *cutting the painting in two* confirms the symptomatic con-   535-B7
flict between the opposing forces of dark and light, of negative and positive,
within him. We find here the psychological explanation for his description
one half is yellow though visually this was not accurate. The impact of the   B 7
"Sower" by the *simultaneous excessive contrast between the violet and yellow*   B 7
was so frightening and exhausting that he sought a resting point for the
irritated eye, for which he wanted to use white. But after all he did not apply
white, which hints at his inability at that stage to find the rest he was seeking,
haunted as he was.

ON THE ROAD TO TARASCON / SUNFLOWERS

In the painting "On the Road to Tarascon" (plate 42), Vincent is again alone on the road. He depicts himself in front of two flourishing trees, carrying his painting equipment and with a yellow canvas under his arm. It is another self-portrait with a canvas, but very different from the Paris portrait. Golden and green fields extend beyond him. In the distance are a house and trees, and some mountains are seen faintly at the horizon.

He continues along the road of the early little drawing "En Route," done shortly after he had left the Borinage. Instead of the lamp, he now carries his canvas, which is bright yellow, the color of love and of the sun and the wheat. The road and fields are bathed in glowing sunshine; Vincent's

251 face under the straw hat and his hands are red from the *toil and sweat* in this burning summer heat of southern France.

The trees on the road are healthy and straight-grown: their branches do not strike fiercely against the sky like those in the little drawing. But a conspicuous feature commands our attention: the deep, dark shadow which Vincent's figure throws on the sunny road. The sharply drawn silhouette is like a black companion who symbolizes his dark side. As if replacing the knotty or bent tree in his other works, it conveys Vincent's struggle and frustration, in somber contrast to the warm sunlight that spreads over the painting. Yet the dark shadow enhances the brightness of this self-portrait in which Vincent is marching resolutely with the gait of the sower on his road of life.

He maintained his terrific volume of work throughout the summer and

543 autumn. In one letter he wrote to Theo: *"I have a terrible lucidity sometimes when nature is so beautiful these days and then I do not feel myself any*

102

42. ON THE ROAD TO TARASCON

more and the painting comes to me as if in a dream." He was engulfed in his
work *"...with a lucidity or blindness of a man in love."*   541

However, he remained alone most of the time. The few friends he made,
such as a postman and a soldier, were simple and straightforward, but there
was not a common spiritual basis for a lasting valuable friendship. In some
depressed letters to Theo about his longing for a home and family, he
reiterated that *art was not the real life*. He described his loneliness: *"A great*   480
number of days pass without my saying a word to anyone except to ask for   508
dinner or coffee, and it has been like that since the beginning."

Ever since he had arrived in Arles he hoped to find a companionship
with someone who would replace Theo. He thought one of the painters whom
he had met in Paris might come to work and live with him. In June he had

103

43. SUNFLOWERS

104

started to write about this idea to Gauguin of whose work he was very fond. Theo as well liked Gauguin and helped him whenever he could by promoting his sales. When Vincent asked Theo to transmit his proposal to Gauguin he made the comment: *"One always loses when one is isolated."*   493

Since then the house which he was so eager to furnish had become a much discussed subject in the correspondence with Theo. He justified his wish by explaining the economic advantages, especially if another painter would share the expenses. He often complained that he was exploited by innkeepers. As he had always stayed in small, austere inns or boarding houses, invariably choosing the cheapest, it was no wonder that he had no comfort or decent food.

With the regular allowance from Theo he could, in fact, have lived much better.[16] He received a minimum of one hundred and fifty francs a month which would have been quite sufficient if he had used it for his subsistence only. By comparison, the monthly pay of his friend, the postman Roulin, was one hundred and thirty-five francs on which his family of five had to live. Although Theo sometimes sent some extra money as well as all the painting materials for which Vincent asked continually, it was never enough. He spent a great deal on buying more paints, canvas, brushes, paper, also for models, and there was not much left for food and clothing.

Unpretentious though Vincent was, the expense of preparing and furnishing the house was too great for Theo to bear, in addition to all his other financial commitments. But when Theo inherited a small legacy, he agreed to meet the costs. Vincent was very engrossed in the prospect and employed all his energy and ingenuity to make the house habitable. He was full of ideas about it, writing to Bernard: *"The decoration of the house absorbs me*   B 18 *terribly,"* and to Theo: *"I really want to make an artists' house of it, but*   534 *not precious — on the contrary, nothing precious — but everything from the chair to the painting having character."* Finally, in September he moved into it; there were four rooms, two on the ground floor and two bedrooms above. The best was to be the guestroom where Theo or a painter friend could stay and which he wanted to make *really artistic like a lady's boudoir.* Many   534 of the paintings he did during that summer and autumn were intended to decorate the house. They include the "Sunflowers" (plate 43), a subject of which Vincent had drawn and painted many versions, both in Paris and in Arles.

Painted in the yellow color and the round shape of the sun, the sunflowers are symbols of his love of man, and their varying compositions reflect

44. SUNFLOWERS

the ups and downs in his relations with his brother and friends. Those shown in plates 43 and 44 are the most widely reproduced. Their vigorous color and form make them particularly characteristic of Vincent's work: whatever the effect on the viewer, it cannot be ignored. He painted the same subject four times in August, starting a few days after he received the good news of Theo's consent to the house. Gauguin had also agreed in principle to join him and Vincent hoped he would soon arrive. He placed two of these canvases in the guestroom, telling Theo: *"The room where you will then stay or which will be Gauguin's if G. should come, will have on the white walls a decoration of large yellow sunflowers. In the morning, when opening the windows, one sees the green of the gardens and the rising sun and the entry to the town. But you will see these large paintings of the bunches of 12, of 14 sunflowers, crammed into this very small boudoir with a pretty bed, with everything else elegant. It will not be commonplace."*

534

106

45. SUNFLOWERS

The house now came into being; it meant to him the realization of his old idea of the painters' home, the beginning of the artists' community. Theo should become a member and direct the business of the society. Vincent was more and more opposed to the existing art trade, and repeatedly told his brother that he never thought of him as belonging to the category of art dealers, whom he knew from his own experience and for whom he felt great contempt.

The key to the meaning of these "Sunflowers" seems to be the place where Vincent chose to sign his name. The signature is prominent inside the contours of the vase, and the canvas thus becomes associated with those works in which he painted his name "into" a certain object. They are the "Potato Eaters" (plate 12), the "Self-Portrait with the Easel" (plate 25), the "Fishing Boats at Saintes-Maries" (plate 38), "Vincent's Chair" (plate 59), and "La Berceuse" (plate 64).

It is hardly accidental that in all the four paintings of "Sunflowers" he placed his name within the vase. It is more likely that in this way he acknowledged his inner tie with its symbolic import. Like a jug, the vase has the same female meaning as a house. Between his trying experiences in the cheap inns, Vincent had lived as a guest in the house of his parents in Holland and also in his brother's apartment in Paris. In each case there had been friction, as his letters from Etten and Nuenen and Theo's correspondence with their sister revealed. Vincent's tenseness, aggravated by his material dependence on the family, often brought out the negative side of his ambivalent attitude towards them, thus causing the painful situations of which Theo had complained.

Now in Arles, Vincent at last had a house of his own in which he could live and work, and where he longed to receive his fellow artists. Those were the thoughts that preoccupied him when he worked at this still life, in which the vase, with his name boldly painted on it, stands for: his house. Out of it grow the sunflowers which, like the sun or the light, are symbols of his love for man, for Theo and for painter friends like Gauguin and Bernard or others to whom he felt close. The painting, all in powerful yellow, symbolizes the dream of his life: companionship, brotherhood, a community of loving and creative men — growing in his house, the home of the painters. The straight line of the horizon is repeated by the circular movement of a line round the vase; it is painted in the same color as his name, which follows its course.

As in his other flower pieces, there are among the thriving sunflowers some which are withering and falling. In all four of these paintings the two lowest flowers, those closest to the vase, fall nearly parallel to each other. At the end of the following January Vincent painted a fifth canvas of these
575 "Sunflowers" (plate 45), which he called *a repetition*. Yet in some respects it is notably different from the four "Sunflowers" done in August: his name no longer appears on the vase — the house — and one of the wilting flowers has fallen so low that it touches the earth at the horizon. In the other four versions, the drooping flowers were all still above the line of the horizon — the life line.

In the meantime, in October, Gauguin had come to stay with him at the house, but he left again at Christmas when Vincent had a terrible mental attack, in which he mutilated himself by cutting off part of an ear. During his recovery he did the "Self-Portrait with the Bandaged Ear" (plate 61), and

108

46. EUGENE DELACROIX, PORTRAIT OF
MR. BRUYAS

shortly afterwards, this fifth painting of the "Sunflowers".

A few days before the outbreak of the illness, he described to Theo a visit he had made with Gauguin to the museum at Montpellier. His reaction to a portrait by Delacroix (plate 46) is remarkable: *"There is a man with a red beard and hair who has a damnable resemblance to you or me, and he made me think of that poem by Musset ... 'Wherever I have touched the earth, an unhappy man, dressed in black, came to sit near us, and he looked at us like a brother'! This would have the same effect on you I am sure."* In this letter he also refers to a painting by Rembrandt: *"I don't know why I always call this portrait the traveller, or the man coming from afar."*

564

The symbolic language in Vincent's letter so shortly before the catastrophe sounds like a foreboding. The *unhappy man in black* who came to sit near them, the *traveller from afar,* is the typical messenger of death. His *resembling him and Theo and looking at them like a brother* affirms Vincent's identification with Theo to whom he extends this impression, asserting *it would have the same effect on him.*

This awareness of death seems to be conveyed in the "Sunflowers" by the parallel fall of the two flowers which are like symbols of the two brothers. The touching of the earth by the one flower in the fifth painting recalls the quotation: *"Wherever I have touched the earth..."* The disappearance of his name from the vase is virtually explained by Vincent himself when he wrote to Theo shortly after he had painted this last version that he *no longer dared to ask other painters to join him after what had happened to him.* About a week later he was taken under constraint to a hospital as a result of a complaint by some Arles citizens, and put in a cell. In a letter from there, he gave a moving description of his anguish, assuring Theo that he was in full possession of his faculties, and not a madman. He concluded with humility: *"We artists in present-day society are only the broken jug."*

564

577

579

47. SUB-LIEUTENANT MILLIET

SUBLIEUTENANT MILLIET / STARRY SKY

One of the friends Vincent had made in Arles was Sub-Lieutenant Milliet, whom he painted in September 1888 (plate 47). The portrait is of a notable simplicity, both in its straight and detailed design and in the clear combination of the three primary colors on a green background. There is a remarkable contrast between the pallid yellow of the officer's face and the bright red of his cap; the ears, too, are peculiarly reddish. In the right hand corner above the figure is a large yellow sickle moon around a star.

When Vincent did Milliet's portrait he wrote to Theo: *"If he posed* **541** *better, he would give me great pleasure and he would have a smarter portrait than I shall now be able to do, though the subject is lovely of his face with a pale and mat complexion, the red soldier's cap against an emerald back-ground."* He also mentioned that *in the back were the arms of Milliet's regiment, the crescent and a five pointed star.*[17] In contrast to the matter-of-fact rendering of the officer's head and uniform, particular prominence is given to the crescent and star. Their impressive size and luminous golden yellow, as well as their place high up on the canvas, strike us at the same time as real and imaginary.

Shortly before, he had written about some portraits on which he was working: *"And in a painting I would like to say something as consoling* **531** *as music. I would like to paint men or women with, I don't know what of eternal, of which formerly the nimbus was the symbol, and which we seek by the very radiance, by the vibration of our coloring."* It was in the same letter that he had spoken of the symbolism in his work such as the *expression of hope by some star.* We also recall his comments on the sun and the light which he could only describe as yellow: *"How beautiful yellow* **522**

111

is!" (page 19). All such associations support the assumption that the imposing crescent and star may have a deeper meaning.

It is the first time that a crescent moon appears in Vincent's works. Later, both in Arles and St. Rémy, it is outstanding on canvases where the subject concerns love between man and woman. In October he mentioned to Theo the painting "Poet's Garden": *"Here is a rather rough sketch (plate 48) of my last canvas, a row of green cypresses against a rose-colored sky with a crescent pale lemon. In the fore, an indistinct ground and sand and some thistles. Two lovers, the man pale blue with a yellow hat, the*

48. POET'S GARDEN

woman with a pink bodice and a black skirt. That makes the fourth canvas of "Poet's Garden" which is the decoration of Gauguin's room."

"Evening Walk" (plate 49), painted in St. Rémy, shows a hilly landscape with small green olive trees. A large sickle moon shines brightly in a green sky above the orange rays of sunset. Two young lovers walk together in the foreground, the man with red hair and beard, again dressed in blue, the woman with dark hair, wearing a yellow dress. The focal point of the painting, however, is the huge silhouette of the radiant yellow crescent.

49. EVENING WALK

While the sun, in its round, complete and never-changing oneness, embraces the whole of mankind and expresses brotherly love, the sickle moon, as an opened part of the round form, is like a weaker image of the sun, a smaller sun with an opening. The horseshoe shape, allowing an entrance as into a sheltering harbor, intimates the female character of the crescent. Shining over pairs of lovers, it symbolizes love between man and woman.

113

A sentence in a letter to Theo, which Vincent wrote while he did Milliet's portrait, may help to clarify the meaning of the star inside the open
542 crescent: *"Milliet has luck; he has as many Arlésiennes as he wants, but you see he cannot paint them, and if he were a painter he would not have them. I myself must now await my time without pressing anything."* Milliet's luck with the Arlésiennes makes him a star of the women, a kind of cock of the walk, a suggestion also hinted at by the glamorous red cap. But Vincent finds consolation in saying that *Milliet cannot paint the Arlésiennes, if he could paint them he would not have them.* Earlier, from Antwerp, he had
442 written: *"The women's figures I see among the people here make an excellent impression on me, much more to paint than to possess them, though*
B7 *indeed I should like both."* And again to Bernard, he wrote: *"Painting and a lot of lovemaking is not compatible; it weakens the brain. And that's quite a nuisance."*

His remarks on Milliet reveal that he compared the lucky officer with himself, who had no luck with the Arlésiennes. They were known as pretty and attractive, yet his own relations with them were limited to visits to the brothels of Arles. The contrast between his profound feeling and thinking on the one side, and on the other his inability to achieve a relationship of mutual love with a woman, for which he longed so much, is symptomatic of the disturbing conflict within him. He himself had referred implicitly to it when
531 he wrote of his *physical frustration* against which he could only set spiritual creation. This condition is as if projected in Milliet's portrait by the over-dimensioned size of the crescent and the star, which brings their symbolic character to the fore.

In this self-portrayal the exceptional color of Milliet's ears also gains significance. By their unusual red they become conspicuous and make us think of what happened to Vincent a few months later, when he cut off a piece of his own ear and gave it to a girl in a brothel.

The self-portraying aspect is, however, not merely negative. The star inside the crescent also expresses his own hopes. He was biding his time,
535 and although he felt isolated *so many ideas came to him for his work that he could not take an interest in anything else.* When he wrote this to Theo he added: *"I am working like a painting steam-engine [Je marche comme une locomotive à peindre]."* These words characterize Vincent's dynamic activity, due to his urge and ability to express himself in his art. They indicate
185, 242 the productive, the positive side of *a great hidden force*, a *fire*, the very

114

source by which his conflicting negative impulses were equally sustained.

The golden yellow of the crescent and star gives a warm light to the appearance of the officer which otherwise would be ashy and cold. Their large silhouette, shining over Milliet in the color of love, does not convey less strongly Vincent's feeling of friendship for him.

50. STARRY SKY

There is more light, though in a different way, in a painting Vincent did simultaneously with the portrait of Milliet. It was the "Starry Sky" (plate 50). For some time he had been greatly tempted to paint at night. As he wrote repeatedly, he found the night was not just dark, but: *"Often* 533 *it seems to me that the night is much more alive and more richly colored than the day."* In fact, he worked a few times outside at night with a small

115

improvised gas lamp. In the "Starry Sky," the night is brightly illuminated by many stars exaggerated in size like sparkling fireworks. The glittering lights of a dark town in the background, along the curved shores of a bay, and the large stars are reflected in the water by long glaring flashes. A young couple walks towards us in the foreground. In the water behind them two boats are moored side by side.

543   Vincent described this work to Theo: *"... at last, the starry sky painted actually at night under a gas jet. The sky is blue-green, the water is royal blue, the land is mauve. The town is blue and violet, the gas is yellow and the reflections are russet gold and descend to bronze green. On the blue-green field of the sky, the Great Bear scintillates green and rose, its discreet pallor contrasts with the brutal gold of the gas. Two little colored figures of lovers in the foreground."*

In the same letter he wrote: *"... I always dream of a painting like this one with a group of living figures of the copains."* However, during his stay in Arles, Vincent did not carry out his idea of such a painting. It was not until the following year in St. Rémy that he painted his great "Starry Night" (plate 79).

HOUSE IN ARLES

Soon after he had moved into his house, Vincent painted the "House in Arles" (plate 51). In the meantime he had continued to correspond with Gauguin, but was not quite sure whether and when he would come. Should he not join him, Vincent thought some other painter might perhaps take his place. In any case he prepared himself to be alone in the house for some time. When he had lived in it for a few days, he wrote to Theo: *"I think* 542 *I shall end by no longer feeling alone in the house and for instance, during the bad days of winter and long evenings, find an occupation which will completely absorb me. A weaver, a basketmaker often spends whole seasons alone or nearly alone with his job as the only distraction. But just what makes these people stay in one place is the feeling of the house, the reassuring and familiar aspect of things."*

He told Theo about his canvas: *"I enclose a sketch of thirty square,* 543 *showing the house and its surroundings under a sun of sulphur, under a sky of pure cobalt. The subject is a hard one! but that is just why I want to conquer it. Because it is terrible, those yellow houses in the sun, and then the incomparable freshness of the blue. The whole ground is yellow too. I shall send you another drawing, better than this sketch from memory; the house to the left is pink, with green shutters, the one in the shade of the tree."*

The painting is dominated by strong yellows, but Vincent's house in the center stands out in an even more intense color. The glaring yellow almost hurts the eye in its tremendous contrast to the deep blue of the front door and windows. He did a second version in water-color (plate 52). In the two

117

51. HOUSE IN ARLES

works a single man is seen in front of the house; in one he is walking and in the other he stands on the pavement. Yet in both cases, his position is exactly between Vincent's house and the next; the line of the wall separating his house from the other is precisely behind the man, as if it were a dividing line cutting him in half.

52. HOUSE IN ARLES (WATER COLOUR)

This position of the man as well as Vincent's emphasis on *the reassuring and familiar aspect of things* make us think of the "Breakfast Table" (plate 34), the still life he had done in the spring, when he was still longing for a house of his own. Then, the orange on the left below his name was partly cut off by the frame which he had painted on the canvas. The symbolic interpretation of the earlier work seems to be reaffirmed by the analogous position of the single man who in both versions of the "House in Arles" appears to be divided by the wall of the house. 542

In each version, a man walks alone in the street on the right, and at some distance from him are women. On the left hand side, there is another woman not far from the man in front of the house. These women, one with a child, bring to mind the domestic objects and lemons in the still life; they again add to the female character of the house. Vincent calls the subject

543 *a hard one,* the same expression he had used once before, when struggling
B 7 with *the simultaneous excessive contrast between violet and yellow* in the "Sower", the painting which had been *cut in two.* Now, the *hard subject*

543 which he *wants to conquer* is his house, with its almost mystically dark holes in the burning yellow. In this struggle for the house — the symbol of woman — the man seems to be as isolated as was the orange in the still life, cut off

53. HOUSE IN ARLES (SKETCH)

by the frame and separated from the other objects. The contrast between the dark blue of the coffeepot and the yellow of the lemons and background is greatly increased in the "House in Arles" by the powerful opposing colors

543 which create the *terrible* impact.

His solitude is further outlined by a lamp-post opposite the man, just included on the extreme left in both the painting and water color. In a rough sketch he made of the "House in Arles" (plate 53), a man stands in the

120

foreground, parallel to the lamp-post. It is the same theme as "Outskirts of Paris," the single street lamp near a lonely man, with groups of people at some distance (plate 18). In the Arles sketch another man moves along the house like a black shadow. To the right and left again are women. The little sketch with the two men adds to our thoughts on Vincent's *hard* 543 *subject*. The solitary man in the foreground and the black figure, which like a ghost paces the sidewalk, are one in the finished painting and water color where he walks or stands. But in the attempt to conquer the house, the man is again divided; like the orange in the still life he symbolizes Vincent's own divided condition in regard to the house — the woman.

In the following year, because of illness, he could no longer remain in the house which he loved so much. While Theo was getting married in the spring, Vincent resigned himself to seclusion in a mental asylum at St. Rémy. On his arrival there he wrote to Theo's wife: *"Well, fortunately* 591 *you are yourself his house,"* thus identifying the house with the woman, the *hard subject* he wanted to conquer.

The gravity of this struggle is intimated by another feature in this painting. A train passes over a viaduct in the background; its movement is suggested by puffs of light smoke. The train implies distance in contrast to the nearness of the house — so close to Vincent's heart and in the center of his canvas. He had referred to a train on an earlier occasion when he had raised the question with Theo *whether life was entirely visible to us or if* 506 *we saw only one hemisphere before death* (page 71). He had then compared life to a one-way journey on a train and continued: *"If we take the train to go to Tarascon or Rouen, we take death to go to a star."* Vincent's symbolic inference preceded the simultaneous portrayal of nearness and distance in the "House in Arles." It is an added contrast to that of the yellow and blue and gives to the impact of light and dark the deeper meaning of life and death.[18]

54. THE BEDROOM

122

THE BEDROOM

The subject of the house remained in Vincent's mind, and soon after the view from the exterior he painted an interior. It was his "Bedroom" (plate 54), one of the canvases with which he wanted to decorate the house. In a long and detailed account of the painting to Theo, he stressed *the simple con-* 554 *ception, the shadows omitted, the flat and frank tones like a print.* The letter begins: *"This time it's just simply my bedroom, only color must do the job here, and giving by its simplification a greater style to things, to be suggestive here of rest or of sleep in general. Enfin, looking at the painting must rest the head or rather the imagination."*

He also described the painting to Gauguin: *"Well, it has amused me* B 22 *enormously to do this interior without anything, with a simplicity à la Seurat: in flat tones, but roughly brushed with a thick impasto, the walls pale lilac, the floor of a broken and faded red, the chairs and the bed chrome yellow, the pillows and the linen lemon-green and very pale, the cover blood-red, the washstand orange, the basin blue, the window green. I would have wanted to express absolute rest by all these very different tones, you see, and where the only white is the little note which the mirror gives in its black frame. (To bring still the fourth pair of complementaries into it.) Enfin, you will see this with the others and we shall talk about it, because I often do not know what I do, working almost like a sleep-walker."*

Vincent had once before called himself a sleep-walker when he wrote about the *metaphysics of colors* in his "Sower." It is worth noting that now, 503 as then, a problem concerning the use of white was involved. In the earlier painting *the white should have rested the eye,* but there was no white in it. B 7

123

554 He now says in his letter to Theo: *"The frame—as there is no white in the painting—will be white,"* while in his description to Gauguin he
B 22 accurately includes *the little white note* in the mirror. He seems to have ignored this fact when he imparted to Theo his deep-lying desire for the rest he hoped to find in his house. Such errors are conceivable by the strength
B 7 of a symbolic impact like that of the *excessive contrast* which *cut the Sower in two* or of the frame—the walls—enclosing his bedroom. In this connection a remark he had once made in Nuenen may be relevant. He had
358 then *preferred to see his work in deep black frames,* the exact opposite of the white frame he now chooses. His seeking these different effects is a sign
347 of an inner development in his striving for *the gentle light—the white ray.*
535 Like the *haunting idea* of the "Sower," also the "Bedroom" must have continued to preoccupy him, as may be concluded from the later versions painted in St. Rémy. When he had recovered from his first attack in January
573 1889, he wrote to Theo: *"When I saw my canvases again after my illness the one which seemed the best was the Bedroom."*

There is also a remote possibility that he added the white to the mirror later, after having written about it to Theo; yet it was in his letter to
B 22 Gauguin, dealing with the "Bedroom," that he asserted *he often did not know what he was doing.* At the same time, his detailed account of the very different tones shows that he deliberately chose his colors and weighed
B 22 the contrasts to *express absolute rest,* although they make the "Bedroom" less an achievement of this rest than an expression of his yearning for it. His wanting the "Bedroom" to hang in his house brings the two subjects, the exterior and the interior, into an even closer relation and thus intensifies their significance.

Another interesting point deserves mention. When Vincent furnished the house he tried to save every franc possible, which may be deduced from his letters and accounts to Theo, and this certainly applied to his own room. It is therefore remarkable that the bedroom where he slept alone was prepared as if for two. This is conspicuously brought out by the two pillows lying side by side on his single-sized bed; nearly all the other objects in the room are also in pairs: the two chairs, the waterbottle and the jug, the other two bottles and items on the table, the pictures on the right hand wall, the mirror and the painting at each side of the window, the doors—practically everything is in pairs.

124

Such doubling and pairing is often seen in his works, but he never mentions it, even in his most exact descriptions. Yet, the frequent portrayal of pairs shows the intensity of his need for a companion — and in this painting for a beloved to share his bedroom. Earlier he had written to Theo: *"As I* 534 *have told you already, my own bed, I am going to paint it, there will be three subjects. Perhaps a nude woman, I have not decided, perhaps a cradle with a child; I do not know, but I shall take my time."* These images indicate the direction into which his longing for companionship went.

The single man on the pavement in the "House in Arles" was divided while in the "Bedroom" the repeated pairing suggests an urge to bring together, to unite. It is the same contrast of division and union which Vincent had portrayed earlier in the symbolic composition of the "Breakfast Table." The three paintings are thus related to one another. They will later be joined by more works with the same motif. The persistence of this pairing not only seems to reflect Vincent's open need for company but to go even deeper and indicate a counteraction against division within himself.

The frame or the wall, either actually painted or intended, is the other symbol which the three canvases have in common. Vincent's association of a nude woman or a child in a cradle with the motif of the interior underlines the symbolic meaning of the walls of the house as confines of the woman — the mother. The female symbolism in the three paintings, in which he expresses his inner division and urge to unite, reveals the link between this exacting condition and womanhood.

55. THE SOWER (OCTOBER 1888)

126

THE SOWER (OCTOBER 1888)

One of the last paintings which Vincent mentioned as a decoration for his house was a new "Sower" (plate 55). It is particularly striking among the many versions he drew and painted of this subject. The outstanding feature is a magnificent golden sun of colossal size. In strong contrast to its warm light are the sower and the tree, both very dark in the foreground. They are similar both in color and in movement. Wide fields of violet and blue with stretches of green and orange spread to the foreground under a light green sky with pink clouds. In the background again is a house between trees. The sower comes towards us, strewing the grain, while within the immense yellow ball of the sun are silhouetted both the sower's head and a young shoot of the tree, which sticks out like a sword. Vincent did a small and a large version of this "Sower" and in the larger painting he placed his name at the bottom, within the contours of the dark trunk.

The powerful "Sower" is a pre-eminent example of his work during the fruitful autumn of 1888. We again see the motif of the early drawing "En Route," though much more pronounced. In this bold work, the man and the tree are more vigorous than ever before. We also find the elements of his "Sower" of the early summer (plate 39) greatly intensified in this autumn painting. The contrast of the colors is even more vehement and the man and the tree still more compelling in their conjoint movement.

The miner's lamp had changed into the rising morning sun in the earlier "Sower" and into the bright yellow canvas in the "Road to Tarascon." Now it has become a huge glowing sun setting in heavy, gravid gold. The miner had started on the road, the light of love in his hand; the painter had marched on with the full weight of his work. Both, in their way, fulfilled

604 the sower's task — sowing the *image of humanity* which the sower now does in an embracing movement in this new painting. The tree as the symbol of struggle, bent but strong and massive and with its shoots striking against the sky, is like a large double of the sower. By his signature within the trunk, Vincent lends added emphasis to his identification with the tree, and thus also with the sower.

The sun in bright burning yellow and the sower, dark violet-green, meet at the level of the horizon. The mighty tree bows towards the sower and the sun, and the pointed twig, extending into the solar disc, accentuates the contrast. The contour of the sun and the line of the horizon seem to go through the head of the sower. The three conceptions — the sun as symbol of light and love, the tree symbolizing struggle, and the horizon as the life line — were all portrayed together with the sower in the earlier painting and sketches (plates 39, 40 and 41). The changing composition of these symbols shows even more that they are not merely casual items of a static background, but rather live elements in a continuous movement which reaches a peak in this intense portrayal. The horizon, the infinite border line of earth and sky, and the light-giving sun are centered as if focused in the sower's head, causing a dynamic impact of simultaneous contrast and union of nature and man.

PART IV

CRISIS AND ANTIDOTE

Arles

PART IV

CRISIS AND ANTIDOTE

Arles

LA LISEUSE (WOMAN READING NOVELS)

Gauguin arrived in Arles in October 1888 and settled down to live with Vincent, both men being financially supported by Theo. It was an important event for Vincent. Throughout the summer he had exchanged views with Theo about the expected association. He repeatedly stressed the point that together they would spend no more than he needed alone. More than the economic factor, however, it was his social and spiritual needs which had deepened his longing for companionship. Gauguin was in a different situation. He worked at that time in Brittany with Bernard and some other painters. He was in no hurry to join Vincent, who tried to overcome his disappointment at Gauguin's reluctance. One of his letters to Theo reads: *"Only 535 understand that if I do not see him coming, I shall not in the least be upset and shall not work less for it. If he comes he will be very welcome, but I see so well that counting on him would just be what would do us in."* He also understood that Gauguin finally accepted the proposition because it promised him relief in his financial difficulties. Nevertheless, Vincent did not lose his esteem for him. These were small matters in his mind compared with the great idea: with Gauguin in Arles he saw his long cherished dream become reality. Their working together would be the beginning of his painters' community. Yet at the back of all these considerations there remained the dominating urge in Vincent to overcome his loneliness after he had parted from his brother.

Shortly before Gauguin's arrival, he wrote to Theo about his work: *"I have pushed what I had in hand as far as I could, with the great desire 556 to show him something new and not to undergo his influence (for he will*

131

56. LA LISEUSE (WOMAN READING NOVELS)

certainly have an influence on me, I hope) before I can show him undoubtedly my own originality." Vincent recognized Gauguin as the more mature, as a master who should become the head of the painters' society. Gauguin for his part later claimed that during his stay in Arles he had greatly influenced Vincent's art and guided its development. In fact he had exercised a certain artistic influence on Vincent, who admitted it frankly.

In November he wrote to his sister that they were working very happily together and added: *"He greatly encourages me to work often from full*   W 9
imagination." He also told Theo: *"Gauguin gives me courage to imagine,*   562
and things from imagination certainly take on a more mysterious character."

57. LA LISEUSE (SKETCH)

He asked for some of his studies which were with Theo in Paris: *"For this*   563
*good reason that everything which I did <u>from nature</u> is [like] chestnuts taken
from the fire. Gauguin, in spite of himself and in spite of me, has shown
me a little that it was time for me to vary a bit; I am beginning to compose
from my head and for this work all my studies will always be useful as they
will remind me of old things I have seen."*

Later from St. Rémy he wrote to Bernard: *"When Gauguin was in Arles,*   B 21
*as you know, once or twice I let myself go to an abstraction, in the Berceuse
and in a Woman Reading Novels, black in a yellow library; and then the
abstraction appeared to me a charming path. But this is enchanted land, my
dear fellow, and soon one finds oneself up against a wall."*

Je viens maintenant de peindre pour le
mettre dans ma chambre à coucher
un souvenir du jardin à Etten et envoici
un croquis — C'est une toile assez grande.

58. SOUVENIR OF THE GARDEN IN ETTEN (SKETCH)

The "Woman Reading Novels" (plate 56), painted in November 1888, shows this influence of Gauguin's. Indeed, it greatly resembles his style, and could almost be taken for one of his works were it not for that vigorous yellow and deep blue-black, partly blended in an intensive green, which could only be Vincent's. When mentioning the painting to his sister he wrote about another canvas on which he was working at the same time. He added

W 9 sketches of both works (plates 57, 58), calling the other painting *a souvenir of the garden at Etten*. There are two women walking in the foreground, while a third woman behind them is working in the garden. He gave a long and detailed description of the "Souvenir of the Garden in Etten", which

134

concluded: *"I don't know whether you will understand that one can express*   W 9
poetry [dire de la poésie] *by nothing but arranging colours well, just as one*
can say consoling things in music. In the same way, bizarre, affected and
multiplied lines, meandering all through the painting, should not give the
garden in its vulgar likeness, but outline it to us as seen in a dream, at the
same time in its character and nevertheless stranger than in reality."

He went on in the letter: *"I have now also painted a woman reading*
novels, a lot of very black hair, a green bodice, the sleeves lees of wine, the
skirt black, the background all yellow, library shelves with books. In her hand
she holds a yellow book." The symbolic contrast of darkness and light is very
pronounced in this painting, done *from imagination:* the deep, dark hair and   562
dress against the brightest yellow all around—of the book in the woman's
hand, of the bookshelf, with some red among the yellow, a yellow ladder
leaning against it. In the background one sees the lower part of a yellow
disk through the window.

Vincent imagined the two women in the "Souvenir of the Garden in
Etten" as *his mother and sister, although they had absolutely not the least*   W 9
vulgar and fatuous resemblance. It may thus be assumed that he also thought
of the "Woman Reading Novels" as his sister, the more so as in his letters
to her he used to discuss the French novels they were then both reading. He
treated the design in this painting less accurately than when he worked with
a model. The contrasting colors, however, are of such violence that even for
Vincent's known powerful colors they have unusual force. Like concentrated
energy this work conveys the atmosphere in his house of which he speaks
to Theo: *"The discussion* [with Gauguin] *is of an excessive electricity; we come*   564
out of it sometimes with the head tired like an electric battery after discharge."

The two men were greatly absorbed by their work and also by their
intense discussions on art and life during which they were, as Vincent said,
in the midst of magic. He wrote to Theo that Gauguin *was a very great artist*   564, 562
and a very excellent friend. In his *Avant et Après,*[19] Gauguin said he found in
Vincent "a rich and fertile soil." He owed to him "the affirmation of his
former ideas about painting, and that in difficult moments he could recall
having found someone more unhappy than himself," but at the same time,
he mentioned Vincent's shortcomings, his untidiness and inconsistent attitudes.
He could not explain the contradiction between his painting and his opinions.
Their judgment on other painters also differed considerably. Moreover, Gauguin was rather critical of what he termed "Vincent's disorderly work with

135

complementaries by which he achieved only soft harmonies, incomplete and monotonous; the sound of the bugle was missing there." But he continued: "Vincent made astonishing progress; he seemed to perceive all that was in him, and from there the whole series of suns upon suns in full sun."

The friendly disposition towards each other did not change the fact that the characters of the two artists were very different. Gauguin had a much more Bohemian nature than Vincent, who could never divorce himself from his solid Dutch background. Although they appreciated each other's work, their strong and contrasting personalities sometimes brought them into controversies which led to the tense *electric* atmosphere. In the relationship between the two men, Gauguin's attitude was obviously much the cooler. As he was lacking in his response to Vincent's unequivocal friendship, the negative side of their feelings was bound to become predominant. He did not have Theo's understanding and tolerant nature. Gauguin could not be a substitute for Theo—and this had been at the bottom of Vincent's desire to live together with him.

When Gauguin arrived, Theo had just sold one of his paintings. Vincent was very glad about this success, both for Gauguin's and for Theo's sake, as the proceeds were to contribute to the common expenses. Yet in the same letter he told Theo about his own work: *"I cannot help it that my paintings do not sell. The day will come, however, when one will see that it is worth more than the cost of the paint and my in fact very meager living, which we put into it."* He deplored that his debt to his brother was so great, *it was anguishing.* The letter he had written about the expected influence he hoped Gauguin would have on him, implied that he felt Gauguin superior to him, a situation which he wanted to counter by proving *his own undoubted originality.* This feeling of inferiority meant an additional conflict in his already strained condition. Moreover, there came an element of jealousy caused by another achievement of Gauguin—his success with the women of Arles. Two days after his arrival Vincent wrote to Theo: *"Gauguin has already nearly found his Arlésienne, and I wish I were already there, but for my part I very easily find the landscape here, and varied enough."* In a later letter he reported that Gauguin had success with the Arlésiennes and although he was married *he did not appear to be very much so.* He added: *"People like us are not clever at that."*

Another characteristic reaction on Vincent's part to Gauguin's apparent superiority is recorded in *Avant et Après:* "One of his rages was that he was

136

forced to credit me with great intelligence, whereas I had a too low forehead, a sign of imbecility." That rage to which Gauguin refers reminds us of Vincent's attitude to Milliet and the officer's *luck with the Arlésiennes*. He could well say *Milliet cannot paint* but in Gauguin's case there was nothing to console him, and his increased feeling of inferiority resulted in aggressiveness. Gauguin continues: "... in the midst of all that a great tenderness or rather an altruism as in the Gospel." The ambivalence of their relationship could not be more clearly indicated. Gauguin seemed to have been aware of the threatening development of which he wrote: "Between two beings, he and myself, one a volcano and the other boiling too, a kind of battle was preparing inside."

542

VINCENT'S CHAIR / GAUGUIN'S CHAIR

Vincent's relationship with Gauguin is portrayed in an exceptional way by two paintings of chairs. They are "Vincent's Chair" (plate 59) and "Gauguin's Chair" (plate 60). After he worked on these canvases in the

563 middle of December 1888, he described them to Theo: *"In the meantime I can at all events tell you that the last two studies are quite curious. Canvases of 30, a chair of wood and rush all yellow on red tiles against a wall (the day). Then Gauguin's armchair, red and green, effect of night, wall and floor also red and green, on the seat two novels and a candle."* However, he completed these paintings only a month later, after the attack at Christmas,

571 when he wrote about them again: *"I should like de Haan to see a study of mine of a lighted candle and two novels (one yellow, the other pink) but on an empty armchair (actually Gauguin's chair), canvas of 30, in red and green. I just worked again today at the companion piece, my own empty chair, a chair of white wood with a pipe and tobacco pouch. In these two studies, as in others, I have sought an effect of light with color; de Haan would probably understand what I am looking for, if you read to him what I am writing you on this subject."*

A year later, in February 1890, he wrote to Albert Aurier, an art critic who had published an appraising article about his work — the first ever to

626a appear — *that he owed much to Gauguin.* He continued the letter: *"A few days before we separated, when my illness forced me to enter a hospital, I tried to paint "his empty place". This is a study of his armchair in dark*

138

brown-red wood, the seat of greenish rush, and in the place of the absent a lighted candle and modern novels." When Vincent used the words *"his empty place"* and put them in quotation marks, he not only suggested that the chair stood for his companion, he thus also pointed out that Gauguin's place had become empty even before their separation at the outbreak of his illness. He filled it with two books and a lighted candle, the symbols which appear repeatedly in his work.

The two chairs certainly have the *character* which Vincent had wanted when he said *everything from the chair to the painting should have character.*   534
Their contrasting nature is so distinct that it is not difficult to accept them as portrayals of the two men.

Gauguin's chair is shaped in an easy, curved movement and painted mainly brown-red and violet; it stands as if on a fancy carpet glimmering in lively colors with red and yellow against a green background. The *elegant*   534
armchair well fits Gauguin's room, the *lady's boudoir.* In his descriptions of   534
the painting Vincent does not mention a very obvious item: the large yellow light shining on the wall. The round shape is like a sun, his symbol of love, which in its conspicuous size gives more and warmer light than the small flame of the candle. This full light, in contrast to the flickering candle *in Gauguin's place,* might also express Vincent's insight into the inner dis-   626a
parity of their relationship. The light shining from above recalls the large crescent and star in the background of the portrait of Milliet, while the two books and the candle remind us of the "Open Bible" in his dark period in Holland (plate 15) when they had symbolized his feelings towards his father. Now, in "Gauguin's Chair" of which he speaks as an *effect of night,* the   563
lights and the books stress the portrayal of his emotional and spiritual companionship with Gauguin.

The other painting shows Vincent's chair, which he called *the day*   563
and its *companion piece.* It is in every respect a contrast, painted in pale yellow, a chair of plain, unpolished wood, heavy and rough, straight backed and without armrests. A real clumsy peasant's chair, the sturdy legs straddled, it stands on the bare floor of plain square tiles — very much like Vincent himself in his austerity. On the seat lie a pipe and some tobacco on a crumpled pouch. In "Gauguin's Chair" the symbolic round light on the wall is much stronger than the flame of the candle. But Vincent's pipe lying unlit and cold on his own chair expresses virile inferiority and frustration when compared with the erect lighted candle in Gauguin's place.

59. VINCENT'S CHAIR (THE DAY)

140

60. GAUGUIN'S CHAIR (EFFECT OF NIGHT)

The pale yellow chair suggests Vincent's loneliness in a particularly impressive way. It is painted in his color of love but stands in the middle of the room, without touching anything. A complete vacuum around the chair —between all its contours and the edges of the canvas—accentuates the isolation, as if to convey his solitude in his own house.

It was in connection with Gauguin's coming that he had written to
493 Theo: *"One always loses when one is isolated."* We may also remember his
351 words *isolation is like a prison* in a letter from Nuenen (page 36). At that time he had placed his name within the chair of the young man in the "Potato Eaters" (plate 12). He now adds a coffin-like box to his chair and writes his name in dark letters within its contours. It is like a reiteration that
133 *the prison,* of which he had complained in the Borinage and Holland, was still latent in him, the same prison which in the "Fishing Boats at Saintes-Maries" was indicated by his name inside the box on the beach. Yet in "Vincent's Chair" too, there is still hope, expressed by the onion sprouting from the box, his cage of imprisonment.

While Vincent portrayed himself in his own chair, in the companion piece he painted his friend — as he saw him. Thus also "Gauguin's Chair" is a self-portrayal of Vincent, conveying his own urges and thoughts. Although the chair was used by Gauguin during his stay in Arles, it belonged to Vincent. He had bought it for the house and one may assume that he had sometimes sat in it.

When he wrote to Theo in December about the two chairs, he mentioned
563 *he could not return to the Goupils with an innocent painting like the "Blossoming Pear Tree."* Love and frustration were then depicted together by the young, charming tree with the trunk in violet and brown-red contours, and the stump in yellow. He now uses the same contrasting colors, though
534 much stronger, for Gauguin's arm chair in the *lady's boudoir,* and his own severe and isolated chair. The three paintings are examples of the recurring portrayal of these contrasts, much as the subjects of his work may vary. The opposing nature of the two chairs was actually a reflection of Vincent him-
563 self, at which he hinted when describing them as *day* and *night.* The complementary contrasts of light and dark were naturally within him, and therefore, the companion pieces taken together portray his inner condition — and the relationship with Gauguin as an immanent part of it — at the outbreak of his illness.

142

SELF-PORTRAIT WITH THE BANDAGED EAR

Vincent's attempt to find a substitute for Theo — and thus to alleviate his inner dependence on his brother — had failed. The acute disappointment over Gauguin threw him even more strongly back on Theo, but a great change was then taking place in Theo's life. A few days before Christmas he had become engaged, and he and his fiancée intended to go to Holland for the holidays. Vincent's reaction to this event may best be understood by a later letter in which he asked Theo *to transfer the affection* [which he had 585 for Vincent] *to his wife*. Theo, his only stronghold, now no longer belonged to him, just when he was in so great a need. No wonder this could have brought to a climax his feeling of loneliness and abandonment which his overstrained nerves would not bear.

For some time he had complained about his health, and shortly before Gauguin's arrival, he wrote to Theo that *he must beware of his nerves*. He 556 had worked relentlessly and under enormous stress during that hot summer in Arles, with its harassing mistral wind. He was not used to such burning heat; his eyes gave him trouble and he also suffered from an old ailment of the stomach. He had lived very austerely, with no relaxation, and there was nobody to look after him. In the same letter, he had expressed fear that *he would without doubt fall ill if he did not take good strengthening food and stop painting for a few days. If he had not somewhat of a double nature like that of a monk and of a painter, he would long ago have been completely and utterly reduced to madness.*

According to Gauguin [20], the night before Christmas Eve they were in a café when Vincent suddenly threw a glass of absinthe at his head, but missed him. He took Vincent home, where he immediately fell asleep. Next morning

143

61. SELF-PORTRAIT WITH THE BANDAGED EAR

Vincent very calmly offered his apologies, which Gauguin readily accepted, telling him, however, that such a scene could happen again and if he were hurt he might retaliate. Therefore he had decided to advise Theo that it would be better for him to leave. In the evening, after dinner, he went for a stroll alone. Suddenly he heard quick steps and saw Vincent rushing towards him with an open razor in his hand. Gauguin continues his report: "My look at that moment must have been very powerful because he stopped and, lowering his head, ran back to the house. Was I a coward in that moment, and should I not have disarmed and tried to quieten him? I have often asked my conscience and never reproached myself. Throw the stone whoever wants to." While Gauguin went to sleep in a hotel, Vincent returned to his house and, with the razor, cut off part of his left ear. He wrapped it in paper, took it to a brothel, and left it for a girl there; in the ensuing tumult his friend, the postman, rushed him home and put him to bed.

Gauguin then describes his visit the next morning to Vincent's house, outside which the police and a crowd of people had gathered. The two rooms on the ground floor, as well as the stairs leading up to Vincent's bedroom, were soiled with blood, and so was the bedroom, where many blood-stained towels were lying about. He did not wait to speak to Vincent who was asleep, and was later taken to a hospital. Gauguin sent for Theo, but he himself left Arles after some days without seeing his friend again. Theo, instead of going to Holland with his fiancée, came to Arles and stayed a few days with Vincent, who was able to leave the hospital about two weeks later. Shortly afterwards Vincent painted the "Self-Portrait with the Bandaged Ear" (plate 61), which he mentions in his letter to Theo of January 17, 1889.   571

We are at once caught by the gripping sadness of his eyes. The distance between them seems narrower than usual, as if strain and pain had drawn them closer together, thus increasing the expression of suffering that his grave, straight look transmits to us. Contrasted by the dark blue fur cap which is deep-set on his forehead, and the white bandage over the wound, the face is very pale. The mouth firmly holding a pipe between the lips shows tense determination. He wears a green jacket outlined in yellow and black. The background is divided in two, the lower part red and the upper orange ; the line of the horizon is exactly at the level of his eyes. The tension in this portrait is greatly increased by the extraordinary rendering of Vincent's breath and of the smoke from his pipe. They are in yellow spirals which rise above the horizon. His recurrent motif of struggle is apparent in the dark strokes from the fur cap in front and above the bandaged ear, stabbing against the sky.

The line of the horizon separating earth and heaven, the infinite life line of circular movement, so prominent in some of Vincent's other paintings, acquires a rare significance by running precisely at the height of his eyes. As if going through them, it becomes a symbol of transcending lucidity, of his deep perception of the incident; an insight arming him with almost superhuman strength and courage to present himself in this condition.

145

Whenever Vincent painted a self-portrait, it was in order to place before his own eyes, and thus to make more objective, his search into himself. In this portrait he renders an uncompromising and merciless account of what he saw, and so documents this momentous experience on his road of life: the appalling affliction which had befallen him. It is an image of his suffering — his own Ecce Homo.

The spiral symbol appears in this painting for the first time. From now on it is often repeated in curls or waves, most strikingly in the St. Rémy landscapes (plates 70, 71) and particularly in the "Starry Night" (plate 79). One may perceive the meaning of the spiral in Vincent's portrait if it is kept in mind that in several basic languages the words meaning breath and soul are the same: in Greek psyche, in Hebrew neshama, in Indian atman. As his breath crosses the line of the horizon, his soul rises above the life line to the sky. It is of great importance that this takes place at the level of his eyes, of sight and consciousness, at the very level where the blood-red earth threatens to submerge him. This red contrasted by the green of the coat, recalls an earlier letter saying that *by red and green he sought to express the terrible human passions*. But against the negative act of destruction imparted by the bandage is the positive reaction of the rising spirals. Their bright yellow, Vincent's color of light and love, lightens the blood-red of the earth and changes it into the orange of the sky. Yet the spirals have one more function. They link the lower and upper parts of the divided background. They symbolize his spiritual force, and their uniting movement signifies the beginning of a tenacious battle against the disintegration which the divided background conveys. They emphasize Vincent's rising into his spiritual sphere, with the life of the soul becoming ever more predominant.

He undertook this fight against disintegration in full consciousness and with the greatest determination. The three hundred paintings and many hundred drawings and sketches he did in the nineteen months from the first attack of his illness until his death are proof of this fight. Many of these works have had extraordinary influence and have attained wide fame in the generations which followed his own. There can be no doubt that the import and greatness of his art was not diminished but fully maintained, if not increased, after the outbreak of the illness. Vincent's spiritual and physical control of his creative capacity, which was indispensable for achieving his magnificent work, certainly makes his case an uncommon one; it still challenges medical diagnosis.[21]

146

In the over one hundred letters he wrote during that time we often find unusual judgment and foresight. In many of them he dealt with his illness. Some extracts from these passages will not only show his own attitude towards this fateful phase in his life, but may throw some light on the nature of his predicament. At first, when he was still in the hospital, he tried to minimize the severity of the illness. His principal object apparently was to reassure Theo about his health. But when the attacks recurred, he often became very depressed and his letters vary from optimism to despair.

"*The worst thing to fear,*" he wrote when he had left the hospital, "*would be insomnia ... the doctor has not spoken to me about it, nor have I spoken to him about it yet. But I am fighting it myself.*" He hoped he had just suffered *simply an artist's fit.* A few weeks later, in another letter to Theo, he expressed astonishment about his getting so well: "*Before, I well knew that one could break one's arms and legs and recover afterwards. But I did not know that one could break one's brain and recover from that too... If I am not mad, the hour will come — when I shall send you what I have promised you from the beginning. Now, the paintings will perhaps inevitably be dispersed, but when you for one will see the whole of what I want, you will perceive, I dare hope, a consoling impression of it.*" 570
569
574

Another though minor attack in February brought him again for a short while to the hospital. It was after he had recovered from this and had resumed work with vigor that the mayor of Arles gave way to some towns-people who demanded his confinement because they feared they might be harmed by possible new outbreaks. This forcible detention was quite unwarranted as Vincent was in full control of himself.

For over a month he was kept in a hospital cell. Although he felt greatly humiliated, he proved himself above the situation and showed outstanding self-restraint throughout that agonizing experience. The first three weeks he maintained complete silence and then wrote to Theo: "*Yet the fact is that here I am shut up for long days under lock and key and wardens in a cell without my guilt being proved or even provable. Needless to say, in the inner forum of my soul I have much to say against all that. Needless to say, I shall not get angry and it seems in that case to excuse myself would mean to accuse myself.*" He continued in a second letter: "*As far as I can judge I am not mad, properly speaking. You will see that the canvases I have done in the intervals are calm and not inferior to the others. I miss the work more than it tires me... If they should continue, these repeated and unexpected emotions*" 579
580

147

may change a passing and momentary mental disturbance into a chronic disease. I am sure, if nothing intervenes, I should now be able to do the same and perhaps better work in the orchards than I did last year."

Vincent felt certain that the best weapon against his illness was his work. Again and again he stressed this conviction, between many intermittent periods of great depression; in one of them he wrote to his friend Signac, an Impressionist painter he knew from Paris who had visited him while he was still detained in the Arles hospital: *"But at times it is not all too easy for me to begin living again, for there remain with me inner despairs of quite big caliber. My goodness, those anxieties ... who can live in the modern world without catching his share of them. The best consolation, if not the only remedy, it seems to me, are still the deep friendships, even though they have the disadvantage of anchoring us more firmly in life than would appear to us advisable in the days of great suffering."*

In a following letter to Theo he expressed fear of losing his ability to work if he were to force on himself the burden of a studio, again living alone, while sharing it with another artist had proved so difficult that he would not even think about it. For the time being he wished to remain confined, *"...as much for my own quietness as for other people's. What consoles me a little is that I am beginning to consider madness as an illness like any other and accept the thing as such, while during the attacks themselves, it seemed to me that everything I imagined was real."* Yet in the same letter he pointed out that *he would not exactly have chosen madness if he had had a choice.*

Theo had just got married. His fiancée had asked whether Vincent could not live with them or with his mother and sisters in Holland, but previous experience had proved this to be impossible. Vincent himself was uncertain what he should do, go into a mental hospital or perhaps join the French Foreign Legion: *"If I talk about enlisting for five years, don't go thinking that I am doing this with the idea of sacrificing myself or of doing a good deed. I have been "in a hole" ["mal pris"] all my life and my mental condition not only is but also has been abstruse [abstrait] ... I cannot think out how to balance my life. Where I have to follow a rule as here in the hospital I feel quiet. And in the army it would be more or less the same. Now if here I would certainly run a great risk of being refused because they know that I am mad or epileptic probably for good (according to what I have heard, there are 50,000 epileptics in France of whom only 4,000 are confined, and so it is not extraordinary), perhaps in Paris I should soon be arranged [casé]."*

When he had entered the asylum at St. Remy, he wrote in one of his first   592
letters from there of his observation that *other patients too had heard strange
sounds and voices and that things seemed to change for them during the
attacks.* He continued: *"And that lessens the horror that I retained at first of
the attack I had and which, when it comes on you unaware, cannot but
frighten you beyond measure. Once one knows that this is in the illness, one
takes it like anything else... Most epileptics bite their tongue and injure themselves. Rey told me that he had seen a case where someone had injured his
ear as I did... I dare think that once you know what it is, once you are
conscious of your condition and of being subject to attacks, then you can do
something yourself in order not to be overtaken so much by agony or fright."*
Two weeks later he wrote again: *"It is strange that each time I try to reason*   594
*and to give an account to myself of why I have come here and that, after all,
it is only an accident, a terrible fright and terror seizes me and prevents me
from thinking. It is true that this tends vaguely to diminish but it also seems
to me to prove that there is definitely something, I don't know what, deranged
in my brain, but it is stupifying to be so afraid of nothing and to be unable
to remember things. But you can count on it that I shall do all I can to become
active again and perhaps useful, at least in the sense that I want to do better
paintings than before."*

After a spell of attacks in the asylum, he asked Theo: *"You will perhaps*   601
*do well to write a word to Dr. Peyron to say that the work at my paintings is
somewhat necessary for me to recover, for these days, without doing anything
and without being able to go to the room he has allotted to me for my painting,
are almost unbearable for me."* *"The work distracts me infinitely better than*   602
*anything else and if I could once throw myself really into it with all my
energy, that would possibly be the best remedy."* He later reiterated: *"I am*   604
*struggling with all my energy to master my work, saying to myself that if
I win, that will be the best lightning conductor against the illness... And
what's to be done, there is no cure, or if there is one, it is to work with
ardor... And altogether I would rather have a downright illness like this
than to be as I was in Paris when this was brewing."* After a year's experience
in the asylum he expressed a poor opinion on the therapy, or rather lack of
therapy, given to the patients there: *"Besides, I should make a change in any*   632
*case as I prefer to be in an asylum where the patients work, to this horrible
idleness here which really seems to be simply a crime."*

When Vincent had written to Theo, before Gauguin's arrival at Arles,

that he *should beware of his nerves* and about his *double nature of a painter*
556 *and a monk,* he had added: *"Yet, even then I do not think that my madness
would be one of persecution since my feelings in the state of exaltation lead
me rather to preoccupations with eternity and eternal life."* A year later he
605 wrote to him from St. Rémy: *"Well, with the mental disease I have I think
of so many other artists who suffer morally and I say to myself that this does
not prevent one from exercising a painter's profession as if nothing were
amiss. When I see that here the attacks tend to take an absurd religious turn,
I should almost dare to think that this even necessitates a return to the North.
Don't talk too much about that with the doctor when you see him ... but I
don't know if this doesn't come from living so many months in the hospital
of Arles and here in these old cloisters. Enfin, I must not live in such surroundings; in that case the street would be better. I am not indifferent and
in the suffering itself sometimes religious thoughts greatly console me."* At
W 14 that time he told his sister: *"Sometimes I also feel inwardly as having the
soul very troubled..."*

The domination of Vincent's life by emotional and spiritual forces rather
than by material factors had been implied in his repeated assertions, such as
226, R 43 his art was the means *for expressing his feelings* or *art welled up from a
deeper source out of our soul,* also when he spoke of *a great hidden force*
185 *of working and creating, which once roused was roused forever.* These were
intimations that he was following an inner lead, the origin of which he did
not know: the unknown source of creativeness. It may be assumed that this
driving force, because of its enormous strength in Vincent's case, had broken
through the limits of human nature and thus had become a main cause of
his crisis. But this great *hidden force* also gave his art that amazing vitality,
the impact of which we feel today, as we share, consciously or unconsciously, the very elements that governed his life.

The affinity between his self-awareness and our own, as it seems to have
developed in recent years, is evident in a statement which he made during
581 his detention in the Arles hospital: *"Must I suffer imprisonment or the
madhouse, why not? Didn't Rochefort, Hugo, Quinet and others give the
eternal example by suffering exile and the first even a convict prison? But
all I want to say is that this is beyond the question of illness or health...
And that is what the first and last cause of my aberration was. Do you know
this expression of a Dutch poet: 'I am bound to the earth by more than
earthly ties.' That is what I have experienced in much anguish—above all—*

150

in my so-called mental illness." His approach to his inner condition as to something *beyond the question of illness or health* in fact went in the direction of today's psychological thinking in extending beyond the regular framework of medicine where answers to psychological problems have so far remained palliative.

Vincent's longing for a greater depth of insight is borne out by further letters. In 1882 he had written to Theo from The Hague: "*I mean, something* 252 *depresses me because I feel a force in me which by the circumstances cannot develop as at other times, and this results in my often being miserable. A kind of inner struggle about what I must do.*" After his separation from Christine in the following year, he again wrote to Theo: "*I must once look into my* 332 *own past for what might have been the cause that for years I have been in this stony, arid mood, and although I tried to get out of it, it always became worse instead of better. Not only did I feel hardened towards nature instead of being perceptive but much worse still the same towards people. They told me I was mad but I myself felt that I was not because deep within me I felt my suffering and tried to remedy it.*" At Nuenen he had impressed on his friend Van Rappard: "*And always I believe that in the depths there are* R 41 *things which would distress us if we would know them.*"

At the end of his stay in Arles, he admitted to Theo: "*I feel deeply that* 586 *this has been working in me for a very long time already and that others, noticing symptoms of derangement, have naturally had apprehensions better founded than the certainty I thought I had of thinking normally, which was not the case.*" Later, in St. Rémy, he repeated: "*You will tell me — what I say* 602 *to myself too — that the fault must be within me and not in the circumstances or other people. Enfin, it is not funny.*" Yet soon afterwards he contradicted himself: "*You understand I have tried to compare the second crisis with the* 605 *first, and I only tell you that it seems to me to be I know not what influence from the outside rather than a cause coming from within me. I may be wrong but whatever it may be, I believe you will find it right that I have got a slight horror of all religious exaggeration.*" And to his sister he wrote from the asylum: "*We know life but little, we are so unaware of what lies beneath it.*" W 13 All these observations would seem to exemplify that *tendency to analyze* 237 *things* of which Vincent had written to Theo.

Shortly before his death he said he wanted to do portraits *which would* W 22 *appear to the people of a later century like apparitions.* This certainly applies to the "Self-Portrait with the Bandaged Ear." As one of his most outstanding

151

and stirring works, it has aroused the concern and stimulated the imagination of many. An interesting comment made a few years ago by J. Olivier of St. Rémy warrants attention because of its typical nature.[22]

There were bull fights in the Roman arena in Arles, to which Vincent went sometimes. He wrote to Theo about the scene, and once made a painting of the crowds. According to Monsieur Olivier, after the matador had shown particular skill in the killing of the bull, he was awarded one of the bull's ears. He carried it around the arena as his trophy and presented it to a lady of his choice in the audience. Monsieur Olivier concludes: "I am absolutely convinced that Van Gogh was strongly impressed by this custom. So that the two acts (cutting off the ear and then offering it to a lady) are in no way incoherent, but follow very well a normal linking for someone who knows this custom. Van Gogh cut off the ear, his own ear, as if he were at the same time the vanquished bull and the triumphant matador. A confusion in one person of the vanquished and the victor. This is often the case with all of us. It was certainly the case with Van Gogh that night when he was over-excited by Gauguin, but when he rejected his domination. Personally I see in this a thrusting back and then a courageous and magnificent exaltation which ends in calm and appeasement of which the portrait of the man with the severed ear is a testimony."

A 13

However, when Monsieur Olivier drew his convincing conclusion he seemed to have ignored the fact that the bulls were not killed in the fights as the time Van Gogh was in Arles. Consequently, he could not have witnessed that Spanish custom which was introduced there only later. He may have heard about it but there is no mention of it in his letters. On the other hand, he had written to Bernard in June 1888: *"Then ... I feel quite an ox — being a painter — and I admire a bull, an eagle, a man, with a veneration that will prevent me from being ambitious."* In earlier letters he had referred to St. Luke as the protector of the painters and to the ox as his symbol. Vincent's identification with an ox — the castrated animal — who admires the bull is symptomatic of his feeling of inferiority.

B 9

For an analysis of the effect of the self-portrait, it is quite irrelevant whether Vincent had knowledge of the described custom or not. What is important is whether the beholder's impressions reflect the inner situation prevailing in Vincent when he painted this portrait.

The assertion that two such opposites as aggression and submission can exist in one person is in line with general experience; like elements of love

152

and hate, they are traceable in every ambivalent attitude. Moreover, aggression in itself contains the seed of self-destruction, and these two contrasts also are closely connected.

Notwithstanding Monsieur Olivier's mistaken reference to the bull fights, he accurately perceives Vincent's inner condition, which had shown itself in aggression against Gauguin, in self-mutilation and submission to a woman by offering her the sacrificed ear. His impression of a magnificent exaltation brings back the symbolic meaning of the spirals in the self-portrait, of Vincent's rising above the level of bodily limitations. It is remarkable that one should say that cutting off the ear and giving it to a woman is a normal linking and that confusion between the vanquished and the victor is often the case with all of us. These words express Monsieur Olivier's identification with Vincent's conflict, at a time when confusion marks the state of mind of our whole age. His generalization is all the more interesting as it connotes a widespread sympathy in the world with Van Gogh, the painter, and to no less a degree with the man.

Further passages from the abundance of Vincent's letters seem to be relevant here. In May 1888, when he was painting the flowering orchards in Arles, he had written to Theo about the harassing life in Paris from which he had emerged a few months earlier. *"My poor friend,"* he said, *"our* 481 *neurosis etc. certainly also comes from our somewhat too artistic way of life, but it is also a fatal heritage, since in civilization, one is getting weaker from generation to generation."*

Vincent was convinced that they belonged to those *suffering from a* 481 *neurosis which came from far back.* A few weeks after his release from the hospital, when he had recovered from the incident with Gauguin, he wrote: *"Everybody one day will perhaps have neurosis, the horla, St. Vitus's dance* 574 *or something else. But the antidote, does it not exist? in Delacroix, in Berlioz, and Wagner? And true, our artistic madness, of all of us, I don't say that I especially am not hit by it to the very marrow, but I say and shall maintain that our antidotes and consolations can with a little goodwill be considered as amply prevailing."*

62. STILL LIFE ON A DRAWING BOARD

154

The *antidote* in the artist, Vincent's creative release in his art, armed him   574
with the strength to fight against the increasing threat of mental disintegration. The day he returned from the Arles hospital to his house, where
he was alone once more, he wrote to Theo: *"I am going to set to work again*   569
tomorrow; I shall begin by doing one or two still lifes so as to get into the
habit of painting again."

In "Still Life on a Drawing Board" (plate 62) a big yellow and orange
drawing board is shown with a variety of familiar objects. In the center lie
some onions in and beside a soup plate. Behind is a large green earthenware
pot. A lighted candle near the right hand upper corner and a bottle in the
extreme left foreground stand diagonally opposite each other. Below the
candle, at the side of the dish, lie a book and in front of it a letter. A box of
matches and a stick of red sealing wax are next to the candle. To the right
of the bottle are Vincent's tobacco pouch and his pipe.

This still life is an outstanding example — like the "Breakfast Table"
and the "Bedroom" — of how Vincent, in some of his most characteristic
works, painted subjects of equivalent symbolic meaning in pairs of alternative
forms: the pot and the deep dish, the candle and the bottle, two onions in
the dish, another two, one at either side, the book and the letter, the pipe
and the sealing stick, the tobacco and the matches. Apart from the conspicuous
male symbols, such as the candle and the tall bottle, and the female symbols
— the pot and the deep dish — all the other objects too are in analogous
positions. The accuracy of the doubling and pairing is so striking that we
cannot help feeling that we have before us one of Vincent's most compelling

155

portrayals of his ever-persistent yearning for companionship, and even more so of his inner urge to bring together those divided elements within him that the symbols convey.

Vincent's approach to symbolism has been noted from previous quo-
531 tations (pages 17, 69, 71.) When he interpreted *the ardor of a being by the radiance of a setting sun,* he did not make use of *delusive optical realism.* It was in a different way that he expressed *something really existing.* His thoughts about symbols and reality were even more directly imparted in a letter to Theo from Nuenen: *"As to Poussin he is a painter who thinks in*
425 *everything, and who makes one think, in whose paintings all reality is at the same time symbol. Also in the works of Millet and Lhermitte, all reality is at the same time symbol. They are something different from what one calls realists."* He never ceased to admire Millet and when he re-created other painters' works he mostly chose his. In decided contrast are Vincent's remarks
444 on Rubens, of whom he said: *"Nothing grieves me less than Rubens as regards the expressing of human sorrow."* Much as he liked his combination of colors he strongly criticized him: *"You will understand what I mean, that for instance his piece of 8 bloated figures of fellows, who perform a tour de force with a heavy wooden cross in the "Elevation of the Cross" seems absurd to me as soon as I take a standpoint of modern analysis of human passions and feelings."*

The existence of symbolism, which Vincent recognized in the art of
623 painters like Millet, whose drawings he later *translated into the language of*
425 *color,* made his own work no less *different from the realists,* in spite of or perhaps because of its apparent simplicity. The way Vincent worked is significant of the close tie between the symbols in his art and his inner condition. He repeatedly touched in his letters on this essential quality of his work. In his early Dutch period when he was still only drawing, he had already
181 stressed " ... *the direct and fatal connection between the inner struggle of the artist's private life and the peculiar difficulties which the producing of a work of art brings with itself."* He had then compared the work of an artist with
181 *a woman in childbirth.*

233 Shortly after he had started to paint he wrote to Theo: *"I believe that one thinks much more soundly if the thoughts arise from direct contact with things, than if one looks at things with the aim of finding this or that in them. It is the same with the question of coloring. There are colors which of themselves do beautifully against one another, but I do my best to make*

156

it as I see it before I set to work, to do it as I feel it. And yet feeling is a great thing and without it one would not carry out anything. Sometimes I long for harvest time, that is, for the time when I shall be so imbued with the study of nature that I can myself create something in a painting. However, analyzing things is no burden to me nor something I don't like to do."

In another letter at that time he asked: *"What is drawing? How does one get at it? It is working oneself through an invisible iron wall that seems to stand between what one feels and what one can do."* Dealing with the intricate relation between imagination and reality he said: *"I see no other way than to work with a model. One should be sure not to extinguish one's power of imagination, but just the constantly having nature before one's eyes and wrestling with it sharpens the power of imagination and makes it more right."* Working from life was Vincent's basic principle. The few experiments when, under the influence of Gauguin, he painted from imagination alone were soon discontinued. In the asylum at St. Rémy, whenever he could not work outside nor have models, he preferred to paint after the works of other artists to whom he felt close, rather than from mere imagination.

To work from life meant for Vincent actually to experience, to live, the subject — the *motif,* as he called it. In this respect his disputes with the teachers at the Academy in Antwerp *who wanted to mechanize* him are characteristic. He drew and painted from the center and was decidedly opposed to the academic routine approach of working from the contours, producing *correct but dead drawings.* For him the center was the essential, not the contours; the heart of the matter, not the periphery, was his principal concern and a determining factor in his art as it was in his life.

We recall his repeated claim that it was *life he wanted to achieve in his work.* In the autumn of 1883, when he worked in the countryside of Drenthe, he had told Theo: *"You see, I merely grab into it and catch hold of one thing or the other; it will later by itself get in order and be clarified. But I do not want to begin here with a predesigned plan, but on the contrary, I want my plan to clarify from my studies."* Earlier he had written from The Hague: *"And one must be so deeply absorbed in it that within a short time something is created on the paper or the canvas, where at first there was nothing, so that later one hardly knows oneself how one hammered it off. The time for reasoning and deliberating must go before the resolute action. During the doing itself there is little room for deliberating and reasoning."*

237
238
450
452
408, 418
332
197

Particularly enlightening is a statement he made at the time he painted
427 the "Open Bible" in Nuenen: *"That is something different from feeling,*
i.e., undergoing impressions; it lies between experiencing impressions and
analyzing them, i.e., one takes them apart and puts them together again —
and that perhaps very often. But it is pleasant to dash something off on the
wing." The apparent contradiction may be understood by what he had said
507 after painting the "Sower," that *the canvases were done quickly and followed*
quickly one after the other but they were calculated long in advance. One
should also not forget his assertion that in the beauty of nature the painting
543, B 22 came to him *as in a dream* and that *he worked almost like a sleepwalker*
(pages 76, 103, 123). As a matter of fact, in dreams one particular situation or
experience may appear in repeated symbolic pictures of varying but equivalent
forms and expressions. Similarly in art, different symbols of the same meaning
can portray one and the same motif. In both cases such repetitions underline
the importance of the experience or the motif. This applies in an extraordinary
manner to the "Still Life on a Drawing Board."

From Vincent's letter of January 7, 1889 one must assume that he painted
this canvas before he resumed work on the two "Chairs" and also before he
did the "Self-Portrait with the Bandaged Ear." As one of his very first works
upon his return from the hospital, the painting is especially indicative of his
state of mind at that crucial stage. Against this background a still closer study
appears to be called for, to ascertain to what extent the simple, everyday
objects in this still life mean more than their material origin and purpose.

The large green earthenware pot behind the board is complemented by
the tall bottle in front, which is like its counterpart and painted in the same
color. They both stand outside the board; in fact neither is wholly inside
the painting, but both are cut off by its edges. This symbolic pair of female
and male is repeated on the board by the deep dish and the candle. Their
main colors are white and blue and unlike the other pair they are both
entirely within the composition. It is notable that the candle is lighted,
although broad daylight spreads over the canvas from the left, as seen by
the shadows.

In a distinct contrast to the two large male symbols, the erect bottle and
the lighted candle, are their smaller counterparts — Vincent's unlit pipe and
the stick of sealing wax, both of which lie flat on the board. Likewise the
female symbols, the tobacco pouch and the box of matches, are much smaller
than the soup plate and the pot. Thus not only the male symbols, as well as

158

their female counterparts, are seen in equal numbers in both a large and a small scale, but the pipe with the pouch and the sealing stick with the match-box are again repetitions of the large male and female pairs, the bottle and the pot, the candle and the dish.

The dish in the center of the board holds two sprouting onions. They are repeated at both sides and their sprouts are shooting upward in a motion similar to the flame of the candle. After his destructive attack on himself, Vincent's acute problem, survival and recovery, is portrayed by the central subject: the dish with the onions in full growth, with their lively sprouts symbolizing motive force derived from the urge to live. But the onion on the right is small and undeveloped in comparison with the other three large, vigorous onions. It lies near-by on a book dealing with matters of health, the *Annuaire de la Santé* (Annual of Health).[23] By its position and stunted size the little onion seems to complement his inner picture of simultaneous vitality and impediment. This portrayal is repeated by the composition of the other objects: the large but cut-off pair of bottle and pot, the small inferior pairs lying at the foot of the lighted candle, symbol of virility, and next to the dish with the onions symbolizing fertility.

The definition of the doubled and paired objects as male and female symbols follows the interpretation already given of works like the "Almond Twig," "Pear Tree," "Breakfast Table" and the "Bedroom". The terms male and female should not, however, be taken in the limited sense of sex alone, but to connote other qualities — corresponding to male and female — such as active and passive, productive and receptive, positive and negative; they may well be extended to light and dark, conscious and unconscious, body and soul. Further examples for such portrayal of contrasts were the two versions of the "Sower," the "House in Arles," and the "Self-Portrait with the Band-aged Ear."

The "Still-Life on a Drawing Board" not only joins all those works but, by its downright — one could almost call it mathematical — exactness of doubling and pairing, reaches a peak in the portrayal of Vincent's fundamen-tal plight: the uniting of his inner contrasts. His statement *to perhaps very*   427
often take apart and put together again impressions undergone — between
experiencing and analyzing them seems to indicate his awareness of this task.
It bears out his *seeking behind the curtains, just the quality a painter must*   237
have (page 76), namely, to seek that *great hidden force of creating and*   185
working to which he had referred by saying *art wells up from a deeper*   R 43

159

source out of our soul. These conceptions are remarkably close to recent psychological research that sees a correlation of symbolism in art and myth with images and motives in the human psyche, and recognizes elements of male and female in every being.

In this still life the book and the letter also are of symbolic importance. Their position on the drawing board reminds us of the Nuenen painting with the Bible and the *Joie de Vivre.* Now the topic of the book is health, and the letter from Theo touches it on a common line, thus suggesting an association of the two objects of a literary nature. They again are like a pair, both painted in the same minute detail: the book cover with the full title and the name of the author, the envelope with Vincent's address in Theo's handwriting and all the stamps and postmarks of a registered letter. A burnt match lies on it as if in derogatory contrast.

Health, the book's subject, is vividly discussed in Vincent's correspondence with Theo. In the letter of January 7, 1889, advising Theo of his
568   return home, he wrote: *"Thanks for your last letter, indeed I feel you always present, but you should know also on your part that I am working on the same thing as yourself."* He apologized for all the trouble and expense and for having *perhaps involuntarily* been the cause of Theo's delaying his trip with his fiancée, and continued: *"You have no idea how much I regret that your journey to Holland has not yet come off. Write me soon and be entirely reassured about my health, it will completely cure me to know that things go well with you."*

Two days later he wrote that he was physically well but that he had been afraid to sleep alone in the house because of insomnia. He had suffered from it in previous years, and it had become worse while he was in the
570   hospital. He tried to *combat it himself by placing strong doses of camphor in his pillow and mattress,* recommending Theo to do likewise in case of need. This remedy was actually prescribed in the *Annuaire de la Santé.*

In the next letter, dated January 17, he accounts for an increase in expenses due to his illness. He complains that since January 8 he had been left
571   without money: *"I hoped for a letter from you about the tenth, now as this letter did not arrive until today, January 17, the time between has been a most rigorous fast, all the more painful as my recovery was impossible under such conditions."* This had added *some more suffering and anguish; he felt weak and somewhat disquieted and fearful but hoped it would pass if he would regain his strength.* In the same letter he repeated his complaint when

160

63. PORTRAIT OF DR. REY

he mentioned a meeting with the physician of the hospital: *"Rey told me that to be very impressionable was enough for the attack I had and that I was actually only anaemic, but that really I must get nourishment. But I took the liberty of telling Mr. Rey, if at present the first thing for me had been to regain my strength, if by a great chance or misunderstanding moreover a rigorous fast of one week had just happened to me, if in similar circumstances he had already seen many madmen fairly quiet and able to work, and if not, that he should deign to remember occasionally that for the moment I am not yet mad."*

By January 17 Vincent had completed three new canvases, most likely still lifes, as they were all done in the studio. He had also painted a "Portrait of Dr. Rey" (plate 63) as well as the "Self-Portrait with the Bandaged Ear," and had further started to work anew on the two "Chairs." This output
569 proves how quickly he *got into the habit of painting again.*

On January 9 or 10 he had entirely run out of money and borrowed a trifle of five francs while waiting from day to day for Theo's letter. He later admitted that the unfortunate delay was not Theo's fault. But the reproaches in his letter of January 17 reflect his contrasting feelings when compared with the regrets he had expressed in the earlier letters. Nevertheless he
571 repeated: *"I was distressed that just at this moment you should have these expenses which did nobody any good."*

The close connection between the regaining of his health and a letter from Theo was quite clear in Vincent's mind; there was still more to it, for another embarrassment awaited him on his return to his house. He heard that during his absence the proprietor had made arrangements to let it to someone else. When he wrote to Theo about this, he tried not to appear too
570 worried. In any case he was determined to oppose *his being almost shamefully turned out of the house.* This threat was an additional blow, just at the time when Theo was about to make a real home for himself with a wife — Vincent's foremost ideal which he himself could never attain.

As he anxiously awaited Theo's supporting letter, one can well understand
573 that he was *somewhat disquieted and fearful.* Had Theo gone to Holland and forgotten to send the money? After all, it was only natural that his interest should now turn more towards his fiancée and their own future. When Vincent later wrote to wish Theo happiness in his marriage and
585 stressed *how good he had always been to him,* he not only made the suggestion, already quoted, that Theo should *transfer this affection as much as*

162

possible to his wife, but even added that *if they would correspond a little less he hoped she would console him.* Such thoughts were bound to be on Vincent's mind in those days when he was again alone in the house and preoccupied with his situation after Theo's engagement. Sincere as his wishes for Theo were, they only showed one side of his feelings whose ambivalence was again evident in the accusation implied in his letter of January 17. Vincent's *involuntarily* delaying his brother's departure with his fiancée can perhaps best be understood if the word "involuntarily" is read as "unconsciously." In his unconscious, nothing less was at stake than Theo's breaking away from their symbiotic tie, which could not but shake Vincent's existence and contribute profoundly to the crisis. This ambivalent situation is portrayed in the still life in an amazing way: Theo's letter — symbolizing his affection and support — is turned away.

The background, behind the drawing board, is light blue and cut into two parts by a dark blue line. It is covered with many small vertical strokes, yellow above and red below the dividing line. Completing the unity of the three primary colors, they are like countless flakes in a continuous flow from heaven to earth. They give an air of timeless rhythm to the background against which the dramatic composition on the drawing board is recorded.

568

64. LA BERCEUSE

164

LA BERCEUSE

Vincent's inner condition is further brought out by another painting which, like the two "Chairs," he had started before the outbreak of his illness but which he completed only after his return from the hospital. It is "La Berceuse" (Woman Rocking the Cradle), (plate 64). The model was the wife of his friend Roulin, the postman. He did more portraits of Madame Roulin than of any other person. From January to March, 1889, he painted her as the Berceuse five times. Moreover, he did three paintings of her with and without her baby; she also appears on other canvases painted in Arles and St. Rémy. Besides, he had often portrayed her husband and the children.

The Berceuse is a rather stout woman with a fair complexion and orange hair. She wears a green dress and sits in a red armchair. In her hands, clasped on her lap, she holds a yellow cord. At the back of the chair, which resembles Gauguin's armchair, is a red ground, below a green wallpaper with pink dots and gay flowers in pink, yellow and white.

Vincent wrote to a friend that the Berceuse held the cord of the cradle 571a in her hands. In all five paintings the cord lies in the same position, on her lap. It seems to extend out of the frame towards us like a link between the portrait and the beholder as it was between the painter and his model. Whether the cord is used for rocking the cradle or later to guide the infant's first steps, it symbolizes the bond between mother and child. It could even indicate a still closer tie between them, their original unity through the umbilical cord.

There is a pecularity in all five versions of the painting. The line of the horizon lies on two different levels; it suggests the rocking of the cradle or the movement of the horizon as seen from a ship at sea. At the time he was working on "La Berceuse" Vincent wrote to Theo: *"I just said to Gauguin* 574 *about this canvas that when he and I were talking about the fishermen of*

Iceland and their melancholic isolation, exposed to all dangers, alone on the sad sea, I just told Gauguin about it that following these intimate talks the idea came to me to paint such a picture that sailors, who are at the same time children and martyrs, seeing it in the cabin of an Icelandic fishing boat, would experience a feeling of rocking, reminding them of their own lullabys."

582   When he did the portrait for the fifth time he wrote again: *"But after all, I seek to make a picture such as a sailor, who could not paint, would imagine when on the high seas he dreams of a woman on land."*

Vincent often compared himself to a sailor. Once he told Theo that he had been examined by a doctor in Amsterdam who had asked him whether he was a steelworker. He was very proud to have been taken for a workman 442 and added *he looked like one or a boatman,* although the doctor had not 437 said that. He also wrote that the girls in Antwerp had thought he was a seaman. In the Borinage when he had gone down into a mine, he had written 129 *it was like a feeling of being for the first time in a ship at sea.* Now the 574 Berceuse — the mother — was to remind the seamen, *the children and martyrs,* of their infancy in the cradle with *their lullabys.* It is yet another sign of his intention to personify motherhood in "La Berceuse."

Two of the portraits are signed; Vincent painted his name within the contours of the arm of the chair on which the Berceuse is sitting. Earlier works had conveyed his isolation when his signature was enclosed in certain objects like a box, a vase, a frame — all female symbols. The place where he now signed the painting is particularly revealing. In small letters, compared with the large inscription "La Berceuse," the word "Vincent" in the arm of Madame Roulin's chair brings him as close as possible to her, to a mother whom he portrayed so many times. Though not physically inside her body, Vincent is here even more distinctly in an enclosure, immediately at her side. It shows his marginal position in relation to the mother which previous paintings had indicated in a similar manner: the orange cut by the frame in the "Breakfast Table" and the man divided by the wall in the "House in Arles." We also recall the "Potato Eaters" when for the first time we saw Vincent, "enclosed" in the chair, directed towards the mother.

The link between Vincent and his model through the cord, his idea of being a sailor to whom the Berceuse was a mother, and finally the closeness of his name to her body, throw light on his inner situation concerning Madame Roulin. It is as if he wanted to be her child. He had painted all her children, the two sons twice and the baby not less than five times.

166

Towards the end of January, just a month after the catastrophe with Gauguin, he wrote to Theo about "La Berceuse": *"I have in hand the portrait* 573 *of Roulin's wife at which I was working before I was ill... If I could finish it, it would give me great pleasure, but I am afraid that she will no longer pose with her husband absent."* He compared the Roulins with their own parents: *"Whatever I think about them in other points, our father and mother* 573 *have been exemplary as married people. And I shall never forget mother on the occasion of our father's death, when she said only one little word, which, for me, made me recommence to love the old mother more after that. During my illness,"* he went on, *"I saw again every room in the house at Zundert, every path, every plant in the garden, the views of the surrounding fields, the neighbors, the graveyard, the church, our kitchen garden behind — to the magpie's nest in the high acacia in the graveyard. It is because I have still earlier recollections of those first days than any of the rest of you; thus there is no one left to remember all that but mother and me. I do not insist as it is better for me not to try to re-establish all that went through my head then."*

64a. LA BERCEUSE (DETAIL)

The idea of motherhood which "La Berceuse" conveys to us, receives more support from the fact that Vincent's own mother was so much on his mind at the time he worked on these portraits. This directs our interest to his relations with his mother. From his early youth he had been closely attached to the father, but nothing is known about any passionate feeling for the mother. The letters he wrote her, usually only in reply to hers, show a respectful, conventional attitude not to be compared with the deep affection and idolizing admiration he had had for his father. When he took such good care of her

167

during her disablement in Nuenen, he did no more than he had done before for the wounded miners in the Borinage or for anyone who needed help.

Factual knowledge about Vincent's childhood is scarce. The limited information available from various sources is conflicting, except in one respect: he was a difficult child, moody and willful. Generally he did not seek the company of other children and was often alone. He loved plants and animals. His uncongenial behavior may have been a reaction to his early experiences in life, when his first human contact was the mother. He was born exactly one year, to the day, after a first son, also named Vincent, who had died soon after birth. It could well be that this fact had an adverse effect on both mother and child. The stone with an inscription to the dead Vincent was in the graveyard by their house and Vincent may have looked at it frequently. This is assumed by Theo's son, who further comments that, "it must have made a deep impression on the child that he had the same birthday and name as his dead brother; when four years later another son (Theo) was born it might have been like a relief to him, as he showed unusually warm feelings for the little brother. It could have laid the basis for their later friendship." However this may have been, his mother's condition, burdened with the loss of her first son, certainly had a bearing on Vincent's early childhood when his character began to form.

Vincent's sister-in-law wrote in her introduction to the letters that he took more after his mother than his father, and that he had inherited the piercing look of her eyes, her energy and will-power. She seemed to have loved the amiable Theo more than Vincent and her other children. Yet there is no sign of jealousy on Vincent's part.

A passage in one of his letters to Theo from The Hague may have a psychological bearing in this respect. He wrote about Christine, with whom he then lived and whom he wanted to marry, that she reminded him *of a nursemaid who was in their house at Zundert,* when they had been small children. His choice of Christine as his partner and future wife, notwithstanding the fact that she had been a prostitute, was apparently influenced by her likeness to that maid whose name he had not forgotten even after so many years. In another letter from The Hague, referring to their connections with women, Vincent said of a friend of Theo's: "...*she will take your thoughts back to the period ten or twenty years ago, and even further. Enfin, in her you will find yourself again, a piece of your life that you had quickly forgotten, that is to say, the earlier* [piece]."

201

262

168

One of the most remarkable drawings which Vincent had done of Christine at the time he had portrayed her in "Sorrow" (page 28), is seen in plate 65. From a dark background her figure emerges as if it were a design for a

The Great Lady

65. THE GREAT LADY

marble sculpture. She is in an imposing, almost a majestic pose. Her head and the contours of her bust are drawn in sharp, accentuating lines. In contrast to her naked body she wears a hair-dress, rendered like a covering head-cloth in rigid style. Very pronounced are her large, full breasts, stressing the maternal character of this portrait which appears at the same time archaic and modern. Its great difference from "Sorrow" is underlined by an inscription at the bottom, by which Vincent calls his model: The Great Lady.

212 He had then described his relationship with Christine: *"I have a feeling of being* <u>*at home*</u> *when I am with her, a feeling as if she brought me my 'own hearth,' a feeling that we are grown together. It is a tender, deep feeling, earnest and not without a dark shadow from her and my rather somber past. A shadow of which I have already written to you, as if something somber, against which our life should be a constant struggle, were threatening us further."* One may also recall his letter to Theo from Nuenen, in which he

347 wrote that his youth was *somber, cold and sterile under the influence of a black ray* (page 100).

212 These words disclose an inner anxiety of *something somber and threatening,* and his *feeling at home and grown together with her* intimate an unrelieved yearning for the mother. In Vincent's eyes, Christine, in her resemblance to the nursemaid, had evidently assumed the rôle of a successor

262 to the maid, in bringing back to him a *forgotten earlier piece of life* — the replacement of a maternal shelter, or the longing for it, or both. His remarks

573 that he *would rather not try to re-establish the even earlier recollections of those first days that only mother and he could remember,* point to a none too happy early childhood. In those first stages, warmth and security, replacing the pre-natal complete unity with the mother, assist the child to find his way into life. In the course of the child's upbringing, the weaning from the mother, as one of life's inscrutable phases of fate, may both further and hinder the child in processing his manifold heritages and developing his own individuality. When — often for no apparent reason and in spite of the efforts by both child and mother — the emancipation from the mother does not proceed in a harmonious and reassuring manner, an element of fear, arising naturally in a child, may become more firmly implanted. A frequent result is the kind of reactions reported of Vincent's childhood.

The consequences may reach far into the life of the adult who somehow has remained in an inner dependence on the mother. His potentialities do not seem to unfold fully within himself, as if he were not quite freed from the maternal confines, a condition which impedes congruous development. It concerns man and woman alike, since for each of them the first contact in life is with the mother. This original dependence can assume an autonomous state and remain an inherent character trait throughout life. It enters

170

into the relations with other persons; they may be father, brother, sister, husband, wife, child, and other relatives or friends, qualified by and in accordance with the degree of intimacy. No close relationship can then be achieved without that intrusion. In this situation one may try to identify oneself with the person on whom one is dependent in such a way, by putting oneself partly in his place and thus adopting some of the other's qualities, possessions and needs.

But it is an inadequate compensation for the shortcomings emanating from a compulsory inner dependence, and typical of symbiotic associations. An unmistakable sign of their ambivalent nature is a kind of love-hatred, in which the other person is hated, and blamed for one's own deficiencies and difficulties. Such hate is sustained by helplessness and fear of being either absorbed or abandoned by the other person. Yet at the same time one loves him because of the need to lay on some one else the burden of one's own failure which would be too heavy to carry alone. This, however, is more a desire to be loved than love itself, in which the well-being of the beloved is the lover's prime concern. On the contrary, in such a relationship one expects the other to fill the gap in one's own impaired development instead of looking to oneself to attain a higher degree of maturity.

In Vincent's case a symptom of this condition was evident in the ambivalence of his symbiotic tie with Theo. The exuberant admiration he had for his father — who also had to be the first substitute, so to speak, for the mother-ideal — had been a sign of his fervent urge to be like him. It had exceeded in intensity the usual identification between son and father. The stronger this is, the greater the conflict during the process of emancipation. We may recall its symbolic portrayal in the "Open Bible" (plate 15). Vincent alluded to this burdening condition when writing from Nuenen about the nature of his differences with his father: *"I believe that father as well feels it is something of a fatality rather than willful intention ..."* In an almost identical way he wrote about Theo and himself: *"But know that it always appears to me that it is more a fateful difference between us than one for which we ourselves are alone guilty."* He had referred repeatedly to *fatality* in the long letter to Theo from the Borinage, in which he had described himself as *an imprisoned bird.* Later in Arles he tried to explain to Theo *the regret of leaving one's prison* (page 80) by adding: *"... because the grinding daily task of earning one's living hardly leaves any freedom."* In fact, since his ordeal in the Borinage, Theo had increasingly become his provider and the father's

380

379

133

478

171

315 substitute. In some letters Vincent put them together as *you and father,* also
358 saying *he wore Theo's clothes as he did his father's.* A few times he actually
388b called Theo *father No. II.*

His attempts to find happiness with Ursula, Kornelia and Christine were bound to fail, if only because of the pre-eminent maternal aspect the three women had for him. In a letter from London in 1874 [24] he had stressed as his deepest impression of Ursula the tie with her mother: *"I have never seen or dreamed anything like the love between her and her mother."* Kornelia was a mother to a son. Also Christine was a mother and, moreover, had the described particular maternal qualification for Vincent. Once he had written
349 to Theo: *"I see in her a woman, I see in her a mother..."*

It was soon after his separation from Christine that he so persistently and irrationally implored Theo to give up his job so that they could live
338 together in the country as *two painter brothers* (page 45). Some months later
358 he exclaimed in a letter from Nuenen: *"A wife you cannot give me, a child you cannot give me, work you cannot give me. Money, yes."* By this assertion
476 he directly blamed Theo for his own inability to achieve the *true life* with a wife and children. He also expressed his uneasiness about being Theo's protégé
358 and reproached him for not selling his paintings: *"You never sold a single one of mine—not for much or for little—indeed you have not even tried."*

Theo, on his side, had deplored in the letter from Paris that "it was as if two men were in Vincent, one wonderfully gifted, fine and tender, and the other egoistic and hard-hearted; he was his own enemy, making life difficult for others and himself." Vincent admitted later in a letter to his
619 mother from St. Rémy: *"And now I am telling this to you and not to him, it is only good that I did not remain in Paris because we both, he and I, became too lost in each other."*

When Vincent replaced his father by Theo, extending his state of depend-
358 ence from father to brother, the women with whom *father No. II* associated were unconsciously taken by him as "mothers"; as such he was drawn to them, and in his identification with Theo he shared his brother's attachment.
460 A significant detail of their stay in Paris was his suggestion that he *should take over* Theo's girl friend who was very unhappy after Theo had broken
460 with her. He would even enter into a *marriage of convenience* with her. The rational explanation was that he would thus save her as well as Theo.

It has been noted that the outbreak of his illness had coincided with Theo's engagement. The marriage, the pregnancy of Theo's wife, and the

172

birth of their son were events in Theo's life which again seemed to have a direct influence on Vincent.[25] Signs of such inner reactions are the subjects of several later works, e.g., the "Reaper" (plate 82), "Watch at the Bedside" (plate 88), "First Steps" (plate 89), "Almond Branches in Blossom" (plate 90). When he had recovered from the first crisis, he wrote to Theo: *"Now your wife will come who has a good heart and rejuvenate us a little, us old fellows."* He added *he believed Theo and he would still have successors.* An indication of how involved he was in Theo's marriage could be seen in his strange suggestion that Theo *should transfer his affection from him as much as possible to his wife.* Shortly after the wedding he stated how *very, very happy* he was about the marriage, but it was in the same letter that he said of himself that he felt *a storm of desire to embrace something, a woman, a kind of domestic hen* (page 87). And again, the day after the birth of Theo's son, he wrote: *"May Jo remain a long time for us what she is."* Finally, in his last two letters, a few days before his suicide, he shows his concern with Theo's marriage, saying *it was threatened by storms* and that he had seen *its good as well as the other side of it.* In a preceding letter he speaks of the *danger hanging over all of them together*, and of *their fragile existence.*   574 585 587 625 651 652 649

Theo's characterization of Vincent "as if two men were in him," had pointed to his ambivalent, divided inner condition. This had also been implied by Gauguin (page 137). Vincent could not live with others, he could be with them only at a distance as if his physical presence were a barrier. Since his youth, he had shown a tendency to overcome his body like someone who did not feel well in his own skin. He had resigned himself to a hard and austere life, notably after disappointments in love, first in London, then in his self-punishment of replacing Kornelia by Christine, and in his withdrawal into solitude when he later left her. At the age of twenty-four, when he was engaged in the theological studies in Amsterdam, his self-chastisement went so far as sleeping on the floor and flagellating himself.[26] His Spartan privations in the Borinage, the placing of his hand in the flame in the desperate scene with Kornelia's parents, his self-mutilation and at last suicide were all acts against his body. They show that he was again and again driven into the same predicament, which was symptomatic of the gravity of his inner conflict.

He once admitted to Theo that *it was not without his own fault if many people considered him an unpleasant character*, and continued: *"I am often terribly burdensome, melancholic and excitable. I demand sympathy with a kind of hunger and thirst, and if I don't find that sympathy I show myself*   212 *indifferent and sharp and pour more oil into the flame myself. I don't enjoy company, and associating and talking with people is often embarrassing and difficult for me."* He thus described himself in the very same condition which had been reported of his childhood. As a grown-up, he still demanded sympathy with a kind of hunger and thirst — a typical childlike behavior, showing the persistence of his state of dependence on the mother. It was his central problem, which is reflected in the numerous portraits of Madame Roulin, particularly in his mother image, "La Berceuse."

66. BERCEUSE WITH SUNFLOWERS

574   Vincent continued to write about this work to Theo: *"I imagine these canvases just between those of the sunflowers which thus form lampholders or candelabra beside them of the same size, and the whole is thus composed*
575   *of seven or nine canvases."* In the following letter he confirmed that he had put the "Berceuse" between the "Sunflowers." Later still he wrote from
592   St. Rémy: *"You must further know that if you place them in this manner, say the Berceuse in the middle and the two canvases of the sunflowers to the right and left, this forms as it were a triptych."* His insistence on this arrangement shows how important it was to him. He even made a sketch in the letter to illustrate clearly how he wanted the paintings to be hung (plate 66). It is notable that in the small sketch the vases, in which the sun-

174

flowers are placed, are considerably larger than in the paintings themselves (plates 43, 44, 45). Evidently, their volume has grown in proportion to the rest of the canvas. The female significance of these vases thus appears more pronounced in the close neighborhood of the imposing mother image in the middle of the triptych.

The "Sunflowers" had symbolized Vincent's dream of life and work with friends in his house. The placing of "La Berceuse" between these canvases consistently links their symbolic content. As in his life the mother problem — so in his art the mother symbol takes the central position.

67. FRUIT BASKET WITH GLOVES

FRUIT BASKET WITH GLOVES / THE POSTMAN

Towards the end of January 1889, a month after his first attack, Vincent mentioned to Theo a still life "Fruit Basket with Gloves" (plate 67): *"I have just finished a new canvas which has an almost chic little air about it, a wicker basket with lemons and oranges, a branch of cypress and a pair of blue gloves; you have already seen these fruit baskets of mine."* 573

Like the "Sunflowers," these fruit baskets with the lemons and oranges in yellows, his color of love, symbolize his house with his painter friends. He himself had implied an affinity between the two subjects when he compared them in a letter to Theo in August 1888: *"I am now at the fourth painting of sunflowers. This fourth is a bouquet of 14 flowers, and is against a yellow background, like a still life of quinces and lemons which I did some time ago."* 527

The two gloves in front of the basket are a peculiar feature. As was seen in other still lifes, it is the specific composition of such simple, everyday articles in a painting that gives them their distinctive meaning. The domestic objects in works like the "Breakfast Table," the "Bedroom" and the "Still Life on a Drawing Board" were pertinent examples. The shoes in the Paris paintings had represented their wearers; here, the way one glove lies on the other suggests two hands. Their position could signify friendship and at the same time rivalry — the ambivalence of Vincent's relationship with Gauguin, who had forgotten his fencing gloves in the house. While Vincent was recovering, Gauguin wrote for these gloves twice within a few days. Vincent could not help expressing to Theo his disappointment that Gauguin had left

177

him alone in the distress of his illness, and wrote rather ironically about the importance his friend attached to the masks and fencing gloves.

The fruit basket lies between the gloves and two cypress branches in the background. In the "Breakfast Table" the dark blue coffeepot, surrounded by the domestic items and lemons, was inside the house; now the gloves, also in dark blue, are outside the basket. The spout of the coffeepot had pointed directly at the rim of the milk jug; now a conspicuous broken twig between the cypress branches moves in the same way, but, unlike the spout, strikes into the air.

The whole composition seems to show Vincent's vacillating state of mind. The main subject is the basket with the yellow and orange fruit in the center, portraying his longing for love and friendship in his house which he does not want to give up. At the same time the threat of having to abandon it is implied by the gloves, symbolizing Gauguin and himself no longer in the house.

572   Shortly before he did this still life he said of Gauguin: *"The best thing he could still do, and the very thing he will not do, would be quite simply to return here."* But when about three weeks later he had again been in the
577   hospital for a few days, he wrote: *"I dare no longer urge painters to come, after what has happened to me"* (page 109). All his thwarted hopes are expressed by the broken twig above the basket, where it stands out as his symbol of frustration, recurrent in the broken branches or tree stumps in so many of his works.

The continuation of his struggle is conveyed by the upward movement of the broken twig and the sharp cypress needles stabbing at the sky. The signature, "Vincent Arles 89," is large and pronounced, as if to stress that
573   *he had resumed his work with that nerve of metal,* as he wrote when he described the painting, adding: *"So many contrarieties certainly make me somewhat disquieted and fearful, but I do not despair as yet."*

In those first months of 1889 Vincent could not speak highly enough of his friend, the postman Roulin. While Gauguin had left him to himself, Roulin showed true friendship at that critical time when help was most needed.

He painted the postman three times after the outbreak of his illness. He had also done some portraits of him in the preceding August and had then
517   written to Theo: *"So now I am working on two figures, a head and a half-length with the hands of an old postman in dark blue uniform. He has*

178

a Socratic head interesting to paint. There is no better or shorter way of improving the work than doing figures. And I always feel confidence when I am doing portraits, knowing that this work is much more serious — that is perhaps not the word, but it rather is what permits me to cultivate the best and most serious in me." This statement will be understood by the fact that when he painted portraits Vincent was directly confronted with other persons. *"I would like to put my appreciation, my love which I have for him, into the* 520 *painting,"* he wrote about another portrait he did at the same time and continued: *"I don't know whether I shall be able to paint the postman as I feel it."* As he was *putting his thoughts into his work,* his own attitude towards 248 the model was expressed; always at the bottom of it was his complex relationship with other people, manifest in his loneliness. To cope with a portrait therefore meant very particularly to work at himself and thus *to cultivate the* 517 *best and most serious in him.*

In his solitude in Arles, when *a great number of days passed without his* 508 *saying a word to anyone* (page 103), the call of the postman who brought the letters from Theo and friends was a welcome interlude. Roulin was the messenger, the link with the world outside. One can well imagine how often Vincent looked out for the postman and how glad or relieved he was when Roulin handed him the expected mail. One friendly word led to another, and a cordial relationship developed between the two men during that summer, which Vincent later described: *"Roulin, though he is not quite* 583 *old enough to be like a father to me, has nevertheless a silent gravity and a tenderness for me such as an old soldier might have for a young one."*

Unfortunately, at the end of January, Roulin was transferred to Marseilles and could come to Arles only occasionally; in February Madame Roulin also left. Vincent thus remained quite alone and without assistance against the provoking behavior of some local people, especially youngsters who molested him even in his house. When these affronts finally led to his enforced detention in the hospital — Dr. Rey was not in Arles at that time — the only person who took an interest in him was a Protestant clergyman, M. Salles. He reported a few times to Theo about Vincent's condition.[27] He was of the opinion that "the neighbors had excited one another; the acts on which their reproaches were based, even if they had exactly happened, did not justify charging a man with insanity or depriving him of his liberty. Unfortunately the act of madness which necessitated the first entry into the hospital had put a wholly unfavorable interpretation on all slightly singular actions which

68. THE POSTMAN (1888)

this poor young man might occasionally have performed. With another man they would not have been noticed, but in his case they at once acquired particular importance." Vincent greatly appreciated M. Salles' attitude. Notwithstanding the general antagonism he had against the clergy since the Borinage, he repeatedly mentioned his high esteem for M. Salles and his gratitude for the help he had received from him both in Arles and St. Rémy.

When he was released by the end of March and felt unable to return to

69. THE POSTMAN (1889)

the house, he rented two small rooms belonging to Dr. Rey. He wrote to Theo: *"How these last three months seem strange to me. Sometimes inde-* 582 *scribable moral anguish, then moments when the veil of time and of the fatality of circumstances seemed for the wink of an eye to open a little. Certainly, after all, you are right, damn well right, even allowing for hope one has to accept the probably very distressing reality. I hope to throw myself again completely into my work which is behindhand."* He deplored *the*

588 *wrecked studio* and the failure of his idea, the house for the painters: *"It was to fight against force majeure or rather it was weakness of character on my part as I am left from that with grave remorse, difficult to define. I believe that this was the reason I cried out so much during the attacks, that I wanted to defend myself and could no longer succeed."*

Yet Vincent had emerged from the attacks with growing spiritual strength. It could be seen in the exemplary way he had controlled the situation during his detention in the hospital cell when he spoke of his state of mind
581 as being *beyond the question of illness and health*. Many of his works in the last year and a half of his life and also the portraits of Roulin are characteristic in this respect. In the earlier paintings of August 1888 (plate 68) one sees a down-to-earth portrait with the postman's stately beard in naturally flowing lines. The portraits done after he had fallen ill are on an animated, colorful background with a variety of flowers (plate 69), in one version almost identical with that of "La Berceuse". Roulin's beard now bulges profusely in involved curls and spirals, a remarkable example of the increasing prominence of the spiral symbol. Since they first appeared in the "Self-Portrait with the Bandaged Ear," when they symbolized his spiritual energy, these curves and spirals were becoming ever more vigorous and dominating.

182

His ensuing work, in particular the landscapes of St. Rémy, gives evidence of his rising spiritual force. There had always been movement in Vincent's landscapes, in the orchards, the drawbridges, the wide open fields. But it was a natural movement, rather serene and cheerful compared with his later works when the trees, clouds, olive groves and wheatfields fluctuate and toss in a spiral motion as if a high wind were moving them.

Vincent left Arles for St. Rémy in the first half of May 1889, and entered the mental hospital there, where he was to spend a year as a voluntary patient. His first impressions were quite favorable and he commented upon his surroundings, the inmates, and management, not without a sense of humor. Most important of all, he felt he would be able to work there; in addition to a bedroom he had been given a room in which to paint.

One of his first subjects was the view from his bedroom. He wrote about it to Theo: *"Through the iron barred window I see a square field of wheat*   592 *in an enclosure, a perspective like van Goyen, above which in the morning I see the sun rise in its glory."* As he frequently had to remain indoors, he painted this view many times, at all hours of the day, with the sun rising in the morning or in bright daylight, or with the evening moon, and even in the rain.

The first version was "Wheatfield after Storm" (plate 70) which he described: *"In the foreground a field of wheat ravaged and beaten down*   594 *after a thunderstorm. An enclosure wall and beyond the grey foliage of some olive trees, huts and hills. Then at the top of the canvas a large cloud, white and grey, drowning in the azure."* He called this landscape *a companion piece*   594 to the "Bedroom" (plate 54). The two paintings are of a completely different nature, one the interior of his bedroom in Arles, the other a wide open landscape. There could hardly be greater contrasts, yet as he perceives the wide view *through the barred window of his bedroom,* both motifs are simul-   592/4

183

70. WHEATFIELD AFTER STORM

taneously experienced by him. Seeing them as companion pieces, the painter
links the opposites of near and far; he writes to Theo: *"This morning I saw
the country from my window a long time before sunrise, with nothing but
the morning star which looked very large. Daubigny and Rousseau have done
that, however, with the expression of all the intimacy and all the great peace
and majesty it has, adding to it a feeling so heartrending, so personal. Such
emotions, I do not hate them."* He painted the huge white cloud in the sky
and the wheat in the field in a forceful, billowing motion as if to convey a
counteraction — to blast the bars of his confinement.

The surging movement continues and is intensified in other landscapes.
Shortly after the "Wheatfield," Vincent did "Olive Trees with White Cloud"
(plate 71), where the soil and the mountains swell in high waves and the
olive trees whirl impetuously between them. Unlike the manner in which he
had rendered landscapes until then, this work appears less "realistic". Earth,

593

184

71. OLIVE TREES WITH WHITE CLOUD

trees, mountains and clouds are ruled by the spiral symbol which brings forth the spiritual character of the canvas. It is one of the paintings which he called *"exaggerations from the point of view of arrangement, the lines contorted* 607 *like those of old woodcuts."* Moreover, in this case one may apply with even greater relevance the description he had given of an earlier work, saying that *bizarre, affected and multiplied lines, meandering through the painting, should* W 9 *not give the* subject *in its vulgar likeness but outline it to us as seen in a dream, at the same time in its character and nevertheless stranger than in reality* (page 135).

Olive trees and cypresses were Vincent's favorite subjects in the country-side of St. Rémy. *The cypresses always preoccupied him,* he wrote to Theo, 596 and he painted them many times. *Big and massive* trees dominate his first 596 "Cypresses" (plate 72), which he did in June. Curly waves and spirals spread all over the painting; from the brush in the foreground they continue in the

185

72. THE CYPRESSES

mountains and rise with the trees up into the undulating clouds in countless
curved lines. High above a voluminous pink and white cloud on the right is a
slim yellow crescent, clearly visible in the bright daylight of a transparent
greenish-blue sky.

The vigorous cypresses are dark green but intermingled with many
brighter shades in light browns, greens, and yellows; their branches and
twigs dart at the light clouds and like licking flames strike at their oval
shaped lines. The large transcending sickle moon is an unusual sight in

186

73. THE CYPRESSES (DRAWING)

the sunlit sky and brings out the symbolic significance of this landscape: the tall, upright cypress which stands for the man struggling and holding his own, under the aegis of the open moon, the female symbol.

Vincent also made a large drawing (plate 73) and added a sketch of the painting when he commented on it to Theo: *"I think that of the two canvases of cypresses the one of which I am making the sketch will be the best. The trees in it are very big and massive. The foreground very low with brambles and brushwood. Behind some violet hills a green and pink sky with a crescent* 596

187

74. CYPRESSES

moon. The foreground especially is painted very thickly, tufts of brambles with touches of yellow, violet and green."

597   Of another canvas "Cypresses" (plate 74) he wrote: *"They are painted with a thick impasto like the Monticellis... the blue sky like a piece of Scotch plaid."* He sent only a drawing to Theo (plate 75); the painting itself he kept until the following year. In February 1890 he dedicated it to the art critic, Albert Aurier, as a token of thanks for the article he had published,

75. CYPRESSES
DRAWING

telling him: *"I am working on it again at this moment, wanting to put a*   626a
little figure into it." In fact there are two women in the foreground who are
not in the drawing. In every other respect the painting and the drawing are
practically identical: the imposing row of the cypresses, flanked front and
back by the light fields, with the two houses and the hills in the distance.
It was unusual for him that after *keeping it for nearly a year,* as he wrote to   626
Theo, he should take the painting up again to add the two women — just as
if he had felt it incomplete without them.

He continued in his letter to Aurier: *"Until now I was not able to do*   626a
*them as I feel it; the emotions which seize me in front of nature go with
me as far as fainting, and then there results from this a fortnight during
which I am incapable of working. Nevertheless, before leaving here I count
on coming back once more to the charge to attack the cypresses. The study
I have designated for you represents a group of them at the corner of a
wheatfield on a day of summer mistral. So it is the note of a certain unnamed
black in a blue which moves through the circulating, wide, open air, and
in contrast to the black note is the vermilion of the poppies."*

189

76. ROAD WITH CYPRESS

626 a   Vincent's last *attack on the cypresses* was "Road with Cypress" (plate 76), which he did in May 1890, the month he left St. Rémy. He wrote from **Auvers**
643   about it to Gauguin: *"I still have a cypress with a star from down there, a last attempt—a night sky with a moon without brilliance, the slender crescent barely emerging from the opaque shadow cast by the earth—a star with an exaggerated radiance, if you like, a soft brilliance of pink and green in the ultramarine sky, where some clouds are hurrying. Below, a road bordered*

190

with tall yellow canes, behind these the blue Lower Alps, an old inn with orange lighted windows, and a very tall cypress, very straight, very somber." Between the sickle moon in yellow-orange and an enormous star, radiant in yellow, green and white, big as the sun, stands the *very tall, straight, somber* cypress. A road flows as though in continuous motion to the foreground where two men, side by side, walk towards us; they are followed at some distance by a horse-drawn cart with a man and a woman in it. A few more cypresses, near the house in the background, repeat the spiral soaring of the large tree in the center.

These landscapes, done at the beginning and at the end of his stay in St. Rémy, are related by the same symbolic meaning. What the crescent is in the first version, the women are in the second: the female complementing the male, the tall cypress. This symbolism appears more pronounced and as if reaffirmed in the "Road with Cypress." Here the large open moon above the cypress symbolizes love between man and woman as it shines in tender gold over the yellow cart with the couple inside. The huge, brilliant, sun-like star, symbol of brotherly love, and another star following behind, correspond to the two men marching together on the road.

The symbolic affinity connecting these paintings of cypresses is widened in scope by Vincent himself. When he started to paint them in June, he wrote to Theo: *"The cypresses always preoccupy me; I would like to make* 596 *something of them like the canvases of the sunflowers because it astonishes me that one has not yet done them as I see them. It is as beautiful in lines and proportions as an Egyptian obelisk. And the green is of such a distinguished quality. It is the black spot in a sunny landscape, but it is one of the most interesting black notes, the most difficult to hit off exactly that I could imagine."* In November he wrote to him again: *"You know the willows are* 615 *most picturesque; although it may appear monotonous, it is the tree in the character of the country. Now, what the willow is at home, the olive-tree and the cypress here have exactly the same importance."* In February 1890, he reverted to the idea with still greater emphasis: *"You need a certain dose of* 625 *inspiration, a ray from above which is not ours, to do the beautiful things. When I had done those sunflowers I looked for the contrary and yet the equivalent and I said: this is the cypress."*

In relating the willows, the sunflowers, and the cypresses to one another, Vincent implicitly refers to his own life and to the leitmotiv of his work: the struggle for love. The willows he had once interpreted as *orphaned men* 242

191

77. ROAD WITH CYPRESS (SKETCH)

(page 17), or as those deprived of parental love. In the canvases of the sunflowers he had portrayed brotherly love and friendship, with the mother symbol of the Berceuse in their center. Their equivalent now was the cypress to which he again had to add a female counterpart.

596
626a
The black spot in the sunny landscape, the most difficult he could imagine, did not cease to preoccupy him and made him reiterate to Aurier *the certain unnamed black in the blue.* It was the same challenge he had felt in the beginning: the dark in the light. The contrast now seems reversed, as one should assume that the cypress in its tall, upright stature, if it stands for the male principle, ought to be light and not the *black* spot of traditional female meaning. But the male cypress has, so to speak, its dark inside, while the female open moon is light, in the color of love. Moreover, the many strokes of light color in every dark tree show the opposites of light and dark in one. The evidently compulsory simultaneous portrayal of these contrasts tends to show their inseparability. One may recall the "Sower," where Vincent had
B 7
expressed very similarly his struggle with the *simultaneous excessive contrast.*

192

78. CYPRESSES

It may be noted that the large tree in the first painting seems to have two trunks, which is not evident in the drawing. In the "Road with Cypres" this peculiarity is even more conspicuous: only one cypress is recognizable but it unmistakably has two trunks. If they are to indicate two trees these must be so grown together that they appear as one. When describing the painting to Gauguin, Vincent made a sketch showing one tree (plate 77) and also speaks 643 of one cypress only. These repeated discrepancies seem to hint at an inner problem. Might the two trunks, rooting in the earth, intimate a duality in one tree — *a drama in every tree, in each figure,* as he once wrote (page 22). 319

193

626a   We remember from the letter to Aurier that he wanted to add *a little figure,* but he actually painted two women. In another similar painting (plate 78), again two women are in the same position. In "Road with Cypress" (pl. 76) this doubling is repeated by the two men, the two stars, the moon and the cart, and the couple in it. Finally the tree with the two trunks has its counterpart in the road itself, which divides the foreground into two, just where the men are walking. The two wanderers with their arms touching each other might recall Vincent's "Two Shoes," which could well have fitted these men on the road. The pair of shoes were like twin brothers, yet they belonged to one person, a quality they seem to have in common with the two trunks of the tree. The repeated pairing and the portrayal of two in one are added to the simultaneous contrast of dark and light in the cypress, which stands

596   as a symbolic landmark, *beautiful as an Egyptian obelisk,* at the roadside where man marches on.

One more observation may be made: in all these paintings the *big and*
596   *massive* cypress is cut off by the upper edge of the canvas. The top seems to disappear in the heights of the sky. It becomes invisible as the tree — symbol of the struggling man — reaches for the infinite.

194

PART V

...CONSOLING PAINTING

St. Rémy

79. THE STARRY NIGHT

196

THE STARRY NIGHT

After six weeks in St. Rémy Vincent reported to Theo *a new study of*   595
a starry sky. The "Starry Night" (plate 79) is painted to a great extent in
waves, curves and spirals. A dark greenish-blue is the main color with many
ranges of strong yellows and white. The greater part of the canvas is taken
up by the sky. In the center two vast clouds are locked together and swirl
in a gigantic movement, surrounded by bright radiant stars. On the right
is a big chrome-yellow sickle moon within a resplendent orb of brightest
sulphur, large as the sun. A light layer of clouds stretches across the sky
above a ridge of blue mountains surging in the background. At their foot
are rows of trees in continuous spirals, and in front is a village with a church.
Yellow lights shine from the village. On the left an enormous cypress rises
from the foreground in a flaming motion high up into the sky. Only the
upper part of the cypress is seen; its imposing form, the striking tapered
contours and the forceful color are of such strength that the village and the
church are quite overshadowed by it.

The "Starry Night" is the canvas which Vincent had *always dreamed of*   543
doing, as he had written when painting his earlier "Starry Sky" at Arles
(page 116). Since then decisive changes had taken place in his life. They are
reflected in the "Self-Portrait with the Bandaged Ear" and in the ensuing
development of the waves and spirals in his work. These symbols of Vincent's
rise into his spiritual sphere reach a high point in the "Starry Night." Here
his soul reigns in its own domain and the life in the sky becomes real life.
The night sky is turned into bright light, while the village down below is

197

like a faint reminiscence of the church spires and houses in the old Dutch

593, 608 villages. Despite the different treatment of the two *night effects*, as Vincent called these canvases, they have important traits in common. Both in the more realistic painting of Arles and the visionary night of St. Rémy, the oversized stars are the prominent symbols of brotherly love. The two lovers in the foreground of the Arles painting are symbolized in the "Starry Night" by the two dynamic clouds, interfluent as in a passionate union — as of man and woman.

The symbolic impact of this work is exceptionally strong. The sharp top of the giant cypress strikes like a soaring flame at the swirling stars and clouds, echoed by the distant church spire. This unbridled symbol of virile striving is in decided contrast to the bent trees, broken branches and tree stumps in Vincent's other paintings. Not frustration but fulfillment of love is portrayed here. The sickle moon, in symbolizing love between man and woman, is like an affirmation of the uniting movement of the two clouds. All the radiant stars have a point in their center similar to a kernel in a seed. They are scattered around the interlocked clouds, which become a huge symbol of procreation. The yellow crescent is as if englobed in a large incandescent sun. In its overwhelming light the sun, symbolic of love in mankind, powerfully stresses the significance of the radiating stars as symbols of loving friends. The composition in the sky is like a love scene on the bed of clouds which extends above the mountains; the agitated motion stresses the sensual nature of the scene.

All this takes place in Vincent's spiritual domain. In this portrait of a vision the tree top has attained the height of the stars for which he was yearning. It is now the trunk that has become invisible. Vincent has reached the infinite sky, and from here he looks down to the earth.

W 8 In a letter to his sister after he had painted the earlier "Starry Sky" at Arles, he wrote about his impressions of the poet Walt Whitman: *"He sees in the future, and even in the present, a world of health, of carnal love, great and frank — of friendship — of work with the great starry firmament, something which in short one can only call God and eternity placed again above this world. It makes you smile at first, it is so candid and pure; it makes you reflect for the same reason."* Nothing could better show the background against which he wrought the "Starry Night" than these words inspired by poetry. It was to be the realization of his dreams in Arles when he went out to paint the stars.

198

He is now in the realm of *the great starry firmament one can only call*   W 8
God and eternity, and here the clouds, the stars, the moon and the sun
unveil their timeless spiritual aspect. The unique interjoined movement of
the two central clouds, brings to mind a very old Chinese symbol, the Yin
and Yang (plate 80). It stands for the unity of dark and light, female and male,

80. YIN AND YANG

of negative and positive, non-being and being [28]. The two parts enter into
each other in a synchronous motion. They are inseparable and together they
become one in a perfect circle of wholeness. In each part is a nucleus as in a
cell, the equivalent of the kernel in the seed recalling the point in the star
that symbolizes man's original oneness and individuality. The black nucleus
in the center of the white field and the white nucleus in the black indicate
the basic existence of Yin within Yang and Yang within Yin, of darkness in
light and light in darkness. Therefore, each element also possesses the quality
of its opposite and thus at the same time contrasts with and resembles the other.

Darkness and light, though not directly shown in the two clouds, are
not missing from the painting. They are conveyed by the deep, dark cypress
opposite the glaring stars and the brightness of the moon and the sun in the
dark sky, and again by the blue-black silhouette of the mountain just below
the light cloud. The extraordinary position of the moon within a sun strikes
us once more as ancient Chinese symbolism. In "The Secret of the Golden
Flower" [29] based on "I Ching, the Book of the Changes," [30] it is written:
"Li is the sun, K'an the moon; the marriage of K'an and Li is the secret
magical process which produces the child, the new man." Thus conceived,
the moon and the sun conjoint in Vincent's painting repeat and endorse the
symbolic meaning of the interlocked clouds in an astounding spiritual confirmation.

The Yang and Yin principle of the union of two different elements makes us think of Vincent's continuous urge to unite within himself the conflicting light and dark factors (pages 76, 159). Their inseparability in the Chinese symbol refers to the inner structure of the individual, to his relations with his environment and to the cosmos as a whole. Male and female, productive and receptive, conscious and unconscious, body and soul, day and night, sky and earth are not in conflict but complement each other. One is unthinkable without its counterpart; there is no rivalry between them and no evaluation of one part against the other. Light is perceived by the existence of darkness as the positive by a negative, soul is expressed through the body like substance through its form. To recognize the complementary nature of these elements would mean to understand and accept them in their polar relationship as constituent rather than opposing forces. This seems to indicate a way in which the individuality and thus the integrity of the human being may be attainable.

In the stupendous exertion against his mental affliction, Vincent gathered and developed the spiritual strength that enabled him to create a painting like the "Starry Night." Here a theme finally was given shape which had preoccupied him for a long time, but his inner vision had to ripen before it could reach its ultimate form.

Preparatory stages are recorded in many letters. When he was still in Nuenen he had spoken of *"expressing light by opposing it to dark"* and *"... sky and earth form one whole, they belong to each other."* But these stages are particularly evident in his previous *realistic and at the same time symbolic* works. One of them was the "Sower" with its *simultaneous excessive contrast* of opposing colors, which Vincent had connected with black and white (page 98). In the "Self-Portrait with the Bandaged Ear" the spiral symbol had for the first time signified, in an outstanding and specific way, his growing spiritual strength. In the "Still Life on a Drawing Board" the doubling and pairing reached a peak in his fight against disintegration. "La Berceuse" surrounded by the "Sunflowers" was a source from which Vincent and his working friends would draw their sustaining force. Her central position might also be a sign of a trend in him towards matriarchy as a reaction to the prevailing patriarchal system with its traits of revenge for man's dependence on the mother.

In the "Starry Night" he goes an important step further as the interlocked clouds become the central motif. It no longer symbolizes a return to

200

matriarchy. In the evolution of the old conflict between these two opposing principles, his vision is crystallized of equality of man and woman in creative love. We recall his earlier views concerning *the collaboration between man* 388 *and woman with equal rights and equal freedom* (page 39). On another occasion he had written: *"Two good people, man and woman united, with* 275 *the same intentions and aims, imbued with the same seriousness, what could they not accomplish!"*

His comment on Whitman's poetry, *carnal love, friendship, work, the* W 8 *starry firmament one can only call God and eternity,* coincided with his letter to Theo from Arles in which he wrote of his intention of doing another painting like the first "Starry Sky": *"That does not prevent me from having* 543 *a terrible need of — shall I say the word — religion. Then I go out at night to paint the stars, and I always dream of a painting like that with a group of living figures of the copains"* (page 116). He applied the expression *copains* exclusively to his fellow painters; never did he include in this term other friends like Roulin or Milliet. This implies that he referred to colleagues, comrades with whom to share life in the work they had in common. The interpretation of the stars in the "Starry Night" as loving friends who work together thus seems affirmed by his own words. The equivalents of the stars — the sunflowers flanking "La Berceuse" — had formed the triptych symbolizing working friends and womanhood; it had preceded the portrayal of an ideal community of productive love, now finally achieved in the "Starry Night" with the symbol of procreation in the center.

When Vincent painted the "Starry Night," he wrote to Theo about the canvases he had in hand that *they would give him, perhaps, better than* 595 *words, some idea of the things he used sometimes to talk about with Gauguin and Bernard, and which preoccupied them.* He emphasized: *"This is not a return to the romantic or to religious ideas, no."* What had preoccupied him and his copains was progress in their work as a pioneering way of human striving. In this way he had seen the task of the Impressionists. He was not sure whether they would succeed — in fact he sometimes criticized impressionism and reduced its importance — and yet they would not give up, perhaps they were *to console, or to prepare for painting that would be more consoling.* 595

While he was working on the "Starry Night," he received a letter from Theo regarding his last paintings: "But how your head must have worked T 10 and how you have risked the extreme point where vertigo is inevitable. For that reason, my dear brother, when you tell me that you are working again which rejoices me on one hand, because there you find a way to avoid the state into which many of the poor wretches fall who are taken care of in the establishment where you are, I think of it with some anxiety because before complete recovery you must not risk yourself into those mysterious regions which apparently one may touch on the surface but not penetrate with

595   impunity." Vincent assured him that *he would not of his own will risk dizzy*

81. STARRY NIGHT (DRAWING)

heights, and indeed, a lost drawing of the "Starry Night" (plate 81) bears witness to this statement. Evidently done shortly before the painting, it shows this work in an earlier stage of evolution into its final shape. The convulsive vibration of the huge interjoining clouds indicates that his daring into these *dizzy heights* was of a more compulsive than voluntary nature. The long stretched upper cloud moves irregularly from the left in the direction of the other cloud which winds towards it from below. The lower cloud is still linked with the earth by clearly visible lines that continue the waving movement of

202

smoke pillars rising from the chimneys of a few houses. Some of the soaring waves of smoke above the horizon actually flow into the cloud — again reminding us of the symbolic spiral in Vincent's "Self-Portrait with the Bandaged Ear" (page 146). These pillars of smoke rise parallel with the church spire; all in one row, they repeat the flaming motion of the immense cypress on the left that reaches the sky. In the final painting the smoke pillars are omitted, only the giant cypress with the church spire, and the interlocked clouds, the central motif in the sky, remain.

No less than the two clouds does the unusual design of the moon in the drawing reveal Vincent's struggle with his subject. The sharp contours of the sickle continue beyond both its ends until they meet in a thin line which virtually closes a circle. The open crescent thus becomes a part of a round form (page 112/13); it is either a full moon or more likely that pre-eminent symbol in Vincent's work: the ever-round sun. These recurrent symbols, the sickle and the sun, are here together in one field, sharing it, if not even rivalling, in the painter's effort to attain a greater volume of light. In the final painting the sickle reverts to a normal form; its chrome yellow color, however, is outdone by the surrounding much stronger white-glowing sulphur yellow of the sun.

This glaring yellow recalls a letter which Vincent had written a few months earlier upon his release from the Arles hospital cell: *"... in order to attain the high yellow note which I have attained this summer, I had somewhat to force the dose [monter le coup]."* Notwithstanding the assurance he now gave about the dizzy heights, Theo's anxiety for his brother was well justified. To be in his spiritual sphere Vincent certainly risked losing ground in worldly affairs. He himself confirmed such fears repeatedly. In Arles *after a session like the work of the Harvest he had become absolutely absent-minded and incapable of a lot of ordinary things* (page 88). Later in St. Rémy he said: *"... a painter as a man is too absorbed by what his eyes see and does not sufficiently master the rest of his life."* 581 507 620

After receiving the "Starry Night," Theo wrote to him: "I quite feel what preoccupies you in the new canvases like the village in the moonlight or the mountains, but I find that the search for style takes away from the true sentiment of things." Vincent's reply was: *"But then I don't know too well if you would like what I am doing now. Because in spite of what you say in your last letter that the search for style often does harm to other qualities, the fact is that I feel greatly impelled to seek style, if you like,* T 19 613

203

but I mean by that a design more male and more willful." He ended the
613   discussion: *"Enfin, I'll do as I can."* Neither of them would have thought
that some generations later the "Starry Night" would become famous as an
outstanding religious work. In fact, in 1954 it was chosen as a representative
masterpiece of religious art in the nineteenth century.[31]

This is the more interesting because of the poor opinion Vincent had
of religious art. Broadly speaking, the only exceptions he made were for
Rembrandt and Delacroix. He was decidedly opposed to most other religious
615   painting, including works by Bernard and Gauguin *who had enraged him
with their Christs in the garden,* as he wrote to Theo. He asserted: *"Of
course for me there is no question of doing something from the Bible — and
I have written to Bernard and Gauguin too, that I considered thinking not
dreaming was our duty, so I was astonished looking at their work that they
615   let themselves go like that."* Such religious paintings gave him *a painful feeling
of downfall instead of progress.* In a letter to Bernard he accused him of
B 21   having *no sincere conviction behind the attempt to renew the tapestries of the
Middle Ages* and implored him *to become somewhat himself again.* He was
extremely upset about this defection of his friends because it touched on the
foundation of his own work and his very conception of life. No compromise
could be tolerated here.

To make Vincent's opposition to religious art still better understood, a
letter may be quoted which he had sent to Theo in 1882, at Christmas time.
He had spoken about some drawings he had made such as the "Old Man"
248   (page 30), to express a feeling of *quelque chose là-haut* [something above],
without even knowing what it was and independent of a religious form.
253   After citing Victor Hugo's words, *"Religions pass but God remains,"* he
continued with a quotation from Gavarni: *"It is a matter of grasping what
does not pass in that which passes."* Vincent went on: *"One of the things
which will not pass is that something above and the belief in God too, though
the forms may change, a change that is as necessary as the renewal of the
green in spring. But you understand from this that in the drawings it is not
my intention to pay homage to the form — but to show that I highly respect
the Christmas and New Year sentiment. And if some sentiment or expression
went into them, it is because I myself also feel it."*

242   A little earlier he had written: *"But when one feels the need for something great, something infinite, for something in which one can see God, one
does not need to look far; it seems to me I saw something deeper, more*

204

infinite, more eternal than the ocean in the expression of the eyes of a small child when it wakes in the morning, crows or laughs because it sees the sun shining into its little crib. If there is a rayon d'en haut [ray from above] perhaps one can find it there."

These repeated affirmations of God can hardly be reconciled with his emphatic declaration: *"In life and in painting too I can well do without a good Lord"* (page 13). The apparent inconsistency however, is resolved by a letter to Bernard denouncing an *infamous society whose empty words like "le bon Dieu" no longer had an effect on him.* He added: *"To study, to analyze society, this always says more than moralizing."* Here is another illustration of how Vincent was committed to the heart of the matter. He would neither accept nor himself make use of empty words because he felt the substance in words — his own and others' — as he did in art. Indeed, art was meaningful to him only if its content was experienced in life. This was one of his basic qualities, borne out by his attitude that *thoughts should arise from direct contact with things and one should not look at them with the intention of finding this or that in them* (page 156). It sustains his unprejudiced search for truth *behind the curtain* and without rationalizing.

Rigorous analysts was his term for the progressive contemporary French writers who greatly influenced him. He especially admired Michelet, Hugo, and Zola, whom he often quoted. When he stayed with his parents in Etten and Nuenen he deplored the *lasting, deep-rooted misunderstanding with his father.* He reproached him for *Jesuitism,* for *an icy coldness,* and saw in him *a prejudiced, a narrow-minded man, not wrestling with the naked truth.* His father thought of the French writers as *thieves and murderers,* and he would not even look at their books as Vincent had asked him to do. All that his parents would concede was the reading of Goethe's *Faust* because it had been translated by a minister. Yet they considered it *nothing but the fatal consequence of an ill-timed love.* La Joie de Vivre opposite the open Bible in the Nuenen painting reflects Vincent's frame of mind in those years.

The conflict portrayed in that still life was so much stronger because his own father, towards whom he had such intense ambivalent feelings, had also represented the church. Many contrasts and outright contradictions reveal the seriousness of the problem. On the one hand he had *a terrible need of — should he say the word — religion;* on the other he was determined there should be *no return to religious ideas.* In one passage he could write that *his attacks of illness tended to take an absurd religious turn* and in the same

531

B 9

233

237

451

161
347/8

159

164

543

595
605

205

letter *religious thoughts sometimes greatly consoled him.* Sometimes he
602 thought that the cause of his illness came from within: *"... the fault must be*
605 *within me ...",* but then again: *"... it seems to me, I do not know, what*
influence from the outside rather than from a cause coming from within
myself." He linked this with *religious exaggeration* (page 151). Vincent was
607 quite aware of these anomalies and wrote in another letter that *he was astonish-*
ed that with his modern ideas and admiration for Zola, and with so much
feeling for art, he had like a superstitious man confused and dreadful religious
ideas. No doubt his contempt for the religious paintings of Gauguin and
B 19 Bernard was genuine, yet in Arles he had himself done *an important canvas*
—a Christ with the angel in Gethsemane—and mercilessly destroyed it,
because the form had not been studied on the model. Notwithstanding his
615 decision in St. Rémy that *there was no question of his doing something from*
the Bible, a few months later he copied there two Biblical subjects by Delacroix, a "Pietà" and a "Good Samaritan." All these contrasts show the struggle
involved in his deep-rooted concern with religion. His very negations no less
than his doubts confirm the existence of a challenging issue.

His long study of the Bible had also left a divided impression on him.
He was struck by the discrepancies and human shortcomings which he found
in it and severely criticized them. The consolation was Christ, whom he
B 8 accepted unreservedly as *"... an artist greater than all artists, disdaining*
marble and clay and color, working in living flesh. That is to say, this artist,
unequalled and hardly conceivable with the obtuse instrument of our modern,
nervous, brutalized brains, did not make statues, nor paintings nor books:
253, 411 *he affirmed it boldly, he made living men, immortals."* Hugo's *"religions*
pass, but God remains," which he quoted repeatedly, may perhaps best impart
161 Vincent's belief. At times he was very outspoken: *"To believe in God (that*
does not mean you should believe all the sermons of the clergy and the
arguments and Jesuitism of the bigoted prudes with stand-up collars, far
from it), the belief in God to me is to feel that there is a God, not dead or
stuffed, but alive, who with irresistible force urges us towards aimer encore
[to love more]—well that is my opinion."

He had written this at Etten, when he was engaged in the struggle with
his and Kornelia's parents—her father was also a clergyman (page 26). But
in a distinct contrast, later in the Hague, when he lived with Christine, he
expressed his desire to paint a poor village clergyman *on the path through the*
299 *heath,* someone like his father: *"Leaving aside the less important differences*

206

in religious opinion, the figure of a poor village clergyman, in type and character, is to me one of the most sympathetic that exists, and I would not be myself if I did not attack it [the subject] *one day."*

He wrote again from his father's house in Nuenen: *"Oh, I am not a* 378 *friend of the present Christianity, though the <u>founder</u> was sublime. The present Christianity — I looked too well into its cards. It fascinated me, this icy coldness, in my youth, but I have taken my revenge since — how? by worshipping the love which they, the theologians, call sin, by respecting a whore, etc. and many would-be respectable pious ladies not! For the one party, woman is always heresy and devilish. For me it is the contrary."* This had been after his friend Margot Begeman had been driven by her mother and sisters, *the would-be respectable ladies,* to attempt suicide (page 39).

When he broke with religious tradition and the church, an unabating urge, a dire need for love, both spiritual and physical, remained in him. His conflict with the clergy had actually been caused by the zeal he had shown on his humanitarian mission with the miners in the Borinage and his ensuing conclusion that the church did not implement the love it preached. The following letter to Theo from the Hague is typical for his conception of love between men: *"I have already said a few words about humaneness ... I have* 219 *no humanitarian plans or ideas as if I could do so for everybody, but I am not ashamed to say (though I know very well that the word humaneness is in bad repute) that for my part I have had and always shall have the need to love another creature. Preferably, I myself don't know why, an unhappy, an outcast or deserted creature. I once nursed a miserable burned mine-worker for six weeks or two months. I shared my food for a whole winter with an old man, I do not know what more, and now Sien [Christine]. But so far I did not believe that something like that was foolish or bad; I find it something so natural and self-understood, that I cannot understand that people can usually be so indifferent to one another. I add that if I did wrong, then you too were wrong to help me so loyally — that something like that should be wrong is really absurd. I always believe that 'love thy neighbor as thyself' is no exaggeration, but the normal situation. Enfin."*

Vincent's simple description shows that his humane approach was not a matter of vague ideas but something tangible which he practiced in the reality of everyday life. This consideration for other people touches a central problem in human relations that certainly extends to our time — the alternatives of an impersonal attitude and indifference on one hand, of personal

207

concern and love on the other. Vincent took a poor view of a society which
259 opposed *the hidden forces of sympathy and love in man and his acting*
194 *according to his feelings and impulses.* Explaining that *sentiment and senti-*
mentality were two different things, he pointed to the conventional shallowness
of society which since his time has developed to a degree of mass behavior
endangering the best qualities of the human being. He alluded to this con-
218 dition when writing to Theo: *"Now that I have such a large and wide feeling*
for art and life itself, of which art is the essence, it sounds so shrill and false
to me when there are people who are only on the hunt."

This ever-increasing drive to run and speed shows itself in our age by
unprecedented achievements in the field of physical movement. At the same
time we experience the paradox that the greater the speed and efficiency
we achieve, the less these successes benefit our inner well-being. In contrast
to our material gains is the reaction of the soul, which tends to take its
revenge, as nature does when mishandled or neglected. One aspect of our
emphasis on expediency is our indifference. It covers an attempt to escape
from the confusion in the relationship between men, that reflects the dis-
harmony existing within the individual. In connection with this expediency,
313 it is noteworthy that Vincent's standpoint was *"at the exact opposite of the*
principle: 'the end justifies the means'." This attitude implies recognition
of the fact that it is always the means which characterize the aim as well as
306 the society that employs them. *"Conscience is for me the highest reason — the*
reason within the reason," was his credo.

His turning away from the prevailing materialism was first seen in the
deliberate jeopardizing of his position with the art dealers, and his devotion
to a religious vocation. His next step was to abandon his theological studies.
326 He could, as he later wrote to Theo, *well have mastered the miserable bit of*
Latin, but the theological faculty seemed to him an inexplicable mess, a
breeding place of Pharisaism. That he did not lack courage was proved by
his going to the Borinage instead of remaining a student.[32]

After he had become a painter, he did not relax in his opposition to the
218 conventional standards of life with the hunt for success, *that sounded so*
shrill and false to him. In the course of his work as an artist he came
increasingly to the conviction that success was no criterion for quality with
either art or man; in fact at the peak of his creative summer in Arles he
524 wrote that *he had a horror of success.* If he had not been so embarrassed
by imposing a continuous financial burden on his brother, he would rather

208

not have seen his canvases sold; he often gave them away as presents. In any case, all he wanted was *that they should get the money back which the* 626 *painting had cost, the rest would leave him cold.* Upon his return to his parents' home in Nuenen, he had to make the decision either *to do what he* 347 *was told was his duty, to earn money,* or to be a painter which meant to him *wrestling with the truth. "I tell you, I have chosen the dog's path in question... I shall remain a dog, I shall be poor, I shall be a painter... I want to remain human — within nature... Since rejecting their systems altogether, I have a certain hope that my striving will not be in vain. And that before my eyes will close, I shall see the rayon blanc [white ray]. Whatever might be the struggle of the soul for what has not yet been found..."*

At that time he had laid down some of his fundamental thoughts in the discussions with his friend Van Rappard: *"Art, although produced by man's* R 43 *hands, is something not created by hands alone, but something which wells up from a deeper source out of our soul, and in the cleverness and technical knowledge with regard to art, I find something that reminds me of what in religion one would call self-righteousness. My sympathies in the literary as well as in the artistic field are drawn most strongly to those artists in whom I see most the working of the soul."*

When reading Shakespeare in St. Rémy, he wrote to Theo: *"But what* 597 *touches me, as in some novelists of our day, is that the voices of those people, which in the case of Shakespeare reach us from a distance of several centuries, do not appear unknown to us. It is so alive that one believes one knows them and sees it. And so, what Rembrandt has alone or almost alone among painters, that tenderness in the eyes of beings [dans les regards d'êtres], which we see, whether in the pilgrims of Emmaus or in the Jewish bride, or in some strange figure of an angel such as the painting you have had the good fortune to see — that heartbreaking tenderness, that glimpse of a super-human infinite which then seems so natural, in many places one comes upon it in Shakespeare."* By his subsequent statement that he *read books to look* W 14 *for the artist who had written them* (page 52), he again stresses the human element in art, the inner tie between art and man.

As a matter of fact, when one is confronted with a work of art one reacts with sympathy, indifference or dislike, almost as when meeting a person. A painting, sculpture, music, poetry, or drama may touch something responsive in us and evoke emotional impressions, even causing mental stimulation. Whatever our reaction, the effect alone is felt, but we do not know its origin. It is not unlike certain other experiences in life, such as intuitions, impulses, presentiments, visions, spontaneous notions, sudden flashes of remembering and spells of forgetting, sensations sometimes of a split second. We tend to ignore these perceptions as we are too busy with our routine occupations. They are like greetings from an unknown sphere, a kind of waves between our unconscious and conscious being. On this level of sensibility art affects us as an inner experience, an intuitive rather than logical knowledge.

R 43   In the letter to Van Rappard in which Vincent wrote *art wells up out of our soul,* he also speaks of *"...the positive consciousness of the fact that art is something greater and higher than our cleverness or knowledge or science."*
439 Later he said to Theo: *"...the painted portraits have a life of their own*
597 *which comes radically out of the painter's soul..."* His *glimpse of a super-*
625, 543 *human infinite — the ray from above — a painting coming to him as if in a*
503 *dream — working like a sleep-walker — falling into full metaphysics of color,*
all these utterances refer to the non-technical side of art. When he saw *in*
R 43 *the cleverness in art something reminding him of self-righteousness in religion*
and thus depreciated the value of technique in both, he deliberately connected art and religion. There is in fact hardly a religious rite or service which dispenses with art — music or poetry, painting or sculpture — and this is by no means accidental. Art, by its spiritual quality, is not only related to religion, but both of them have in common that they express the very nature of man: the union of matter and spirit. As man is an image of God, art is an image of man.

      Of Vincent's many letters on art and religion the following is partic-
542 ularly significant: *"I have read another article on Wagner, love in music — I think by the same author who wrote the book on Wagner. How we would need the same thing in painting. It seems that in the book "My Religion," Tolstoi suggests that however violent a revolution there may be, there will also be an inward and secret revolution in the people, from which a new religion will be reborn or rather something quite new which will have no name but which will have the same effect of consoling, of making life possible, which the Christian religion once had. It seems to me that this book ought to be very interesting, in the end one will have enough of cynicism, of scepticism, of humbug, and one will want to live more musically. How will that come about, and what will one find? It would be curious to be able to predict it, but it is even better to have a presentiment of it instead of*

210

seeing in the future absolutely nothing but the disasters which, anyhow, will not fail to fall on the modern world and civilization like terrible lightnings through a revolution or a war or a bankruptcy of the worm-eaten states. If one studies Japanese art, then one sees a man undoubtedly wise and philosophic and intelligent who spends his time doing what? studying the distance between the earth and the moon? no, studying the policy of Bismarck? no, he studies a single blade of grass. But this blade of grass leads him to draw all the plants, then the seasons, the wide aspects of the landscapes, at last the animals, then the human figure. He thus passes his life, and life is too short to do it all. Look, is this not almost a true religion which these simple Japanese teach us who live in nature as if they themselves were flowers? Earlier he had written: *"And who has retained a faith in God sometimes hears a soft voice of conscience which one then perhaps does well to follow with the naïveté of a child."* 259

These reflections as well as actual experiences that he had in his own work such as *"...during the doing itself, there is little time for the deliberating and reasoning"* (page 157), are remarkably close to the following 197 concepts of Zen Buddhism: "Man is a thinking reed but his great works are done when he is not calculating and thinking. 'Childlikeness' has to be restored after long years of training in the art of self-forgetfulness. When this is attained, man thinks yet he does not think. He thinks like the showers coming down from the sky; he thinks like the waves rolling on the ocean; he thinks like the stars illuminating the nightly heavens; he thinks like the green foliage shooting forth in the relaxing spring breeze. Indeed, he is the showers, the ocean, the stars, the foliage." [33]

Vincent's interest in the East, particularly in Japan, was extraordinary. Far in excess of the vogue Japanese prints had at the time, he was deeply impressed by Japanese art. It was, he wrote, *in decadence in its own country,* 510 *but took roots again in the French Impressionist artists.* He also found that the co-operation between artists, their exchanging paintings, etc., which he B 18 had always advocated, was practiced by the Japanese. In his first letter from Arles, he spoke of the snow-covered countryside in the south of France as *very much like the winter landscapes which the Japanese had painted.* In 463 other letters he wrote *one saw with a more Japanese eye there,* and further, 500 *nature under a brighter sky could give him a better idea of Japanese feeling* 605 *and drawing.* His moving to the South was *an equivalent of going to Japan* 500 and he once told his sister: *"For me, I do not need the japonaiseries [Japanese* W 7 *art objects*] *here because I always say to myself that here I am in Japan."* The identity of his thoughts with Zen Buddhism is so striking that his feeling as if *he were in Japan* may appear a little less strange. It is worth noting that in none of his letters does he mention ever having read about Zen.

545　His earlier avowal that he did not intend to express any particular form of religion in his art (page 204) is borne out by his veneration of Christ and at the same time of *the eternal Buddha.* He thus tends towards the universality of God, common to men of all races and above their individual religious systems. On a similar basis is his admiration for Tolstoi, as well as for Socrates

306　in whom he saw *"... the same phenomenon as in Jesus, who had raised himself to a personality so full of pity, love, goodness, earnestness, that one is still drawn by it."* In that letter to Theo, at the end of his Hague period, he wrote further: *"One should arrive at leading one's conscience to a state of development so that it becomes the voice of a better and a higher self of which the ordinary self is a servant."* Vincent's words *a higher self* were

545　followed later in Arles by the expression *enlarging* himself and still later in

625　St. Rémy by *a collective self*; they indicate trends in his mind preceding the use of similar terms in modern psychology.[34]

On the occasion of the exhibition in 1954, which showed the "Starry Night" as a religious masterpiece, an essay was published entitled "Authentic Religious Art." [35] It contained the following passage: "If religion be defined as man's ultimate concern for Ultimate Reality, all art which reflects, however partially and distortedly, this ultimate concern is at least implicitly religious, even if it makes no use whatever of a recognizable religious subject matter or any traditional religious symbols." If this approach means that the churches accept man's "ultimate concern for Ultimate Reality" as their highest principle, over-riding all other doctrines, they would, within their own realm, have extended the road to the professing of genuine religiousness.

218　On this very road Van Gogh's art is a milestone, portraying *the essence*

626　*of life* in his unceasing struggle for truth—*the truth which was so dear to him,* as he wrote five months before his death. His question whether in *his*

543　*terrible need he should say the word religion* almost imposes a thought about the affinity of the word "religion" with the Latin terms "religare" and "relegere" (as used in "to bind back" and "to gather together"). Obviously in Vincent's mind, the ominous word religion was a stirring challenge. It struck at the core of his life, his constant attempt to gather together the separate, to reconcile body and soul, finally to become a whole—by uniting the primordial contrasts as Yin and Yang had symbolized in the circle of perfection.

212

It was in the midst of this spiritual struggle, so pre-eminent when he wrestled with the colors of the "Sower," *the image of humanity* which was cut in two, that he had suddenly exclaimed: *"But when shall I do the starry sky, the painting that always preoccupies me?"* (page 98). Although no connection is visible between the two works, there is fulfillment in the "Starry Night" of Vincent's yearning in the "Sower" for the *rayon blanc* (the white ray). His starry sky is now all lit by rays of light.

Yet a significant feature does not escape our attention. Yellow light is shining from houses in the village, as if it were a reflection of *the ray from above,* the light of love. But one of the exceptions is a large building in the center, the church. In contrast to all the light in the painting, it is unlit, bringing to mind the *icy coldness,* the term Vincent used in his letters. Light from a church or a house was no accidental or minor matter for him. When he studied in Amsterdam he had written to Theo: *"I think the sun never shines more beautifully than in a parsonage or in a church."* And further: *"The light in the little Sunday school room in Barndesteeg is only small, but let me keep it burning."* In the early little drawing "En Route," the house threw its light into the darkness of night. Even some of his dark Dutch cottages had a light, however small, in their windows. From his solitude in the north of Holland in 1883, he described to Theo *a village, mighty companionable with the reflections of its lighted windows,* and shortly before his death, when he speaks of his "Road with Cypress", he again stresses the *lighted windows* of an old inn.

Could the remarkable choice of the "Starry Night" as a religious painting mean that the church too, in a dark urge from within, is searching for light? Should the church itself be destined to fulfill Van Gogh's hope that this painting might be *consoling?* And should the clergy who helped to select this work have been inspired by it to become instrumental in spreading his faith: the belief in God and eternity, lived and practiced by creative men and women in equality and love of soul and body. In this *badly reputed humane* sense the "Starry Night" can be called religious. It is Vincent's spiritual testament, his message of a conception that *does not pass in the passing,* communicated in a change of form, a metamorphosis, as he wrote: *"...as necessary as the renewal of the green in spring."*

604
B 7

347

242

348, 378

103
121

330

643

595

219

253

253

82. THE REAPER

THE REAPER

About the end of June, Vincent wrote to Theo: *"The latest started is the* 597 *wheatfield where there is a little reaper and a large sun."* The "Reaper" (plate 82) shows a wheatfield in warm, golden yellow. The ripe wheat waves in blazing sunshine, and some large sheaves lie in the foreground. In the high wheat, on the left, is a man with a sickle. Behind him, beyond an enclosing wall, a single tree stands out against the sky, its movement repeating that of the reaper. In the background are violet and blue mountains, some houses at their foot, and in a pale cloudless sky is a large sun in bright yellow.

While Vincent was still working on the painting, he received a letter from Theo's wife with the good news that she expected a child. They hoped it would be a son whom they would call Vincent after him. He at once sent them his best wishes, yet to their request that he should be the child's godfather, he replied that *he preferred to wait until he had left the asylum.* A few 599 days later he was shaken by a grave recurrence of his illness which lasted several weeks and interrupted his work until September.

When he began to recover, he wrote to Theo in black chalk: *"... it is* 601 *very difficult for me to write, my head is so disturbed [dérangée] ... For many days I have been absolutely lost, as in Arles, quite as much if not worse, and it is to be presumed that these attacks will come back in the future; it is abominable. For four days I have not been able to eat because of a swollen throat."*

In the first days of September he was still unable to leave the house, but he had resumed his work on the "Reaper." During the intervals when he

215

604 was tired from painting, he wrote a long letter to Theo: *"The work is going pretty well—I am struggling with a canvas begun a few days before my indisposition, a reaper. The study is all yellow, terribly thickly painted [empâté]: but the subject was beautiful and simple. I saw then in this reaper —a vague figure struggling like a devil in great heat to come to the end of his task—I saw then in it the image of death, in the sense that humanity would be the wheat one reaps. So it is, if you like, the opposite of that sower I had tried before. But in this death, nothing sad; it happens in broad daylight with a sun flooding everything with a light of pure gold."* He later continued: *"My dear brother—it is always in between the work that I write to you—I am laboring like one possessed. I am more than ever in an insensible fury of work. And I think that this will help to cure me."* Later again he went on: *"Oof—the reaper is finished. I think this will be one of those you will keep at home—it is an image of death such as the great book of nature speaks of it to us—but what I have sought is the almost smiling. It is all yellow, except a line of violet hills, of a yellow pale and blond. I find it queer myself that I saw like this through the iron bars of a cell."*

Vincent painted the "Reaper," one of his best known landscapes, in a state of great emotion. His health had improved since he had fallen ill in December the year before, and although he had suffered some attacks thereafter, they had not been so severe. His often depressed letters to Theo from Arles in March and April became more cheerful, and at the end of May,

592 when he had been in St. Rémy a few weeks, he wrote: *"Now that it has gone on diminishing for five months I have good hope of getting over it, or at least of not having any more attacks of such strength."* But after the

601 agonizing relapse he said: *"You understand that I am very deeply distressed that the attacks have come back when I was already beginning to hope that this would not recur... I no longer see a possibility of having courage or good hope, but after all it is not since yesterday that we knew the profession is not gay."*

It will be remembered that his first attack at Christmas the year before had occurred just at the time of Theo's engagement. At the wedding in

583 April, Vincent claimed: *"It is like a nervous tic with me generally to have difficulties on festive days in formulating a congratulation, but you should not conclude from this that I wish you happiness any less ardently than anyone else, as you well know."* However, on that occasion, only a few days after he had suggested that Theo should transfer the affection he had for him

216

to his wife (pages: 143, 162, 172), he warned him: *"If I were without your* **588**
friendship I would be remorselessly driven back to suicide, and however
cowardly I may be, I would end by going there." Some weeks earlier he had
also written to his sister: *"Every day I take the remedy which the incom-* **W 11**
parable Dickens prescribes against suicide. This consists of a glass of wine,
a piece of bread and cheese and a pipe of tobacco. That's not complicated you
will tell me and you don't believe that melancholy comes to me about as far
as that, however at moments — oh but — ..."

The news of the expected child again seemed to have a contrasting effect
on him. This was brought out when he wrote to Theo: *"I imagine you will* **600**
be well absorbed by the thought of the child to come. I am well pleased that
this should be the case..." But in the same letter he came back to his old
"...ideal of that simpler and truer nature of having a wife and child which
sometimes haunts us." One recalls his earlier complaint: *"A wife, a child,* **358**
you cannot give me..." (page 172). His reiteration at this moment of that
haunting ideal once again points to his feeling inferior to his brother and **600**
to the negative side of his relationship with him. For Theo the expectation
of the child meant consolidation of his own family life, while for Vincent
his solitude and the burden of his *failure* became ever more heavy to carry. **648**

After the new attacks Dr. Peyron of the St. Rémy asylum reported to
Theo: "I add a word to your brother's letter to tell you that he is well over
his attack, that he has regained all his lucidity and resumed his painting as
he did before. His ideas of suicide have disappeared; painful dreams alone
remain which tend to disappear and their intensity is less. His appetite has
come back, and he has resumed his usual life." Contrary to Vincent's allusions
to suicide when writing to Theo and their sister before he had left Arles,
there were no more hints of this kind in his letters following his arrival at
St. Rémy. It is Dr. Peyron's note which throws light on the underlying connection between Vincent's *image of death* and his own drive towards death. **604**
The doctor must have learned "the ideas of suicide" from Vincent's delirium
during the attacks when, in his own words, he had been *absolutely lost.* **601**

From his descriptions of the painting it is evident that Vincent was fully
conscious of the image of death which he wanted to portray in the "Reaper."
His words *"I saw in this reaper a vague figure struggling like a devil in* **604**
great heat to come to the end of his task" have a striking similarity with
"I work like one possessed, I am more then ever in an insensible fury of **604**
work." They endorse his identification with the reaper and the self-portraying
nature of this motif.

217

83. REAPER

It had been in connection with the peaceful, harmonious "Harvest" of
497 Arles that he had previously used the word *kill* (page 88). There was a
reaper in the "Harvest," and in its companion piece, the "Haystacks," a single
tree, the recurrent symbol of the lonely fighter. In these earlier works the
reaper and the tree had been depicted separately. In the "Reaper" their
meaning is confirmed and re-emphasized as man and tree appear together in
the painting. This concentration indicates a different stage in Vincent's life,
underlining his self-portrayal in the task of the reaper and his advancing
towards the end of his road.

218

84. EGYPTIAN WOMAN

The single tree behind the reaper is in an identical position with the tree in the "Sower" (plate 39). Vincent himself connected the two works, saying: *"The canvas of the reaper will become something like the sower of the other year."* It also was *its opposite,* as he termed it later, implying that they were counterparts. While the sower was strewing the seed, symbolic of giving, a positive act, the reaper is taking and becomes the opposite, negative, the two functions complementing each other in fulfillment of the unchanging law of nature.

597
604

219

501a Vincent had been afraid of *the hard subject* of the "Sower," calling the
B 7 sower and the sheaf *symbols of the infinite,* and he had wrestled with the
B 7 excessive contrast of the colors by which the painting was *cut in two.* This
543 torn condition had been repeatedly portrayed, as in his other *hard subject,
the house he wanted to conquer* (page 117). He is still struggling in the
"Reaper," as he will be until the end of his life. But now the figure of the
reaping man and his companion, the tree, are painted in green — the synthesis of the contrasts of blue and yellow, symbolic of dark and light. Vincent
seems to fear the excessive contrast no more, the violet and blue of the
distant mountains are no longer disturbing in their tenderness; golden yellow
604 exuberantly dominates the wheatfield, his *image of humanity.*

604 His idea that *humanity would be the wheat one reaps* brings to mind
the ancient myth of the gods of the corn: "Serving the great Mother-Goddess,
they were killed, cut and reaped when they were ripe, in order to fertilize
the earth." [36] There is a drawing of a reaper (plate 83) which he did on the
back of another drawing of a large mysterious head of an "Egyptian Woman"
(plate 84). This head, drawn in different versions, will occupy us again later.
The reaper here is in a state of utter exhaustion, bearing witness to Vincent's
604 *coming to the end of his task* — in *the image of death.* A single tree behind
the reaping man follows his movement; in this drawing, too, the symbol of
the lonely fighter is not missing.

The warm color and bright light of the "Reaper" convey Vincent's feeling
604 that *"there is nothing sad ... in this image of death, such as the great book
of nature speaks of it to us."* This conception is again akin to that of the Zen
Buddhist who sees death "like the petal of the cherry blossom that loosens in
the ray of the morning sun and, gaily shining, glides to earth." [37] In a similar
way we see in the reaper, Vincent himself, almost absorbed by nature in the
billowing waves of the high golden wheat. His coming to the end of his
task relates two phases: the course of his personal life is approaching its end
as he experiences an ever-increasing solitude. The other phase is on a different
level, transcending the personal. After he had delivered his spiritual message
604 in the "Starry Night," he may find the *almost smiling* in the image of death.

220

OLIVE TREES / ALMOND BRANCHES IN BLOSSOM

85. OLIVE TREES

During that autumn Vincent painted many more harvesting themes. When he could go out to the fields, he again took up olive trees as his subject. They were as meaningful to him as the cypresses, both comparable to the Dutch willows (page 191). *"On the other hand,"* he told Theo, *"the olive trees are very characteristic, and I am struggling to catch that. It is silver, sometimes more blue, sometimes green, bronzed, whitening on yellow ground, pink, violet, up to dull red ochre. But very, very difficult... And one* 608

86. OLIVE PICKING

day I shall perhaps do my personal impression of them, as the sunflowers are for the yellows." A little later he wrote more about this personal impression of the olive trees: *"If I remain here I would not try to paint a Christ in the garden of olives, but the picking of the olives as one can still see it, giving all the same the right proportion of the human figure in it; this might perhaps make one think."*

614

In his many versions of "Olive Trees", such as plates 85, 86, the trees, with their trunks like human bodies and their branches like arms outstretched towards the sky, actually appear as those *living beings* and *figures* in which he had seen *a drama*. Of another painting, "Saint Paul's Park," with pine trees (plate 87), he gave the striking description: *"Now, the first tree is an enormous trunk but struck by lightning and sawn off. A side branch, however, shoots up very high and falls again in an avalanche of dark green*

152
319
B 21

222

87. ST. PAUL'S PARK

twigs. This somber giant — like a proud man defeated — contrasts, when considered in the character of a living being, with the pale smile of a last rose on the fading bush opposite it."

When Vincent was indoors during the winter he continued to paint many harvesting scenes, frequently working after other artists, especially after Millet for whom he had a *very profound and sincere admiration*. Two paintings, "Watch at the Bedside" (plate 88) and "First Steps" (plate 89), show one trend of his thoughts. Depicting young parents with their infant, these canvases convey his preoccupation with the coming event, which he frequently mentions in his correspondence with Theo. *"How beautiful Millet is, the first steps of a child,"* he exclaimed in one of his letters, and closely followed the French master's drawing in his own painted version.

Particularly interesting is his choice of "Watch At The Bedside". From a large round lamp, bright light spreads over the room, over the mother who

623

88. WATCH AT THE BEDSIDE

does some needlework, and the child in the cradle. The father who is directed towards them, is seen from his back and remains in the shadow; sitting on the left side of the canvas he is in a position similar to the young man in the "Potato Eaters", but there is more light in the portrayal of this small family and the atmosphere is friendlier. He is a basket maker, bent over his work, which recalls Vincent's mention of a basket maker when he had moved into his house in Arles. He was alone then and consoled himself with the thought that *a weaver, a basket maker could spend whole seasons alone, with their work as only distraction, because of the feeling of the house.* The adoption of Millet's work as his subject bears out his earlier identification with a basket maker but now he is in the rôle of a husband and father — of Theo to whom his thoughts are going.

542

224

89. FIRST STEPS

The child was born on January 31, 1890. It was a boy, and the parents named him Vincent. In a letter to his mother in February Vincent wrote: *"I would have much preferred him* [Theo] *to call his boy after father, of whom I have been thinking so much these days, instead of after me, but seeing it is now so, I started right away to do a painting for him, to hang in their bedroom, big branches of white almond blossom against a blue sky."*   627

This painting, "Almond Branches in Blossom" (plate 90), is of a sublime tenderness. Large branches expand all over a transparent light blue sky. Many white and some light pink blossoms are bursting out of old gnarled wood. The bare knotty branches in the lower part of the canvas are broken off in various places; they branch out in an upward movement, characteristic of many of Vincent's works, such as the "Cut Sunflowers" (plate 26), where

225

the broken stems lie in the foreground in a similar position. This recurrent symbol of frustration and struggle is conspicuous in both paintings. However, there is an essential difference between them. The cut stems of the sunflowers are carried to death in the stark, lifeless flower heads. In the "Almond Branches," through the young buds, new life emerges from the old, broken wood. The delicate white blossoms of spring beauty flowering on the rugged branches are rendered in an exquisite shape and color, a refined contrast to the gnarled wood. Spread out like a net over the whole canvas, these branches and buds make us think of the barred window in the asylum through which Vincent saw the sky with *the sun rising in its glory*.

592

The little "Blossoming Almond Twig" (plate 28), which he had done on his arrival in Arles after the dark winter days in Paris, had been a message of new hope and a symbol of renewing life. Just as in the little study at Arles, so in the large painting of St. Rémy, the young blossoms spring forth from the broken wood; they are ringing like little bells on a spring morning, joyously heralding love for the newborn.

While Vincent was working on the "Almond Branches in Blossom," he was seized by a new outbreak of his illness, which occurred during a visit to nearby Arles. It was the beginning of a grave crisis with repeated heavy attacks lasting for over two months, the longest he had to endure. At the end of April, he wrote a few lines to Theo, but had to tell him: *"Today I wanted to read the letters which had come for me, but I did not yet have enough clearness to be able to understand them."* He added a postscript in which he said about the painting: *"Work was going well, the last canvas of flowering branches — you will see, it was perhaps what I had done most patiently and the best, painted with calm and a greater sureness of touch. And the next day, done for, like a brute."* In the next letter he repeated: *"I fell ill at the time I was doing the blossoms of the almond tree."* He deplored that he had lost his chance as the trees were no longer in bloom. *"What to tell you of these past two months? It doesn't go well at all; I am sad and worried, more than I could express to you and I no longer know what I am about."*

628

629

629

628

His *most patiently done canvas* of the almond blossoms was the result of an intense effort. His falling ill at the time he painted them, hints at a strain which all the devotion that Theo and Jo showed him evidently could not relieve. On the one side was his feeling of inferiority and the increasing fear of being a burden to Theo, whose family was now complete. On the

226

90. ALMOND BRANCHES IN BLOSSOM

other side remained his longing to be with him, his attachment and affection, which he spontaneously extended to Theo's child, *starting right away to do a painting for him*. This conflict added to his existing tension when he suffered his most severe crisis, which was also to be the last.   627

    Vincent's assertion that this canvas *was perhaps the best* calls for closer attention to its self-portraying character. The ambivalence in his relationship with Theo showed only one aspect of the contrasts within him. The birth of the child, for whom he did the painting, was only the external cause; the motif of the blossoming almond branches was his inner choice. The broken wood does not merely mean his own broken existence, and the young blossoms are not only symbolic of the new life in Theo's child. For the old wood and the new buds belong to each other, and thus, as one inseparable whole,   628 portray Vincent himself in his inner condition of hope rising from despair, of rebirth from death—as young grows from old and morning rises from night.

After the struggling "Reaper" in which he had conveyed his conception of death, the "Almond Branches in Blossom" follow with their joyful message of rebirth. The jubilant blossoms triumph over the old broken wood. As he expresses his love for the newborn child, he also portrays victory in *the struggle of his soul for the white ray.**

347

628   He had painted the almond blossoms *with calm and greater sureness of touch* — in white on an ethereal blue. Perhaps he thought this painting the best because he now applied so gently and calmly, and in broad daylight, the white which had broken through in the wild clouds of the stormy and contorted St. Rémy landscapes (plates 70, 71) and in his visionary "Starry Night"; the white he had so desperately sought as a resting point since the

604   "Sower." The *pure gold* had expressed his seeking the *almost smiling* in the "Reaper," his image of death. Now rebirth, announced by the white spring

628   blossoms, makes Vincent's *perhaps best* painting truly consoling.

---

* An affinity of vision is found in Goethe. By strewing blossoms, the angels saved the soul of Faust from the devil, to whom he had committed it:

Fluttering, quivering,	Blossoms of gratitude,	Truth in its nearness,
Sweetness delivering,	Flames of beatitude,	Ether in clearness,
Branching unblightedly,	Love they are bearing now,	Give the Eternal Hosts
Budding delightedly,	Rapture preparing now,	Everywhere Day!
Bloom and be seen!	As the heart may!	

(Translation by B. Taylor)

PART VI

ENDING THE JOURNEY

St. Rémy and Auvers

91. THE RESURRECTION OF LAZARUS

230

THE RESURRECTION OF LAZARUS

One of the first paintings which Vincent did when recovering from the last and most severe recurrence of his illness was the "Resurrection of Lazarus" (plate 91). It is a fragment after an etching by Rembrandt (plate 92). Christ, the principal figure there, is omitted. In the center of Vincent's composition is a woman in a green dress. She is at the entrance of a cave, bending towards Lazarus in intense animation. Her arms are stretched out to him as if to receive him from the grave. In her right hand she holds a piece of cloth. While there is no sun in Rembrandt's work, a large sun is shining above the woman in Vincent's painting. In the foreground Lazarus lies in an opened coffin; the upper part of his body is raised a little and leans against the wall of the cave. He is in a state of utter weakness and can hardly lift his head and open his eyes. On the right is the profile of another woman.

Vincent described this work to Theo: *"On the other side I have scribbled*   632
a sketch after a painting I have done of three figures who are in the background of the etching of Lazarus: the dead man and his two sisters. The cave and the corpse are violet, yellow, white. The woman who takes the handkerchief off the face of the resurrected man has a green dress and orange hair; the other has black hair and a garment striped green and pink. At the back a countryside of blue hills, a rising yellow sun. The combination of the colors would thus speak by itself of the same thing which the light and shade of the etching expresses. I should still have at my disposal the model who sat for the Berceuse, and the other whose portrait after Gauguin's drawing you have just received, and I would certainly try to carry it out in large size, this canvas, as they are the personalities of whom I would have dreamed as characters."

231

92. REMBRANDT, THE RESURRECTION OF LAZARUS (ETCHING)

Not only is the woman, the central figure in Vincent's work, shown with
the features of the Berceuse, but the face of the resurrected man is unmistakably Vincent's own. The resemblance is all the more striking if compared
with a "Self-Portrait" (plate 93) which he had done immediately after the
earlier crisis, when he was painting the "Reaper." The green color of
Madame Roulin's dress is much lighter in the "Resurrection of Lazarus" than
it was in "La Berceuse." Her unusual orange hair, which had always been
neatly braided on her head, now flows openly over her shoulders in bright
light. She is altogether rejuvenated and appears idealized as an angelic figure.
The woman who had personified motherhood in "La Berceuse" now assumes
the rôle of an angel raising Lazarus from the grave. Vincent's identification

232

93. SELF-PORTRAIT

with Lazarus and the portrayal of Madame Roulin as his saviour reaffirm his underlying relationship with her — that of a son to a mother who in a rebirth delivers him from his nightmare of suffering.

Before his last attacks, when he had just started to do the "Almond Branches in Blossom" for Theo's newborn son, he wrote to his sister: *"Thinking like this but very far away, the desire comes to me to remake myself and try to get excused for the fact that my paintings are nevertheless almost a cry of agony, though in the rustic sunflower symbolizing gratitude."* W 20

233

To whom should gratitude be expressed if not to the Berceuse, the mother, who was to be surrounded by the sunflowers? The triptych thus brought together the symbols of gratitude and motherhood. The *agony* through which Vincent had since gone still lies over him and marks his whole appearance as he is being resurrected by the same mother figure.

A few days before painting the "Resurrection" he mentioned in a letter to Theo that he wanted to do again the "Potato Eaters": *"That canvas must be all black now; perhaps I could do it again altogether, out of my head."* This work, *the effect of lamplight,* as he called it now again, had been the first in which the position of his name had affirmed the self-portraying meaning of the symbolic enclosure. The chair of the sad young man who was looking towards the mother had been obscurely signed "Vincent." His desire at this stage to do the "Potato Eaters" again, to *remake* it, corroborates his urge to *remake himself.* In the "Resurrection," Vincent remakes himself as in a second birth, completing the first which had left him in the inner dependence on the mother. One will recall his remarks about his early childhood that it *would be better for him not to re-establish what only mother and he could remember,* and that his youth had been *somber and under a black ray.* His relationship with Christine, too, he had connected with *a somber past against which life should be a constant struggle* (pages 100, 169).

This state of his mind had been the background of many of his works. In "La Berceuse" his signature, enclosed in the arm of Madame Roulin's chair, had underlined his marginal position to the mother. At that time he had also placed his name within the coffin-like box in his "Chair." The same motif of enclosure was evident in other important paintings, even in such a cheerful work as the "Fishing Boats at Stes. Maries." We remember his stirring letter from the Borinage, that *he felt like a bird in a cage, in the impossibility of doing anything* (page 80), and his thought about liberation from imprisonment when he painted the drawbridges. Though in an obvious contrast, their structure had much in common with the weavers' looms which had conveyed his somber isolation. All these portrayals of enclosure, the earlier ones still in the *deep black frames* (page 124), had symbolized his *being enclosed* and *walled in* within maternal confines. His ensuing condition of both division and the urge to unite was seen in various outstanding works such as the "Breakfast Table," the "House in Arles," the "Bedroom," and the "Still Life on a Drawing Board." The predominantly female symbolism of these paintings had pointed to the connection of womanhood with his inner predicament.

234

Vincent's *desire to remake himself,* which had been announced by the "Almond Branches in Blossom," takes on an eminent form in his "Resurrection of Lazarus." As an actual portrayal of his remaking himself, this painting becomes one of those essential works which he had to do *to come to the end of his task,* as he had said of the "Reaper." In the sense that the "Reaper" was the opposite of the "Sower," the "Resurrection of Lazarus" is the opposite of the "Potato Eaters," signifying the near completion of his road, which he had first depicted in his dark motifs of enclosure in the Dutch period. Now the enclosure is opened, the coffin is uncovered — he can rise from his confinement.

W 20

604

"I need air," he exclaimed, determined to end his confinement in the asylum which *weighed on him more than he could say.* He insisted that he would return to the North, and pertinently called some canvases which he actually had *done from memory* during his last illness "Reminiscences of the North." Plate 94 shows a quivering vision of thatched houses with a red sun setting behind them and spirals flaming to the sky; in the foreground is a man carrying a spade. This work bears out what he had written to his sister: *"Some of my paintings, if I compare them with others, certainly show traces that it is a sick man who has painted them, and I assure you I don't do it on purpose."* The subject resembles the cottages he had done years before in Holland, such as a canvas from Nuenen, "Peasant Going Home" (plate 95).

631

629

W 16

It was in fact in the last phase of his stay in *the old cloisters* of St. Rémy that Vincent painted his "Resurrection of Lazarus." About two weeks later, in the middle of May 1890, he returned to the North. *"Oh yes, it is quite finished, this journey here,"* he wrote to Theo. This was true in more than one sense; in late July the journey of his life was to come to an end.

605

630

We are reminded of the age-old conception of man's return to his origin when the circular road of life is closing (page 71). He is then received by Mother-Earth, *as the great book of nature spoke of it to us* in the "Reaper," the image of death. In the "Resurrection of Lazarus" the meaning of Vincent's rising from the grave as birth, or rather rebirth, is stressed by the central position which he again gives to the now idealized mother figure.

604

Instead of Rembrandt's Christ, he painted a huge sun. This should not be taken as derogatory to Christ, for whom Vincent always felt the greatest veneration. He never wanted to portray Christ, and it may be remembered how vehemently he objected to Bernard's and Gauguin's *Christs in the garden,*

615

asserting that *for him there was no question of doing something from the Bible*. The rising sun, his symbol of love, at the same time conveys the emergence of light, of sight and consciousness. Its radiant brightness is repeated around the head of Lazarus, i.e., his own head; it has dissolved the darkness of the cave and spreads light everywhere.

Besides the sun, there is something very arresting in the position of the raised hand of the Berceuse. While the three figures of the group remain below the skyline, her hand extends above it as a large silhouette against the sky, as if to take the place of the single tree with its darting branches in Vincent's other paintings. Yet her hand does not express the struggling motion of the lonely fighter but rather is testifying and exalting, recalling the hand of Christ in Rembrandt's work, which is also raised high above the group. The prominence of the hand heightens the impact of the scene in the cave, linking it with the sunlit sky.

The hand, an ancient symbol of Bona Dea, the Good Goddess, the life-forming mother, is also an expression of the masculine power to create.[38] In contrast to the shaded and receding hand of the woman in Rembrandt's etching, Vincent painted the hand of the Berceuse upright, in daylight, and large, like the hand of a man. Just as he portrayed his own condition of hope rising from despair in the "Almond Branches in Blossom," so in the "Resurrection of Lazarus" he *remakes himself* by his own creative act. His rebirth is not merely of a mother's making. He himself is the re-creator in the self-portraying resurrection, in which the raised hand of the Berceuse is also his own creative hand and thus expresses union of the male and female factors within him. The woman-angel symbolizes his inner female counterpart, the soul, the "anima," animating the imprisoned body. This second birth amounts to an integrating process in Vincent's deliverance from the *somber past* and his rising to light.

He had been particularly emphatic about that somber past, when he had portrayed Christine in "Sorrow" and "The Great Lady" (plates 7, 65), describing his tie with her as *grown together*. These perceptions have deep roots in the human psyche. They may go far back into man's past, to his earliest infancy when he was grown together with the mother as in her womb. But it was a dark and unknown condition prior to consciousness, almost like a state of pre-life before birth, or of after-life or death. This would explain Vincent's reference to the *threatening somber past and a dark shadow*. His reaction that *life should be a constant struggle against it* suggests an awareness of the nature of these experiences. Although they stemmed from his personal and intimate

212

212

212

life, they have a far broader scope and significance in human evolution as a whole.

A somber past, as the original condition of the world before light came into being, is a general concept of mankind. Since the earliest times, mythology tells of an indistinguishable somberness, neither light nor dark, the realm of an all-embracing figure of a great Earth-Mother who was at the same time woman and man in an undivided state. The contrasts emerged with the advent of light, which qualified its opposite as darkness. Light equally signified man's emergence from chaos and the awakening of consciousness. This was not a process completed at one moment but the beginning of a development of which our time is but a stage, carrying within it the traces of these primordial images.

In this development symbolism fulfills the important function of communicating to us primitive elements and motives which have existed in mankind as far back as memory may reach. These basic motives are experienced in a receptive as well as in a creative way through the medium of symbolic forms and expressions. Their vestiges are found in mythology, religions, cults and traditions, throughout the ages, from ancient graves to works of contemporary art.

The work of Van Gogh is typical of the communicating nature of symbolism. We have followed this all through his paintings, e.g. the "Potato Eaters," the "Blossoming Almond Twig," "La Berceuse," the "Starry Night," the "Reaper." The "Resurrection of Lazarus," now added to those works, deepens their symbolic meaning, which is virtually confirmed by Vincent's own words. When he had designated his mother figure, the Berceuse, as the center of the triptych, he had emphasized the solemnity of this arrangement by calling the "Sunflowers" at either side *lampholders or candelabra* 574 (page 174). In the "Resurrection of Lazarus," the Berceuse is given an even more exalted position. According to various letters, he had deliberately chosen Madame Roulin as the Berceuse. In June 1889, he wrote to Theo: *"...Ah, if I had now and then someone like that* [the model for an Arlé- 595 sienne] *or like the woman who posed for the Berceuse I would do something quite different."* And in another letter: *"Also I tell you—and you see it in* 605 *the Berceuse, however much a failure this attempt may be and weak—had I the strength to continue I would have done portraits of saints and saintly women from life who would have appeared as of another century, and they would be middle-class people of today and yet they would be related to very*

237

94. REMINISCENCES OF THE NORTH

primitive Christians. The emotions which this causes are, however, too strong.
I should stop at that, but later, later I don't say that I shall not come back to
the charge."

In the "Resurrection of Lazarus" he came back to that charge. Here not
only Madame Roulin, the Berceuse, personifies an early Christian, but Vincent
himself has become one in the figure of Lazarus. The early Christians who
had serenely accepted suffering were a frequent theme in his letters. He

238

95. PEASANT GOING HOME

admired them, and he felt compassion for them as he did for every suffering creature. In St. Rémy he once compared old cab horses to the early Christians as they had the same *large, beautiful, heartbroken eyes.* In Nuenen he already 591 had spoken of the long-suffering weavers as *old cab horses,* and when writing 392 from Arles about the artist's life, he said: *"One feels oneself like a cab horse* 489 *... one no longer revolts against things but is not resigned either... There is an art of the future, and it must be so beautiful, so young, that truly if at*

239

present we give up our own youth for it, we can but gain by it in serenity."
His linking the Berceuse, himself, and his fellow artists, to the early Christians should, however, not be seen from the angle of any one creed. To Vincent, suffering was the fate of all mankind and at the same time a very personal experience which he neither sought nor avoided.

Just after Theo's marriage, and before entering the asylum at St. Rémy, W 11 Vincent had written to his sister: *"It is very probable that I shall have to suffer a great deal yet. And to tell you the truth I don't like it at all, because under no circumstances would I want a career of a martyr. Because I have always looked for something else than heroism which I do not have, which I certainly admire in others, but which I tell you again, I do not think is my duty or my ideal."* In the same letter he wrote: *"Not very far from here there is a grave, very, very, very old, older than Christ, on which this is inscribed: 'Blessed be Thebe, daughter of Telhui, priestess of Osiris who never complained of anyone.' I thought involuntarily of this when you told me that ˙the patient you are nursing never complained... Mother must be satisfied with Theo's marriage and he writes me that she appears to be rejuvenating. This gives me great pleasure."*

He had already quoted the old inscription in a previous letter to Theo, when he was painting the "Berceuse" for the fifth time, shortly after the 582 painful detention in the hospital cell at Arles: *"Oh, I must not forget to tell you a thing of which I have thought very often. By mere chance in an article of an old newspaper I found a word written on an ancient grave in the neighborhood between here and Carpentras. Here is this very, very, very, old epitaph of the time of, say, Flaubert's Salambo [sic]: 'Thebe, daughter of Telhui, priestess of Osiris who never complained of anyone.' If you see Gauguin you should tell him this. And I thought of a faded woman; you have at home the study of this woman who had such strange eyes, whom I had met by another chance. What is that she never complained of anyone? Imagine a perfect eternity, why not, but don't let us forget that the reality in the old centuries has this: 'and she never complained of anyone'."* He reverted a few times to the same subject, always repeating the full epitaph eulogizing the acceptance of suffering by the priestess of Osiris.

The extent to which he was seized by the experience of suffering is 597 expressed in another letter to Theo from the asylum: *"To learn to suffer without complaining, to learn to consider pain without repugnance, it is just about there that one risks vertigo, and yet could it be, could one yet foresee*

240

even a vague probability that on the other side of life we shall find good reasons for the existence of pain which seen from here sometimes occupies so much the whole horizon that it takes on the proportion of a hopeless deluge." His looking to *the other side of life* to find out what one cannot see from this side of the horizon is a virtual allusion to the non-conscious origin of his suffering. There may be relevance here in his remark about *some, he did not* 605 *know what, influences from outside* (pages 150, 206).

He also implies a *vague probability* of consolation. Only shortly before 597 he had said of himself and of Gauguin and Bernard that *perhaps they were* 595 *there to console or prepare for a more consoling painting* (page 201). Consolation in pain, misery and death by the belief in recovery and revival sustains the idea of resurrection which has persisted in all religions from the earliest mythology down to our day. Van Gogh's reiteration of the revered name of Osiris and his *imagining a perfect eternity* shows the same universal approach 582 to humanity as his reference on other occasions to Buddha and Christ, to Socrates and Tolstoi. It is revealing to see how his "Resurrection of Lazarus" goes back directly to the primeval Egyptian myth: indeed, it portrays the original story of Osiris with a striking exactness. The dead Osiris had been resurrected by the Goddess Isis who was mother, wife and sister in one person. The resurrection took place in union with Ra, the God of the Sun.

In Vincent's "Resurrection of Lazarus" only the two sisters witness and assist in the revival. The rejuvenated Berceuse who resurrects him now acts not only as a mother but as his sister. When imagining her as one of the sisters, he had thought of the other as an Arlésienne, of whom he had done a painting after a drawing by Gauguin (plates 96, 97). Among Vincent's papers an unfinished letter to Gauguin was found, in which he writes from Auvers about the "Arlésienne": *"And it gives me enormous pleasure that you* 643 *say the portrait of the Arlésienne, strictly based on your drawing, is to your liking. I have tried to be respectfully faithful to your drawing, while nevertheless taking the liberty of interpreting it by means of color in the sober character and the style of the drawing in question. This is a synthesis of an Arlésienne if you like; as the syntheses of Arlésiennes are rare, take this as the work of you and me, as a summary of our months of work together. For my part, I have paid for doing it with another month of illness, but I also know that this is a canvas which will be understood by you, me and by very few others, as we would wish it to be understood."* Of the *very few others* he quoted Dr. Gachet[39] as saying: *"How difficult it is to be simple."* 643

96. THE ARLESIENNE

242

The "Arlésienne," one of his last works before the "Resurrection of Laza-rus", was painted at the time he did the "Almond Branches in Blossom," when the heavy attacks had recurred. He had made several versions of the "Arlésienne," always with two books on the table in front of her. There are no books in Gauguin's drawing, but, as will be noted, in every other respect Vincent *strictly* adhered to it. When Gauguin was with him in Arles, Vin-   643
cent had done the portrait of a woman reading a novel (plate 56). It may be recalled that he had worked on this canvas, under Gauguin's influence, *from imagination* and had in all likelihood been thinking of his sister   W 9

97. PAUL GAUGUIN, AN ARLESIENNE

(page 135). He then also painted another "Arlésienne," and in both portraits books play a prominent part. At that time he had placed the two books on Gauguin's chair, where they symbolized the spiritual tie between the two men. The book meant to him *all books or literature and at the same time*   351
conscience, reason and art, as he had said in Nuenen where he did his first still life with books (plate 15).

By adding the two books to Gauguin's drawing, Vincent stresses not only the spiritual bond between himself and his friend *who should take this*   643
as a work done by them together, but as this symbolism extends to his model, the Arlésienne, a spiritual attitude is also implied towards her. He thus makes her join the ranks of the *copains* and, like a sister, she becomes a positive link between them — a distinct change compared to his other experiences with women in Arles, which had led to jealousy.

Vincent's choice of the Berceuse and the Arlésienne, of whom he had
632   *dreamed as the characters of the sisters of Lazarus,* throws light on the back-
582, W 11   ground of his repeated references *by mere chance* and *involuntarily* to the
ancient name of Osiris. In one of these letters to his sister he compared the
W 13   fate of man to that of the wheatfields: "*... for aren't we, who live on bread,
ourselves wheat to a considerable extent, at least should we not submit to
growing without the power to move like a plant ... and to being mown like*
607   *it when we are ripe.*" Writing in a similar way to Theo, he added: "*... if one
is not sown in the earth to germinate there, what does it matter, one is
ground to become bread.*" These strange reflections gain a meaning from the
old myth, in which Isis had first personified the type of the Mother-Earth-
Goddess to whom Osiris, God of Fertility, was sacrificed so that the earth
should be fertilized. But when he was buried she changed from the Terrible
Mother into the Good Mother who gave rebirth to her son, raising him from
the underworld to new life and to a great kingdom in our visible world. She
thus made him a symbol of consolation, herself also becoming his wife and
sister. The sisterly relation prevailed; Isis and Osiris were even believed to
have originally been together as twins in the mother's egg.

The death and resurrection of Osiris and the change of Isis from the
Mother-Earth Goddess who had to kill, to the reviving Good Mother and
loving wife and sister, symbolize instincts and impulses in human nature
which have a determining influence on the relationship between man and
woman. These impulses were later dramatized in the Greek tragedies and
reappear in the plays of Shakespeare. In our time, psychoanalysis has seen in
the same forces the basis for the Oedipus complex.[40] More recent psychological
research tends to apply the symbolism of the Isis and Osiris myth in a still
broader sense to a transformation of man's character. In one of the latest
works in this field, "The Origins and History of Consciousness", by E. Neumann,[41] we read:

"It is no accident that the many-sided figure of Isis was not only the wife
of Osiris and the mother who bore him anew, but also his sister. The sisterly
side of the man-woman relationship is that part of it which stresses the
common human element; consequently, it gives man a picture of woman
that is close to his ego and more friendly to his consciousness than the sexual
side. It is a typical form of relationship, not a real one. Mother, sister, wife
and daughter are the four natural elements in any relationship between man
and woman. Not only do they differ typologically, but each has its legitimate

244

place in the development — and misdevelopment — of the individual. In practice, however, these basic types may be mixed; for instance, maternal or conjugal traits may be involved in a man's relations with his sister, but the important thing is that the sister, the feminine soul-image who appears personally as Electra and transpersonally as Athene, is a spiritual being, representing the female as a separate, ego-conscious individual who is quite distinct from the feminine-collective aspect of the "Mothers". Once the anima-sister has been experienced through the rescue of the captive, the man-woman relationship can develop over the whole field of human culture."

"His ascension and resurrection reflect a psychic transformation which is mythologically projected as the union of the lower, earthly Osiris with the higher, or the union of the dismembered but reconstituted body of Osiris with the higher "spiritual soul" and "spiritual body". This self-transformation, resurrection and sublimation, which is at once a union with the self, is described as the union of Osiris, God of the Underworld, with the Sun-God, Ra."

"The rescue of the captive" in Neumann's book refers to the "female side" in man, to his unconscious, his soul. Vincent's work, the self-portrayal of *the liberation of the prisoner, of the remaking of himself,* shows his own "experience of the anima-sister". Should these experiences be merely coincidental? Or rather, do they point to the continuous vitality of those age-old symbolic images, which the artist and the psychologist expressed, independently of each other and in different generations, each in his own way. 133, W 20

Apart from his version of the fragment of Rembrandt's "Resurrection of Lazarus" — depicting his revival by a mother-sister figure as it had been symbolized in the resurrection of Osiris by Isis — Vincent has left some little known, yet enlightening large drawings. About the time he was quoting the epitaph on the old grave, he had drawn several times the head of the woman in an ancient Egyptian head-dress. The expression of her face is very unusual: her smile is at the same time mystifying and frightening. In one of the drawings (plate 98) he added a sketch of an emaciated bearded man beside the woman; her head is enormous compared with the small bust of the man. He will be recognized as the reaper whom Vincent had drawn on the back of another portrait of the same woman (plates 83 and 84). Such portrayals as background to the mysterious woman — Egyptian priestess or goddess — are compelling in their affinity with the myth of the Mother-Earth-Goddess. Another version (plate 99) shows the profile of a young woman in the position of the bearded man, again a strong contrast to the huge head. These drawings may indicate Vincent's imagination when *he thought* so *very often* of the old inscription with the name of Osiris. The Egyptian woman, the reaper, and the young woman, seen together in the light of the Isis and Osiris myth, are like an illustration of some of its phases leading to the resurrection.

98. EGYPTIAN WOMAN

The original unity of Isis and Osiris as twins in the mother's egg symbolized male and female elements together in one shell. It was the nucleus of the human being, with all the forces connoted by the terms "male" and "female" (page 200) unfolding within it. Their incongruous development and conflict, of which the confused relationships between men are one symptom, had caused the yearning of the individual for harmony in these contrasts, in an urge to remake himself. The reunion with his sister in the resurrection of Osiris thus conveyed the idea of integration of the male and female, light and dark in man, of body and soul.

The continuance of this process is evident in Vincent's "Resurrection of Lazarus" and its validity is affirmed by another salient symbol, again identical with the old Egyptian myth — the large rising sun which he had painted

99. EGYPTIAN WOMAN

instead of Christ. The resurrection of Osiris in union with the God of the Sun signified his rise from the darkness of the underworld to daylight. Resurrection in the wake of the sun is no accidental concurrence: ascending to light symbolizes man's gaining consciousness.

Vincent's "underworld" is reflected in his enclosures, his dark paintings of the miners, peasants and weavers of his early period, among which the "Potato Eaters" stands out as the counterpart to the "Resurrection of Laza-

247

rus." In the darkness of night the lamp gave only sparse light in the grim hut. But this lamp was the glimmer that was to grow into full sunlight. In the somber hut the young peasant was absent-minded as he looked for the mother; his head did not seem to know what his hand was doing. The resurrection, however, takes place in the bright light of the enormous rising sun. In his last self-portrait (plate 93) his head is like a glowing yellow star emerging from a dark sky. In the "Resurrection of Lazarus", moreover, not only his head and that of the Berceuse are in full light, but also the background of night has changed into daylight which radiates around his rising

629   head like the sun. Now even the cave is sunlit. He thus *remade the "Potato Eaters," the canvas which must be all black now.*

     The two paintings exemplify works which he had at one time charac-

316   terized: *"… however different they may be, they will nevertheless complement each other."* The lamp and the sun, night and day, absent-mindedness and consciousness, imprisonment and liberation, isolation and integration, looking for the mother and finding her as mother-sister: these are the complementary opposites in the two works. They make the "Resurrection of Lazarus" — the second birth — a symbol of maturing life.

     Rising from the darkness of his last crisis, Vincent adopts Rembrandt's "Resurrection of Lazarus" for expressing an inmost experience, almost like *a*

W 20   *cry of agony* — his rebirth into life. He now accomplishes the portrayal of ordinary people as saints and saintly women. One may conceive that this

605   exertion *caused him too great emotions* when realizing that in this portrait of himself and the two women of Arles he personalizes the transcending, timeless theme of resurrection.

     The idea of resurrection had preoccupied Vincent for years. After he had spent his last winter in Holland, he had written to Theo from Antwerp

453   *there was resurrection in the atmosphere of a first spring day.* When, after the shock of his disappointment over Kornelia, he had told Theo that his

193   *love had literally been slain,* he had added: *"But after death one rises from death. Resurgam."* He connected resurrection with man's remaking himself

543   in a second letter about Tolstoi (page 210): *"And if he does not believe in resurrection, he seems to believe in the equivalent — the continuance of life — the march of humanity — man and work almost infallibly continued by humanity in the generation to come. Enfin, it should not be ephemeral consolations that he gives. Himself a nobleman, he turned laborer, can make boots, can mend stoves, can guide the plow and dig the earth. I can do nothing of all that,*

248

but I can respect a human soul energetic enough to reform itself in such a way. My God, we have after all not to complain of living in a time where there would be nothing but idlers, when we witness the existence of such specimens of poor mortals, who do not even believe very strongly in heaven itself. He believes — I have perhaps already written it to you — in a non-violent revolution, by the need of love and religiousness which must manifest itself in the people as a reaction to scepticism and the desperate suffering that makes one despair."

Vincent had not read Tolstoi's book and these views were apparently his own, as may have been the thoughts he had expressed at that time to his sister regarding the poet Walt Whitman. In the same letter he also wrote about the painter Monticelli: *"And what does it matter to us whether there is* W 8 *a resurrection or not when we see a living man rise up immediately in the place of a dead one. Taking up the same cause, continuing the same work, living the same life, dying the same death."* He felt unusually close to Monticelli, who had lived in Marseilles and died a few years before Vincent came to the south of France, and he actually thought of himself as the living man taking up the cause of a dead one. His conception of resurrection thus has a threefold meaning. Apart from his *consoling hope to see another and* 490 *better life than in this world,* as he once wrote to Theo, he saw resurrection in the *continuance of life, the march of humanity in the generation to come* 543 and not least in man's *remaking himself* during his own lifetime. W 20

Seen in this way, resurrection is perhaps not so very far from our daily experience of life and nature when we awake every morning to see light breaking through the darkness of night. Indeed, it may not be less natural.

249

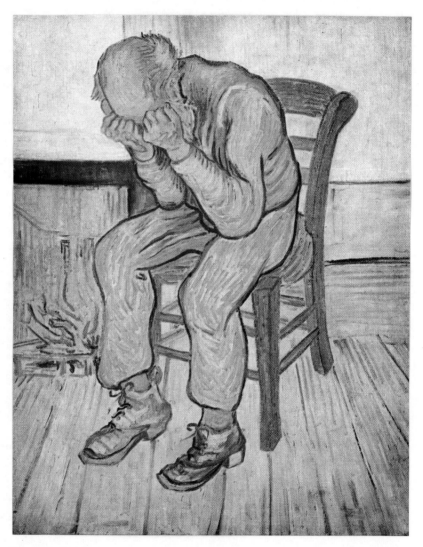

100. OLD MAN

250

OLD MAN / IRISES

In the last days of his stay at St. Rémy, Vincent's health improved rapidly. He worked with great vigor, painting a new canvas practically every day. Between April 29, when he informed Theo that he had resumed work, and May 14, the date of his last letter from St. Rémy, he did at least fifteen paintings in addition to numerous drawings. He later wrote to his sister from Auvers: *"At St. Rémy, the last days I again worked in a rage."* One of his subjects in those last two weeks was "Old Man" (plate 100). No reference can be found in his correspondence to this portrait, which he could have done just before or after, or even simultaneously with, the "Resurrection of Lazarus."

W 21

It is a repetition in colors of the drawing (plate 8), done years before in The Hague. He had then made two drawings and an etching and had written to Theo about the *little old man whose expression revealed something precious, noble, something not destined for the worms, and a frame of mind which gave him the feeling of an eternal home to which he was near* (page 30). He had also mentioned a similar drawing (plate 101) done still earlier at Etten, and which he *always kept because he wanted to make a better one.* At that time he had described it as *"an old sick peasant who sits on a chair at the fireplace, with head in hands and elbows on knees."* In two of several versions of that drawing one finds at the bottom the words *"worn out."*

248

247
150

The fact that Vincent reverted a third time to the portrait of the old, sorrowful man stresses its self-portraying character; the subject obviously had

101. WORN OUT

not ceased to preoccupy him. As he had kept the very early drawing to make
247   *a better one,* he apparently also kept the better one during all those years
until he made a still better version a few months before he himself went to
248   his *eternal home.*

The lonely man looks into himself as if reflecting Vincent's own worn
out condition. Compared with the earlier drawings, the man appears smaller
and weaker. He is sitting on a plain wooden chair; its yellow is contrasted
by the blue color of his clothes. This light blue tone also contrasts with the
distress of the bent body. The shoes are also notable; in their shape and
expression they resemble the "Two Shoes" (plate 16), the painting he had
done in Paris soon after his arrival from Nuenen. They add poignancy to the
portrayal of the tired old man, bearing witness to his walk on the stony road
of life.

252

The drawing done in The Hague had shown him in a downcast position similar to that of Christine, when he had drawn her as "Sorrow" (plate 7). Although he had been separated from her a long time, his identification with her misery must have been still latent in him — just as there had remained in his mind the theme of the "Old Man," which is very much like a companion piece to "Sorrow." The depressed mood of these drawings had been borne out in one of his letters at the time Christine and he were still living together: *"... in some circumstances it is better to be the vanquished than the victor."*   242

At Arles, in his prolific summer of 1888, only about six weeks after he had expressed a special ambition in his work, he had written to Theo: *"I have*   524
a horror of success ... I no longer care for victory ... I prefer to await the   529, 525
generation to come." In the next year when he had completed the "Reaper,"
which had been interrupted by his grave crisis, he wrote: *"And I myself*   605
already foresee the day when I shall have some success, regretting my solitude and my distress here when I saw through the iron bars of the cell the reaper in the field below... To succeed, to have lasting prosperity, one must have a different temperament from mine; I shall never do what I might have done and ought to have wished and pursued."

These feelings are even more transparent in the last version of the "Old Man," done in May 1890. In February he had been still grateful to the critic Aurier and pleased with his article, but after the last attack, at the end of April, he requested Theo: *"Will you ask Mr. Aurier not to write any more*   629
articles on my painting; tell him with insistence that, to begin with, he is mistaken about me since I really feel too overwhelmed with grief to be able to face publicity. To make paintings distracts me, but if I hear talk about them, that gives me more pain than he knows." At the same time he wrote to his mother: *"It goes almost always like that in a painter's life that the*   629a
success is about the worst."

The strained and exhausted body in the "Resurrection of Lazarus" is repeated in the bent, weak figure in the "Old Man." If the earlier drawings in Holland had conveyed his worn out state, the little old man now appears still more overcome with grief and humility. The end seems very near now. The struggle will soon be over; it may last as long as the small broken pieces of wood will burn. The tired man will hardly put fresh wood on the fire. He has no ambitions any more. As Vincent had foretold many years earlier in his letter from the Borinage, *he knew there would be a liberation,*   133
but it would be a late one.

253

604 Vincent had another task to fulfill *to come to the end*. He had to see Theo again. When he wrote *this voyage here is quite finished* he added:
630 "*Enfin, what consoles me is the great, the very great desire I have to see you again, you, your wife and your child and so many friends who have remembered me in my misfortune, since, besides, I also do not cease thinking of them.*"

The forthcoming meeting with Theo was foreshadowed by various inconsistencies, which are found in Vincent's letters ever since the brothers had separated about two years earlier. They recall the strong contradictions in his correspondence from Nuenen and Antwerp before he had joined Theo
476, 600 in Paris for the first time. Notwithstanding his deep longing for the *real life* with a wife and child, he had stated in a letter from his appalling detention
580 in the hospital cell at Arles: "*The best for me would certainly be not to remain alone, but I would rather live forever in a cell than sacrifice another life to mine.*" Shortly after he had withdrawn to the asylum in St. Rémy
594 he had written to Theo: "*It is a great consolation for me to know that you no longer live alone.*" But after learning that Jo was expecting a child, he
603 made the very odd comparison between his life and Theo's: "*Indeed, I am so satisfied that if sometimes there are cockroaches in the food here, in your house there is a wife and child.*" When he raised with Theo the question of
605 his return, he asserted he *would certainly not be with them, that would not*
648 *be possible*. However, later from Auvers, he claimed *they could live together for years*. There was another small but typical discrepancy, just before he left the asylum. Theo had invited him to stay with them in their apartment.
631 Vincent replied that *he would remain only two or three days and then go on to Auvers*,[39] but at the same time, in a letter to friends, he extended the
634a expected stay to *two weeks*.

These contrasts also find expression in his work before he left St. Rémy. In those last days he painted some of his best flower pieces. A large bunch of irises (plate 102) varies in tones from light blue to deep violet. Flanked and interspersed by their sharp green leaves like vigorous swords or flames, the irises are in a vase of chrome yellow earthenware on a stand of similar color. Also the background is yellow, of a lighter shade. In a distinct contrast to the upright bunch, some flowers and leaves are falling to the ground. Their direction downward to the right, behind the vase, is diametrically opposed to the soaring leaves on the left. A few other flowers are tumbling over the rim.

These "Irises" remind us of Vincent's previous flower pieces, from his early works in Holland all through the periods of Paris and Arles, always with

254

the contrast of up and down in them—like a leitmotiv of growth and decline. Even in such an innocent painting as the little "Pot of Herbs" (plate 22) it was not missing. This contrast was conspicuous in his imposing "Sunflowers" (plate 43) of Arles, which are particularly akin to the "Irises." In both canvases the vase is in the same position, as if the line of the horizon were running through it. The yellows of the background and stand are likewise almost identical. The movement of the two falling sunflowers was quite contrary to the flowering growth. This is still more pronounced in the "Irises" to which a further contrast, not less strong is added: the dark violet and blue against the pale and chrome yellow.

Vincent painted these flower pieces while he was waiting for permission to leave the asylum. His mind was fully set on his return to Paris, and he became impatient when an exchange of letters between Theo and Dr. Peyron about his departure caused a few days' delay. The very subject he chose for these last canvases indicates that his thoughts were already more in Paris than in St. Rémy. Throughout his stay in the asylum, he had not even once painted still lifes of flowers, although for long periods he had to remain indoors. In both Arles and Nuenen he had done such still lifes frequently. It was in Paris, however, that he did the great majority of his flower pieces, in fact about twice as many as in Nuenen and Arles together. One of his first works upon his arrival in Arles had been the "Blossoming Almond Twig" (plate 28) of which he had made two versions. Now, on the verge of his return to Paris, he suddenly concentrated again on flower pieces, his favorite subject when he had lived there with Theo. Within a few days he painted five large, magnificent canvases. They seem to be more accomplished than most of the still lifes of flowers he had done before.

633   In one of his last letters from St. Rémy to Theo, Vincent wrote: "*At present the betterment [le mieux] continues, the whole horrible attack has disappeared like a storm and I am working to give a last stroke of the brush here, with a calm and continuous fervor. I have in hand a canvas of roses on a light green background and two canvases representing large bunches of violet irises, one against a pink background where the effect is harmonious and soft by the combination of greens, pinks, violets. On the contrary, the other violet bunch (going as far as carmine and pure Prussian blue) stands out against a background of shrill lemon yellow, with other yellow tones in the vase and the stand on which it rests, and is an effect of the terrible, disparate complementaries which are exalted by their opposition.*"

256

This description recalls Vincent's wrestling with the *simultaneous exces-*   B 7
sive contrast in the colors of his "Sower." After the consoling paintings — the
"Starry Night," the "Reaper," the "Almond Branches" and the "Resurrection" — his struggle with the opposing violet and yellow seems to be
revived; it is like a regression into his fear *whether he would have the strength*   501
to paint the Sower in colors. (page 96) The imminent fulfillment of his *very*   630
great desire to see Theo again and to meet his wife and child brings brusquely
to the fore the other side of his inner contrast, his feeling *frustrated* in the *real*   531
life, which suddenly gives rise to a flare of fear lest the reunion should not
be harmonious. As if by compulsion, he had to contrast the *harmonious and*   633
soft canvases by the *terrible disparate complementaries* of the irises.

This portrayal of his condition at the time he left St. Rémy is corrob-
orated in a remarkable way by Vincent's own words when he continues the
letter to Theo: *"Yes, also to me it seems there is a very long stretch of time*   633
between the day when we took our leave at the station and these days now.
But, strange again, that just as we were so struck by Seurat's canvases on that
day, these last days here again are for me like a revelation of color." As he
faces the return to the North and to his brother's home his *symbolic language*   503
of color speaks even louder in the "Irises" than it did in the "Sunflowers."
By the exalting opposition of the violet-blue and yellow, which had charac-   633
terized his *hard subjects,* the "Sower" and the "House in Arles," the impact   501a, 543
of the "Sunflowers" is vigorously increased. Vincent not only doubles the
effect of the opposing movement of growth and wilting by the *terrible dis-*   633
parate complementaries of these colors, but intensifies this multiple contrast
still more when he sets the "Irises" against the other *harmonious* flower
pieces. Just as he had been *struck* on the day of his parting from Theo, now
as he returns to him, *strangely again these last days his revelation of color*   633
expresses his old inner conflict with threefold strength.

257

103. PORTRAIT OF DR. GACHET

PORTRAIT OF DR. GACHET

In her introduction to Vincent's letters, Jo described his visit to Paris: "I had expected a sick man, but here was a sturdy broad-shouldered man, with a healthy color, a smile on his face and a very resolute appearance; of all his self-portraits, the one before the easel is most like him at that period... 'He is perfectly well; he looks much stronger than Theo,' was my first thought. Then Theo drew him into the room where our little boy's cradle was... Silently the two brothers looked at the quietly sleeping baby — both had tears in their eyes... He stayed with us three days and was cheerful and lively all the time. St. Rémy was not mentioned... The first morning he was up very early and was standing in his shirt sleeves looking at his paintings, of which the apartment was full. The walls were covered with them ... besides they were under the bed, under the sofa, under the cupboards, in the little spare room, huge piles of unframed canvases; they were now spread out on the ground and studied with great attention. We also had many visitors; but Vincent soon perceived that the bustle of Paris did him no good and he longed to set to work again."

Vincent had written from St. Rémy that when he came to Paris he also wanted to work there. He was particularly keen on the idea of painting a bookshop, brightly lit at night, with many books in lively colors and with people passing in the dark street. He would also have to touch up several canvases done in St. Rémy. *It was not work that he would be lacking in Paris,* 626 he asserted. However, he did not carry out these intentions. In fact, he never worked there again. There is neither a painting nor a drawing, nor a letter from his stay in Paris which could amplify Jo's report. But he made up for it in nearby Auvers. His contact with Theo continued by intensive correspondence. Some three weeks after his visit, Theo, Jo, and the baby went to

259

Auvers where they all spent a Sunday together. In early July, Vincent again came to Paris for a day.

Upon Vincent's arrival in Auvers, Dr. Gachet [39] had recommended an inn which would have cost six francs a day, but Vincent found one for three francs fifty. As usual, he chose the cheapest place to stay. It was a poor lodging, a tiny room on the upper floor which did not even have a window, only a small skylight. He was alone once more. A few times a week he visited Dr. Gachet, who showed him great interest and also encouraged him to paint in his own house and garden. He spoke not only as a physician but as a lover of art; he himself drew, painted and etched. The doctor was very fond of the Impressionists, and when Cézanne, Guillaumin, Pissarro and Renoir had been in Auvers, they had become his friends.

Among the first works in Auvers, Vincent painted the "Portrait of Dr. Gachet" (plate 103). Gachet's face looks pale, the head rests on his right hand while the arm is leaning on a red table. He is dressed in a buttoned dark blue jacket, and wears a white cap on his reddish hair. In front of him are two yellow books, and a glass of water with two pale blue and purple foxgloves, with green leaves. His left hand lies squarely on the table. Behind him is a moving silhouette of blue mountains against a sky of a lighter blue. The whole background is covered with white and light blue strokes. Dr. Gachet's face, the look of his deep-set, transparent blue eyes, the drawn lines of his mouth, framed by a moustache and small beard, express intense melancholy.

Vincent added a small sketch (plate 104) when he described this canvas to Theo: *"I am working at his portrait, the head with a white cap, very fair, very light, the hands also in light carnation, a blue dresscoat, and a cobalt blue background, leaning on a red table, on which are a yellow book and a foxglove plant with purple flowers. It is in the same sentiment as the portrait of myself, which I took when I left for here. Monsieur Gachet is absolutely fanatical about that portrait and wants me to do one of him*, if I can, absolutely like that, which I too would like to do."* Shortly afterwards he mentioned in a letter to Gauguin: *"Now I have a portrait of Dr. Gachet with the heartbroken expression of our time."*

638

643

---

* This sentence has been published erroneously *"and wants me to do one for* [sic] *him"* which has given rise to misinterpretations. The original French written text is: *"... et veut que j'en fasse un de lui..."* (not "pour" lui), (plate 104).

260

He also wrote about the painting to his sister: *"My friend Dr. Gachet* W 22
*is decidedly enthusiastic about this last portrait of the Arlésienne of which
I also have one for me, and about a portrait of myself, and this pleased me as
he will push me to do figures and, I hope, will find me some models that
will be interesting to do. What impassions me most, much, much more than
all the rest in my profession — is the portrait, the modern portrait. I seek it
through the color and I am certainly not the only one to seek it in this way.
I would like, you see, I am far from saying that I could do all this, but
enfin I tend towards it, I would like to do portraits which a century later
would appear to the people of that time like apparitions. Hence I do not seek
to do this by the photographic resemblance but by our passionate expressions,
employing our science and modern taste of color as a means of expression
and exaltation of the character. So the portrait of Dr. Gachet shows you a
face in the color of over-heated brick, tanned by the sun, with reddish hair,
a white cap in a surrounding landscape, background of blue hills, his clothes
are blue ultramarine — this brings out the face, and makes it pale in spite of
its being brick color. The hands, the hands of an obstetrician, are paler than
the face. In front of him, on a red garden table, yellow novels and a flower
of foxglove, dark purple. The portrait of myself is also almost like that, the
blue is a fine blue of the South and the clothes are light lilac."*

In another letter to his sister he returned once more to the subject:
"I have done the portrait of Monsieur Gachet with an expression of melan- W 23
*choly which might often appear to those who look at the canvas like a gri-
mace. And yet, this is what one should paint, because then one can render*

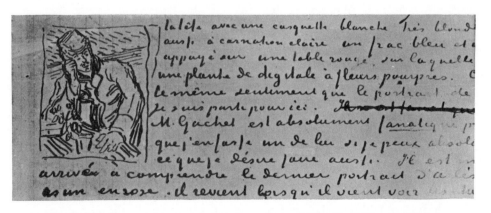

104. PART OF LETTER No. 638 WITH SKETCH OF THE PORTRAIT OF DR. GACHET

an account to oneself, in comparison with the old calm portraits, how much expression there is in our heads of to-day, and passion, like an expectation and like a growth. Sad but gentle, but clear and intelligent, this is how one ought to do many portraits."

Of no other work in Auvers did he write as much as of the "Portrait of Dr. Gachet," which shows the unusual importance he attached to the painting. While Vincent himself is portrayed in all his work, without his having to mention it, in the case of Dr. Gachet's portrait he is specifically outspoken about its self-portraying character. According to his letter to Theo, he had taken with him to Auvers a self-portrait done before he left St. Rémy.

638   He fully concurred with Gachet's wish to do his portrait *absolutely like that.*

This "Self-Portrait" (plate 105), the last he was to do, is among his most powerful works. The penetrating eyes are so strong that they almost hypnotize the beholder. Their tremendously forceful look reflects Vincent's psychic

R 43   energy and lets us sense its unfathomable source which *wells up out of our soul.* The stern expression of the mouth adds to the severity of the eyes. The rigid bearing of the head makes this portrait like a counterpart to the "Old Man" in which the face was buried in distress in the hands. What the bent figure of the *worn out* old man had expressed (pages 251/3) is now brought forth in the infinite desolation of Vincent's upright face, as if in a final impact: he has withdrawn into another sphere and no longer wants anything from this world.

As his first sojourn in Paris had culminated in the "Self-Portrait with the Easel" (plate 25), Vincent again concluded his stay in the South with a portrait of himself. Tense as he had been in the Paris painting, he had then still looked to the future. Before him had been his work, his canvas and easel. In this last self-portrait the piercing look — once directed at himself in

597   the mirror — is now directed straight at us like a challenge from *the other*

W 22   *side of life.* There is no horizon, no life line; he appears virtually *like an*

638   *apparition. In the same sentiment* as his self-portrait, and as that of the distressed old man, the melancholy in Dr. Gachet's portrait expresses Vincent's own state of mind during those weeks at Auvers. In the few days in

489   Paris he had been face to face with the reality of Theo's family, *the true and ideal life,* that to him was denied. Finally realizing that Theo belonged first of all to his wife and child, Vincent must have felt his loneliness weighing ever heavier on him as he climbed the narrow stairs to the cage-like room in the miserable little inn at Auvers.

262

The insoluble conflict between his deep-rooted desire to share Theo's life, and the compelling fact that this was impossible, is evident from his letters at that time. In one of them he wrote to Theo: *"I feel — a failure. — So much for me — I feel that is the fate which I accept and which will not change any more. But all the more reason, putting aside all ambition, we can for years live together without ruining each other."* He had used the term *ambition* on several earlier occasions. Once in the Hague when he had just done his first canvases in color, he had written: *"But this I want to tell you; while painting I feel there are things of color in me coming to light which I did not have before, things of breath and power. Now I shall not yet send you that at once — let it first ripen a little, but know that I am full of ambition there and believe that for the present it is flowing."* In the flourishing summer of Arles, he had again spoken of the ambition he had in his work, which he pointed out was done by Theo and him together. What a difference between that ambition and his discouragement, as he now wrote from Auvers: *"He* [Dr. Gachet] *is just as discouraged in his profession as country doctor as I by my painting."* Another time he had referred to ambition in his letter to Bernard from Arles (page 152): *"I feel quite an ox ... and I admire the bull ... with a veneration that will prevent me from being ambitious."* In that case he had connected ambition with his physical frustration, as he had called it. He now implied that unless *they put aside all ambition they would ruin each other.* This very condition, which he imposed not only on himself but also on Theo, precluded any possibility of their living together, and the reiteration of his desire only reaffirmed his unreleased symbiotic relationship with Theo.

An additional illustration of his frame of mind was an apparent uncertainty whether he would continue to receive Theo's financial support: *"On the other hand, I too fear very much that I am confused and I find it strange that I do not in the least know under what conditions I left — if it is as formerly at 150 francs a month in three payments. Theo has not fixed anything and therefore, to begin with, I left in confusion."* He soon received the first payment of fifty francs, which obviously set him at ease, but his reproach was typical of the ambivalence in his feelings towards Theo.

In many respects the situation in Auvers resembled that of Arles after his arrival there from Paris. He again threw himself vigorously into his work, trying, as he later wrote, to be *of good enough humor.* While his thoughts remained centered on Theo, he tried to find a substitute for him. His hope

648
225
637
B 9
648
648
649

was now set on the new friendship with Gachet, who had received him very cordially, and who had given to him, as well as to Theo his opinion that Vincent's illness would not recur. The day he met the doctor, Vincent wrote to Theo: *"I have seen Dr. Gachet who gave me the impression of being* 635 *rather eccentric, but his experience as a doctor ought to keep him balanced in combating the nervous trouble by which he certainly seems to be attacked at least as seriously as I."*

A little later, when he was working at the portrait, Vincent wrote again: *"He certainly appears to me just as ill and confused as you or I, and he is* 638 *older and he lost his wife some years ago, but he is very much the doctor and his profession and his faith hold him up nevertheless. We are great friends already..."* He repeated: *"Enfin, father Gachet is very, but very* 638 *much like you and me."* These feelings are indeed evident in the portrait. The facial resemblance of Dr. Gachet to the Van Goghs is so striking that one is immediately seized by this self-portrayal. No less does *the heartbroken* 643 *expression of their time* in Gachet's face depict Vincent's own plight.

Once before he had done a portrait of his doctor (plate 63, page 161). It had been that of Dr. Rey, the physician of the hospital at Arles, whom he had painted while beginning to recover from his first attack, in which he had cut his ear. That painting was second to none in its self-portraying nature, a clear example of Vincent's projecting his inner condition into his work. He had painted this canvas when his wound was still fresh, even before the "Self-Portrait with the Bandaged Ear." He signed his name, adding *Arles 89*, in big letters, blood-red. Done in the first days of January, it pointed to his having reached the year 1889 in face of the dreadful attack at Christmas, when he had shed his own blood. Only Dr. Rey's left ear is visible, but in Vincent's identification with the man whom he portrayed, this ear became his own left ear — his burning wound — as he painted it in the same flaming red as his name below.

In the "Portrait of Dr. Gachet," which again is outstanding as a portrayal of two persons, Vincent's feeling of friendship for Gachet is conspicuously symbolized by the two yellow books in front of him. While he was still at work on the portrait, he mentioned only one book to Theo, but in the letter to his sister after he had finished the painting, he writes *novels*. The W 22 two books are too important a motif to be accidentally in the portrait. Their significance has repeatedly been noted in previous works. There are usually not less than two when books are shown on a canvas which portrays or

626a   implies the portrayal of persons or objects *in their place*. The two books in the "Open Bible" at Nuenen were symbolic of the relationship between Vincent and his father. In Paris, as with the subject of shoes, he had done various still lifes with books, which symbolized his contact with Theo and the artists there (plate 19). At Arles, the two books in "Gauguin's Chair" stood for his spiritual companionship with Gauguin, while in the "Still Life on a Drawing Board" the book and the letter had expressed his acute situation in relation to Theo. In all the four versions of the "Arlésienne," done in St. Rémy, the

643   two books stressed Vincent's idea of *the synthesis of the Arlésienne as a work done by him and Gauguin together*.

Now in Dr. Gachet's portrait the two books again convey the spiritual tie between two men, Vincent and Gachet. To his description of the painting

638   to Theo, he added: *"I feel that he will understand us completely and that he will work with you and me without reservation, for the love of art, for art's sake, with all his intelligence."* The yellow, his color of love, emphasizes his

W 22   affection for Gachet, in whom *". . . I found a complete friend, something like a new brother, so much do we resemble each other physically and morally,"* as he reiterated in the letter to his sister. *Seeking the portrait through the color,* he enhances the expression of affinity with Gachet by complementing the blue of the coat and background and the red of the table by the yellow of the books, thus obtaining the unity of the three pure primaries.

The glass of water with the foxglove reminds us of the "Blossoming Almond Twig" (plate 28), one of his first works in Arles. In the "Portrait of Dr. Gachet," it is again a symbol of hope, this time in his new friendship. However, there is a difference: while the young almond buds were full of vitality in their fresh white and pink tones, the foxglove, the medical plant, is mainly in a drooping movement and of a pale subdued color. Compared with the bright yellow of the books, it is almost like a hint of Gachet's and Vincent's discouragement in their profession and of the fragility of their existence as well as their friendship.

Even with the best intentions, Dr. Gachet could not have been a substitute for Theo or alleviate the cause of Vincent's depression, and the relationship with him was bound to take a course similar to that with Gauguin. Vincent was too closely attached to Theo for any replacement to succeed.

635   As, moreover, the *eccentric* Dr. Gachet also seems to have been difficult to get on with, it is not surprising that the new friendship was short-lived. In fact, this had been foreshadowed by Vincent himself. In almost the same

266

phrase with which he had once voiced his warning against "... *counting on*   535
Gauguin" (page 131), he wrote now from Auvers: "*I think that one must in*   648
no way count on Dr. Gachet. First of all he is more ill than I, as it seems
to me, or let us say just as much, there you are. Now if one blind man leads
another blind man, don't they both fall into the ditch?" Such a negative
approach expressed in the same letter in which he even raised doubt about
the future support from Theo, shows a similar ambivalent attitude to Gachet
as had been seen before in his relations with Gauguin — and much more so
in those with Theo. These contrasting feelings towards brother and friends
reflect his inner condition, as if he himself were "cut in two" — in an ambivalence concerning his own self. His torn state of mind is brought out in
that letter by more contradictions. On the one hand he said: "*But I shall still*
do my best to find that everything goes all right," and on the other: "*And*
the prospect grows darker, I see no happy future at all."

The correspondence with Theo during the remaining weeks at Auvers
continues to show discrepancies of this kind. Theo had written to Vincent
that he still hoped with all his heart that he too would one day have a wife.
But there is an intrinsic contradiction in the letter: "*You, you have found*   T 39
your way, old brother, your carriage is already well set and strong, and
I foresee my way thanks to my beloved wife." He could not have touched
their individual problems more directly. Because of his pioneering approach
to art, he could not get satisfaction in his job with the old-fashioned, short-
sighted art dealers. He tried to find happiness in his private life with his wife
and child. He wanted to console and encourage Vincent who must however
have felt an implicit difference of values in the letter. That he should have
found in his art an equivalent for Theo's family life was like an unwanted
confirmation of what he himself once had written to Theo: "*... the family*   604
may be for you what for me are nature, the clods of earth, the grass, the
yellow wheat, the peasant." Now, his answer to Theo is again contradictory:
"*And if my illness came back, you would excuse me. I still love art and life*   646
very much, but as for ever having a wife of my own I do not believe in it
very much. I rather fear that towards say forty — but don't let us say anything
—I declare I know absolutely nothing, but absolutely, as to what turn this
could still take." These words are as if they were an allusion to his early
death.

Soon afterwards, in one of his last letters, Vincent again speaks of his
resignation: "*Often I think of the little one. I believe it is surely better to*   649

267

bring up children than to give all one's nervous energy to make paintings, but what do you want, I am now — at least I feel — too old to retrace steps or to desire anything else. This desire has left me, although the moral suffering of it remains."

This moral suffering lies over the "Portrait of Dr. Gachet." Vincent's *melancholy* and *heartbroken expression of their time* is different from that *something sentimental or melancholy* to which he had taken exception years earlier when he wanted to express *severe suffering in his figures and landscapes* (page 17). He had then just started to paint. It was the beginning of his struggle for color — for light — in the course of which *he fell into full metaphysics of color.* The fight with the symbolic colors of the "Sower" continued with unabating vigor. By color, *by red and green, he had sought to express the terrible human passions,* as he had written from Arles (page 146), and through his color he found in St. Rémy *the white ray,* his ray of light. In Auvers he is at the end of the battle, now his melancholy expresses the *acceptance of fate.*

The fate of Vincent's personal life was *failure.* But as he had told Theo after he had painted his image of death, the "Reaper": *"The difference between happiness and unhappiness! both are necessary and useful and death and disappearance… this is so relative — and life the same."* In the same letter he wrote: *"Do you know of what I think quite often, what I have already said to you in the past, that if I did not succeed, yet I believed that what I had been working at would be continued. Not directly, but one is not alone in believing in things which are true. And what does one matter then personally?"* Here was the other side to his fate which he equally accepted. It went beyond his personal *physical frustration.* In a triumph of his spiritual forces he achieved a higher goal: *the essence of his art — was to strike man — in a later century.*

In the "Portrait of Dr. Gachet," this other side is stressed by the innumerable light strokes, as though to express once more *the ray from above.* They extend all across the sky and over the mountains in the background, touching Gachet's shoulder and following the contours of his arm. Linking the sky, the mountains and the figure, they bring continuous movement to the painting, symbolizing the everlasting unity of cosmos and man.

W 23, 643
218

503

533

347

648

648
607

531
218
W 22

625

268

WHEATFIELD WITH CROWS

"These days I am working much and fast; in so doing I seek to express   W 23
the desperately rapid passage of things in modern life," Vincent wrote in
June to his sister. We are reminded of his *fury of work* at the "Reaper" *who*   604
struggled like a devil to come to the end of his task and again of his *working*   W 21
in a rage in the last days at St. Rémy. During the two months at Auvers,
he worked no less furiously, doing about sixty canvases and many drawings.
When painting Dr. Gachet, he told Theo: *"I feel more sure of my brush*   638
than before I went to Arles," but five weeks later he was so thoroughly
exhausted that the brush was *almost dropping from his hands.*   649

In the spring of Arles, too, he had written: *"I am in a rage of work ..."*   473
(page 72). But at that time it was because the trees were in blossom, not
unlike Vincent's own prolific creativeness. He then recovered quickly from
momentary exhaustions after such absorbing works as the "Harvest." This
was long before he felt he was coming to the end. Long before may sound
exaggerated if one considers that it was actually only two years earlier, but
in Vincent's case a somewhat exceptional approach to time is indicated. His
concentrated speed could almost be compared with the hands and wheels
of an overwound watch whirling round in but a fraction of the normal span
of time. His productive capacity in the eight years of his painting was so
enormous that the physical effort alone would take most other artists several
times as long. The *rage* and *fury,* as he himself described his way of working,   473, 604
are symptomatic of his fierce drive in his art as well as in his life. He once
referred to another painter, who had died at the age of thirty-eight [42], and

106. CHURCH AT AUVERS

309

asserted: *"It is in this way that I see myself—as if within a few years I had to do something wherein there is heart and love and to do it with will-power."*

W 22

In a letter to his sister, Vincent commented on one of the works he had just completed, the "Church at Auvers" (plate 106): *"This is again almost the same thing as the studies which I did at Nuenen of the old tower and of the cemetery, only at present the color is probably more expressive and more sumptuous."* The canvas has much in common with the "Old Tower" (plate 107), of which he had done several versions at home. It is notable that in the "Church at Auvers" the woman wears a Dutch bonnet, as in the Nuenen paintings. Also the building in the "Townhall in Auvers on July 14th" (plate 110) resembles the town-hall in his birthplace at Zundert.

270

107. OLD TOWER

In the last weeks of his life, Vincent's thoughts obviously turned homeward, as they had done when his life had been threatened by his first attack in Arles. He had then *during his illness seen every room in the house in* 573 *Zundert, the graveyard, the church, the magpie's nest in the high acacia in the graveyard* (page 167). Similarly, during the last grave crisis in St. Rémy he had reverted to the subject he had drawn a long time before in his parents' house at Nuenen, "Peasant Going Home" (plate 95). The last versions of the "Old Man," and of a "Sower," after Millet (page 101), showed the same trend, the return to the earliest subjects of his work.

Now in Auvers he again paints those peasant houses which he had done so often at home in Holland. His "Cottage at Auvers" (plate 108) shows a remarkable development of the tree as the branches seem to break away from

271

108. COTTAGE AT AUVERS

it. As dark silhouettes against the white cloud, the loose branches begin to move like birds in the sky. In one of his last works, "Landscape at Auvers" (plate 109), done in July, the trees themselves seem to lose their hold in the soil. Painted in spirals, they rise to the sky as in a releasing motion. The whole vast plain appears to be one great movement as though the huge orb of the earth were visibly turning towards the sky. The *last line of the horizon,* the border line of our world, symbolizes the limit of life as seen from here. From the far distance of *the other side,* large light clouds are coming up in a countermovement as if to meet the revolving globe.

411

597

Vincent wrote about these last landscapes to Theo and Jo (plate 112): *"They are immense stretches of wheat under troubled skies, and I did not have to strain in order to seek to express sadness."* As if to explain this

649

272

109. LANDSCAPE AT AUVERS

sadness, he inserted between the lines: *extreme solitude.* The letter continues: *"You will see this soon I hope — because I hope to bring them to you to Paris as soon as possible, as I almost think that these canvases will tell you what I cannot say in words, what I see as healthy and strengthening in the country."* But his hope to bring those landscapes to Theo did not materialize, nor did his intention of staying a little longer in Paris, which he had mentioned a few times.

On the other hand, there is hardly a letter from Auvers in which he did not suggest that Theo, Jo and the child should join him there. Once he added: *"Then I look forward with pleasure to doing the portraits of all of you in the open air: yours, that of Jo and that of the child."* But during their visit the following Sunday, he did not paint. Instead they all were Dr. Gachet's

638

273

110. TOWNHALL IN AUVERS ON JULY 14TH

guests for lunch and then took a long walk. Shortly after his arrival in Auvers, Vincent suggested — just as he had done in Arles — that a house could be rented at not much higher cost than he was paying at the inn. It would then also be a pied-à-terre in the country for Theo's family. He argued with Theo that during the coming summer vacation, instead of the traditional trip to Holland, they should come to Auvers: *"That is why I would have you think of not going to Holland this year; it is always very, very expensive, the journey, and has never done any good. Yes, it does good, if you like, to mother who will love to see the little one — but she will understand and prefer the well-being of the little one to the pleasure of seeing him. Besides she will lose nothing, she will see him later."*

In the desperate fight against his loneliness, it was as if he competed with their mother for the visit of Theo and his family. His reasoning that *father,*

648

274

mother and child should take a month of absolute rest in the country instead   648
of the expensive trip to Holland was certainly meant well and sincerely. But
that this should be at Auvers shows Vincent's underlying aim to relieve his
own affliction, the *extreme solitude* which he could bear no longer. He even   649
wrote to Gauguin that he thought it *most probable that he would join him*   643
and De Haan in Brittany for a month if Gauguin would permit it, yet he may
have felt the futility of this idea as he did not finish that letter. In any case
it was never carried out.

He continued to plead with Theo and Jo: *"Would there be a way to see*   648
each other again more calmly—I hope so, but the journey to Holland I am
afraid, this will be the last straw for all of us. I always foresee that it makes
the child suffer later to have been brought up in town. Does Jo find this
exaggerated? I hope so, but, enfin, I believe one must nevertheless be cautious.
And I say what I think because you will quite understand that I take an
interest in my little nephew and am anxious for his well-being; as you have
been good enough to call him after me, I would wish that he had a soul less
unquiet than mine which is foundering."

His next trip to Paris seems to have been still more hectic; he went back
to Auvers the same evening. On his return he sent them a short note which
alludes to a strained atmosphere during his brief stay. In fact, Theo and Jo
had been run down owing to an acute illness of the baby, and Theo also had
business worries. A few days later Vincent replied to a reassuring letter from
Jo: *"It is not a slight thing when all together we feel the daily bread in*   649
danger, no slight thing when for reasons other than that too we feel our
existence fragile. When I returned here, I too felt still very sad and had
continued to feel weighing on me too the storm which threatens you. What
is to be done about it—you see, I try usually to be of good enough humor,
but my life too is attacked at the very root, my step too is unsteady."

In those days he wrote his last letter to his mother and sister: *"As for*   650
me, I am entirely absorbed by the immense plain with wheatfields against
the hills, large as a sea, fine yellow, fine tender green, fine purple of a
plowed and weeded piece of ground, regularly checkered by the green of
flowering potato plants, everything under a sky with fine blue, white, pink,
violet tones. I am entirely in a mood of an almost too great calmness, in a
mood to paint this."

The *almost too great calmness* was like a hint of a calm before a storm.
It didn't take long in coming. We see the storm break in "Wheatfield with

275

Crows" (plate 111). A billowing field of wheat in bright and chrome yellow rises mountain high to both sides of a path in the center, which runs from the foreground through the field until it is submerged under the spreading wheat. Two other grass-grown tracks turn to the sides, where they are cut off by the edges of the canvas. Large jetblack birds are swarming over the field. Two light clouds stand out against the deep, almost black blue of a storm-laden sky. The line of the horizon is windswept and flooded by the mounting 650 waves of the blazing wheat, *large as a sea*. The path in the center — as if to symbolize Vincent's own road — has come to a dead end, barred by the fire which has taken possession of the whole field.

The dark silhouettes of the crows were preceded by the loose branches above the house in the "Cottage at Auvers." In their movement against the sky they recalled the gesticulating branches of the tree which, since his earliest drawings, had symbolized Vincent's struggle. They are now completely detached and have become identical with the birds, traditional messengers, which were nearly always somber in his paintings like the thoughts they carried. The few little birds we once saw in the "Sower" (plate 39), the counterpart to the wheatfields, have become the stormy swarm of the huge crows, sinister and foreboding in their intense blackness. In the center of that field was a large furrow. Its position under the enlivening morning sun resembles that of the path, again directly below the light cloud and in the center of this last of his wheatfields. In the earlier painting the furrow had been dug to prepare the earth for the sower's task and came towards us together with the striding man. Now the path goes away and disappears from our eyes.

Vincent painted the "Wheatfield with Crows" in the very fields where, it is reported, he put an end to his life. His leitmotiv of struggle, seen at the outset of his work in the little drawing "En Route," is brought to a climax here. He is at the end of his road and ceases his work in fire and storm. The glimmer of the miner's lamp, the gay light of the blossoming orchards in the spring of Provence, the glow of the summer sun in Arles and St. Rémy have burst their bounds and become a huge wild fire. The overripe wheat 604 is the prey of the raging blaze and the low-flying crows sharply accentuate the *image of death*.

604
242 His drive to the sun ends in his own fire, which consumes him as it overwhelms and burns his *image of humanity*. A letter which he had written to Theo years back, in 1882, comes to our mind: *"I feel a power in me which*

276

I must develop, a fire that I may not quench, but must keep ablaze, though I do not know to what end it will lead me, and shouldn't be surprised if it were a somber one. In times like these, what should one wish for? What is relatively the happiest fate? In some circumstances it is better to be the vanquished than to be the victor—for instance, better to be Prometheus than Jupiter. Well, it is an old saying, Let come what may." It was like a premonition, as was the assumption he made in the following year, that *his body would hold out a certain number of years, between six and ten for instance.* He then commented further on his working capacity: *"If one consumes oneself very much in those years one does not get over 40... My intention is not to spare myself, nor to avoid any emotions or difficulties—for it is relatively immaterial to me whether I live longer or shorter..."*

309

In the "Wheatfield with Crows" another presentiment would seem to have come true, one which Vincent had felt at the time when he painted a cemetery in Nuenen. He then wanted to express in that work *"... how very simple death and burial are, as natural as the fall of an autumn leaf,"* [43] and further: *"The fields around where the grass of the cemetery ends, beyond the little wall—they make a last line against the horizon—like a horizon of a sea."* In Auvers he again compares the fields to *a sea, the fields beyond the little wall,* where he and Theo were to be put to rest.

411

650, 411

Yet in this final painting too, is the vision of resurrection. Vincent is no longer portrayed in his earthly existence—his soul rises to the sky, symbolized by the light cloud just above the road which has come to its end. The two clouds bring to mind the two clouds in the drawing of the "Starry Night" (plate 81), in which pillars of smoke rose from the earth to the sky to flow into the interlocked cloud. Earlier, in the "Self-Portrait with the Bandaged Ear" spirals of smoke and breath had risen above the horizon. As the detached tree branches have become swarming birds, so have the rising spirals— symbols of his spiritual force—left the earth and become the light clouds in the sky.

The death of Theo a few months later is as if foretold by the second, more distant cloud; the crow within its contours enhances the ominous impact. The two clouds may also recall the "Sunflowers" (plate 43), where the two falling flowers had conveyed Vincent's awareness—if not presentiment—of death. By stressing in his last letters to Theo *their fragile existence, his life too being attacked at the very root, his step too being unsteady* he implied that he was afflicted as was Theo.

649

278

When Vincent shot himself he missed the heart and did not die at once. In spite of his bad wound, he managed to walk to the inn and up the steep stairs to his little room. Dr. Gachet sent for Theo, who arrived the next morning to find Vincent calm and smoking his pipe. Theo still hoped that he would recover, as he did after the catastrophe with Gauguin, when Theo had rushed to the hospital at Arles. As reported by Jo[44], he had then been overcome by his brother's suffering and had laid his head on the pillow close to Vincent's while they talked about the old times of their childhood in Holland. But this time Theo's hope was not to be fulfilled. The brothers stayed together all that day and the following night. Vincent remained completely lucid until the end, which came a few moments after he had said: "I wish I could go away like this."

112. PART OF LETTER No. 649

PART VII

AN INTERMEDIARY

281

"*Painters—to speak only of them—being dead and buried, speak to a*   506
following generation or to several following generations through their works.
Is that all, or is there even more?" Vincent had written to Theo from Arles,
and added: "*In a painter's life death is perhaps not what will be hardest for
him.*" In another letter he dealt with the question of life after death:
"*I always feel I am a traveller who is going somewhere and to a destination...*   518
*A child in the cradle too, if one watches it at leisure, has the infinite in its
eyes. In short, I know nothing about it, but just this feeling of not knowing
makes the real life we are actually living comparable to a one-way journey
in a train. One goes fast but does not distinguish any object very closely,
and above all one does not see the locomotive.*" Notwithstanding his belief in
an existence beyond the grave, he stated: "*The future life of artists by their
works, I do not see much in it.*" He thus made a distinction between the
effect of his works on succeeding generations in this world and their value
for a life of the artist after death. He continued his thoughts: "*Yes, the artists*   518
*perpetuate themselves by handing on the torch, Delacroix to the Impressionists,
etc.*" And again he asked: "*But is that all?*"

What did Van Gogh mean by these questions? A passage in a letter to
Bernard may lead to the answer: "*It seems to me that we ourselves serve as*   B 19 a
*intermediaries only. And that it will only be a following generation which
will succeed in living in peace. Well, all this, our duties and our possibilities
of action, could not become clearer to us than by experience itself.*" Ever
since he had worked as an artist he had sought to perceive and express that
experience itself in his art, which was his instrument as an intermediary. Of
what then was he the intermediary?

There is an unusual self-portrait, painted at Arles in September 1888 and dedicated to Gauguin, which might be enlightening (plate 113). Vincent had
545 described it to Theo: *"Here at last I have the opportunity of comparing my painting with that of the copains. My portrait, which I am sending to Gauguin in exchange, holds its own, I am sure of that. I have written to Gauguin, in reply to his letter, that if I too were permitted to enlarge my personality in a portrait, while seeking to render in my portrait not only myself but in general an Impressionist, I had conceived this portrait as that of a bonze [Buddhist monk], simple worshipper of the eternal Buddha. And when I put the conception of Gauguin and my own side by side, mine is as grave but less despairing."*

In the identification with a Buddhist monk Vincent became an intermediary of an *enlarged* self, enlarged by something nameless, called in Zen Buddhism the "It" which is beyond and directs the self. "It" cannot be described or explained. "It" might be imagined as referring to all energies and inner forces which activate our mind, body and soul, and from which we derive the criterion of human beings. "It" can perhaps be assumed as the ultimate reality in man's life. There may be a hint of it in Vincent's repeated
242, 625 mention of *something above,* and in one letter of a creative silence: *"I cannot*
333 *say it exactly: It must be a je ne sais quoi [I do not know what] in man that keeps his mouth closed and makes him active, that is silent even when he speaks ... an inner silence that leads to action."* In his discussion with Theo
613 on paintings such as the "Starry Night," he had stressed *the fact that he felt greatly impelled to seek ...* (page 203/4). By whom or by what could he have
625 been impelled? Would the answer not lie in his exclamation: *"... inspiration, a ray from above which is not ours ...?"* This ray is a sign of the "It" which is not ours. We belong to "It."

506 The *even more* of his question seems to relate to those prime motives which, in mythology and religions under varying forms and different denominations, have for ages occupied the human mind. On the same level is his
B 8 assumption that *"... life is round and much superior in extension and capacity to the hemisphere known to us."*

545 He wanted to render in his portrait *in general an Impressionist.* This is conveyed in some unusual features. His appearance as a Buddhist monk with the closely-shaven head is enhanced by the shape of the eyes which he
545 *slanted a little in the Japanese way.* It brings to mind his statement that
510 *Japanese art was taking roots again in the Impressionists.*

284

113. WORSHIPPER OF THE ETERNAL BUDDHA (SELF-PORTRAIT)

B 18   While he was working on this portrait he was *terribly absorbed* by the furnishing of his house (page 105). He had then written to Theo at great
534   length about *everything from the chair to the painting* in his own room and the guest room where Gauguin or another painter would stay. It may be noticed that Vincent's clothes in the portrait are of exactly the same unusual brown and violet color in which a few months later he painted Gauguin's chair; there is even a similarity in the contours. Yet in none of his detailed
545   descriptions of these paintings did he mention this way of *enlarging* himself when rendering Gauguin, to whom he had dedicated the portrait, and —
489   through him — the Impressionists in general, who made him feel like *a link in the chain of artists.*

The existence of this link disproves the common assumption that Vincent's art was only appreciated long after his death. Apart from Gauguin and Bernard, other painters such as Guillaumin, Monet, Pissarro, Signac and Toulouse-Lautrec had a high opinion of his work. They were, of course, only a small circle, and they, too, had to fight their way, like all the Impressionists, and indeed like every artist or creative person at all times. Already in 1889, only seven years after Vincent had started to paint, the Dutch painter and writer Isaacson, a friend of Theo, wanted to write about his art in Dutch newspapers, but Vincent himself discouraged him from doing so. Shortly afterwards, however, in January 1890, appeared the first article by Aurier in the *Mercure de France,* a well-known Paris journal. At the same time another article must have been published in Brussels, to which Vincent
626b, 640a   refers briefly in two letters. In one of them he also mentions a third article, written a few months later in Holland. Such recognition was rather early, especially if one considers the revolutionary character of his art. He himself
612   had acknowledged that *one needed ten years to learn the profession.*

Aurier's article was written with great enthusiasm, and included such phrases as "At the same time really true and quasi supernatural... The continuous search for the essential sign of everything... A kind of marvelous language to interpret the idea... Almost always a symbolist... A symbolist feeling the continuous necessity to reclothe his ideas in various forms... Simple expressive means as simple processes of symbolizing... The "Sower," this majestic, troubling sower, the boor with the brutally ingenuous forehead, sometimes faintly resembling the artist himself, obsessed by the idea of the coming man, a Messiah, a sower of truth who would regenerate the decrepitude of our art and perhaps of our imbecile and industrialist society...

A conviction of the necessity of recommencing everything in art... Capable of touching the humble... He will never be understood fully except by his brothers, the artists ... and by the happy ones among the small people, the very small people who will by chance have escaped the well meaning teachings of the laity."

Theo had sent a copy of the journal to Vincent, who reacted immediately: "*I was extremely surprised at the article on my paintings which you sent me; no need to tell you that I hope to go on thinking that I do not paint like that, but I do see in it rather how I ought to paint. For the article is very right in this sense, that it indicates the gap to fill, and I believe that really the writer wrote it rather to guide not only me but the other Impressionists as well, and more particularly to make the breach at the right place. Thus he proposes a collective self [un moi collectif] ideal to the others as much as to myself; he simply tells me that here and there is some good, if you like, in my so imperfect work, too, and there is the consoling side which I appreciate and for which I hope to be grateful.*" 625

To Aurier himself Vincent wrote about the article: "*I like it very much as a work of art in itself. I find that you create color with your words; enfin, in your article I find my canvases again, but better than they are in reality, more rich, more significant. However, I feel ill at ease when I think that what you say is due to others rather than to me. For example, to Monticelli above all.*" He underlined the following sentence: "*For the part which is due to me, or will be due to me, will remain, I assure you, most secondary.*" 626a

His insistence does not seem to have derived from modesty alone. The reference to Monticelli was based on a deep affinity Vincent felt with him. His affection for this artist, whom he had never met, was extraordinary, and he described his link with him in a manner which has an almost spiritualistic note: "*I myself think here enormously about Monticelli. He was a powerful man — somewhat cracked, and even very much so — dreaming of sun and love and gaiety, but always worried by poverty — an extremely refined taste as a colorist, a man of uncommon stamp [de race rare] continuing the best old traditions. He dies in Marseilles, sadly enough and probably by passing through a real Gethsemane. Well, I for myself am sure that I carry him on here [je le continue ici] as if I were his son or his brother. We were just speaking of fatality which appears sad to us. But does not there exist another, a charming fatality.*" He had seen this in *the living man rising up immediately* W 8 *in the place of the dead one, taking up the same cause again, continuing the same work, etc.* (page 249).

545   Such perceptions again intimate the *enlarging of his personality* beyond himself; the intense link he felt with Monticelli stresses his rôle as an intermediary not less than the way he painted after works of Millet, Delacroix,
607   or Rembrandt. He explained this way of working: *"I place before myself ... their black and white as a subject and then improvise with color, though of course not being entirely myself ... this is my own interpretation."* He further
613   asserted: *"... it is translating them into another language much more than*
623   *copying them,"* and later taking the matter up again: *"So if one day they are criticized or despised as copies, it will remain no less true that it has its justification in trying to render Millet's work more accessible to the large ordinary public."* He compared himself to a musician who gave his own
607   interpretation to a composer's work: *"... my brush moves between my fingers as a bow would on a violin, and absolutely for my pleasure."*

    Receiving from the past and handing on to the future is a recurrent theme in Vincent's letters. He was concerned with the painters of the future in his frequent exchange of views with Theo about the artists' community
538   which he planned in his house in Arles: *"But my idea would be that in the end we shall have founded and left to posterity a studio where a successor could live. I don't know whether I express myself clearly enough, but in other words we are working at an art, at matters which will last not only in our*
469   *time but which can still after us be continued by others." "That is to say that I always hope not to work for myself alone. I believe in the absolute necessity of a new art of color, of design and — of the artistic life."* He elaborated on
482   that life: *"This painter of the future, I cannot imagine him living in little restaurants, working with several false teeth and going to the Zouave brothels as I do. But I think I am right when I feel that this will come in a generation farther away, and as for us, we have to do what our means permit in that direction without doubting and without flinching."*

    Vincent's influence on *the painter of the future* was once brought out by Picasso. He is reported to have said, in front of the "Bedroom" at a Van Gogh exhibition in 1953, that when seeing Van Gogh's work for the first time in 1901 he felt if someone could paint like that, there were no longer any limits and everything was now permitted in art. The need for new ways of
469   expression — Vincent had thought it *an absolute necessity* — makes modern art, with its apparently deliberate distortion and the disintegration of tradi-

288

tionally realistic form, a mirror reflecting our existing inner condition. It signifies a continuation of the very struggle Van Gogh was fighting and which he had portrayed without compromise in his work. Keeping in mind that changing forms in art stand for changing ways in life, we may see in the future development of art a record of our own struggle for integrity, the vital task of our time, both individually and collectively.

625 The *collective self*, of which Vincent had written to Theo as if it had been suggested by Aurier, was in fact his own idea. The article of Aurier contained nothing of the kind. This new expression adds to the understanding

545 of his self-portrayal as a Buddhist monk in which he had conveyed an *enlarged*

218 self. Whether he had seen in his work *the essence of life* or an *enlarging* of

625 himself or now a *collective self*, all these terms bear out the same conception: the self is extended in his art beyond the limits of passing day-to-day life and

538 becomes collective, accessible to others, *not only in our time*. They all imply the communicating character of his work — the work of an intermediary.

 This task was on his mind until the very last. In an unfinished letter

652 which was found on him after his death, he said to Theo: *"But yet, my dear brother, there is this that I have always said to you and which I say again once more with all the gravity that can be given by the efforts of thought, assiduously fixed to seek to do as well as one can — I say it to you yet again that I shall always consider that you are something other than a simple dealer in Corots, that through my intermediation you have your part in the actual production of certain canvases which even in the disaster retain their calm. For that is where we are and that is all, or at least the main thing that I can have to tell you in a moment of relative crisis."*

 The gravity of these words — they are like an expression of a last will — could not more strongly impress on Theo the rôle of the intermediary which Vincent saw in himself. The communicating link he had felt with other painters had shown a pronounced personal aspect when he had worked

290

side-by-side with Gauguin, and perhaps not less so in his affection for Monti- W 8
celli, whom he *continued like a son or brother*. But the personal character of
this communication was strongest in his tie with Theo. Of his repeated
statements that his work was done by Theo and him together, one of the
most pointed was made by him in the summer at Arles: *"You understand ...* 504
*that I have a certain ambition, not for the <u>number</u> of canvases, but that the
whole [l'ensemble] of these canvases should all the same represent a real labor,
on your part as much as on my part."* When towards the end of his life in
Auvers he suggested to Theo that *they should put aside all ambition*, he was 648
on the very verge of completing *the whole* of his work, of coming to the end 504
of that *real labor*.

At the beginning of this book it was indicated that the extraordinary
effect of Van Gogh's art emanated from a symbolic content. The ensuing
study of his work and writings has shown the course and underlying motives
of his life as portrayed in a continuous thread of recurrent symbols: trees,
flowers and plants growing, cut and wilting; wheat sown and reaped; lamps,
candles, the sun, moon and stars with their light and shade; houses, looms,
bridges, boats, books, pieces of furniture, containers, shoes and other domestic
objects. The self-portraying nature of all these familiar things of everyday
life was brought forth and enhanced by their shape and color, and their
specific composition within a painting, particularly by their pairing and
doubling. Foremost in our mind is his struggle with the colors of the "Sower,"
the image of humanity which was *cut in two*. His portraits of men and 604, B 7
women, individually and in groups, had little of the *delusive optical realism* 531
but were *realistic and at the same time symbolic*. We recall his portrayal of 425
ordinary people as saints and saintly women like the first Christians; his
spiritual message in the vision of the "Starry Night," and the primeval symbolism of the rise from darkness to light in the "Resurrection of Lazarus,"
finally a last image of death and resurrection in his burning "Wheatfield
with Crows."

The attempt to understand Van Gogh's symbolic language renders relevant a further look into the background of symbolism. A great scholar in
this field, J. J. Bachofen, wrote in 1859: "Into the most secret depths of the
soul does the symbol strike its root, language touches the surface of compre-
hension like a light breath of wind. The former is directed inward, the latter
outward. Only the symbol succeeds in combining the most differing into a
uniform impression of the whole. Language ranges single subjects and brings

only piecemeal to consciousness what should be presented to the soul at one glance—in order to be grasped in all its power. Words set limits to the infinite. Symbols carry off the mind beyond the boundaries of the finite, nascent world into the realm of the infinite world of being." [45]

Yet words, despite their inadequacy, can have a symbolic character, for instance in poetry. Their effect is generally less immediate than that of pictorial or musical expression, but their meaning is like the substance within any other form. In fact, the derivation or origin of a word may contribute to a deeper understanding of its significance. Taking the word "symbol" itself as example, its earliest use is found in ancient Greek as identifying two partners to an agreement. It reflected the legend of a man who on a voyage abroad had made a close friend. At the farewell meal he broke a small bone into two pieces, one of which he gave to his friend, taking the other home with the understanding that he would leave it to his son, and his son to his, and so on. His friend would do likewise, and whenever their descendants would meet and produce the two parts of the bone, the fitting together of those parts into one would testify to a bond of friendship and brotherhood. They called this bone the "symbolon."

The uniting action thus indicated by the word symbol is confirmed by its origin. Coming from the Greek symbolon, it is composed of two parts, sym from syn (together) and bolon from ballein (to throw). Symbol, therefore, originally meant to throw together. The general conception of a symbol as something which implies more than its appearance, is qualified by the original throwing together, not only of two parts of a bone, but of the visible part (form or expression) and the invisible (substance or meaning). Their ideal union was depicted by the classic Chinese symbol of Yang and Yin in one simultaneous motion of light and dark and all other connotations of male and female (pages 159, 200). In this way Yang and Yin became an outstanding example of a sym-bol, of two different elements thrown together, complemented and integrated into one whole. This qualifying original meaning of the term symbol has far-reaching implications for its widespread usage in so many fields. For instance, religious symbols such as the Buddha or the cross, derive their existence as visible forms from their communicating an invisible spiritual substance. Only the "throwing together" of both parts, the visible and the invisible, makes them a symbol. Idolatrous worship of a form alone had certainly been one of the main reasons for the Jewish commandment: "Thou shalt make no image...".

292

The deepest root of the uniting function of the symbol may be in the myth of the great Earth-Mother, the primordial, pre-conscious undivided male and female. One might perhaps even look for the source of human creativeness in the urge to unite these elements, in an inherent energy of throwing them together to attain integrity and oneness, as it is experienced in the act of procreation.

There is a fundamental analogy between symbol and integrity, whose Latin origin "integrare" means to make a whole, to renew, to restart, to restore. What could primarily be restored to wholeness if not the separate which were once united — as handed down to us by that primitive myth of the great Earth-Mother at the cradle of humanity? However, it would not be a return to indistinguishable chaos, but an integration of our positive and negative, our conscious and unconscious forces into a congruous motion. It would be a task of human insight, which might be called religious in the integrating sense of gathering together body and soul (page 212). As integrity simultaneously denotes honesty and moral soundness, it implies their inter-dependence with wholeness; in other words, man's ethical quality is relative to his state of integration. This relativity is borne out by the meaning of integrare — to renew, to restart — which suggests a continuous renewal of effort and so development rather than accomplishment. How relevant in this respect seem Van Gogh's assertions: *"Though I fall 99 times, I shall stand the* 160 *100th,"* and *"to study, to analyze society, this always says more than moraliz-* B 9 *ing"* (page 205). As man's relations with others are closely interwoven with his inner structure, his striving for wholeness, for integrity, is at the same time a struggle for love.

This inner situation underlies Vincent's art, on which the original meaning of the term symbol sheds additional light. His leitmotiv had literally been a throwing together, namely, the struggle to unite his inner contrasts. This made the sum total of his work one gigantic symbol in the profoundest sense of the word. When he *wanted to grasp life in its depths* and *was looking* 197 *for the root or origin of so many things at the same time, taking apart* 255 *impressions and putting them together again, dashing it off on the wing,* 427 when his *symbolic language of color* expressed *the simultaneous excessive* 503, B 7 *contrast of violet and yellow,* of dark and light — all those statements show his keen awareness of the dynamic nature of symbolism in his art.

He did not ignore the consuming effect which this symbolic work had on himself. One recalls his *falling into full metaphysics of color, being* 503

605
626a, 595
614a   *absent-minded like a sleep-walker, his too great emotions, to the extent of
fainting, the dizzy heights*, etc. Once he wrote about the olive trees of the
South: "... *in front of such nature I feel impotent, my northern brain having
nightmares in those peaceful spots ... Yet, I did not want to remain without
at least making an effort ... with the cypresses and olives."* He concluded:

614a   *"May others, better and more powerful than I, express their symbolic language."*

He was referring to the canvases painted in St. Rémy (pages 185, 189),
but at that time he had not yet given up. He still had to complete the last
phase of his work from the "Almond Branches in Blossom" and the "Resurrection" to the final "Wheatfield." Since his early beginnings he had stressed
309   the character of wholeness of his works: *"I do not consider my studies as
made for their own sake, but am always thinking of the work as a whole."*
316   In another letter he said: *"Above all, my thoughts are these: a drawing of
mine will also in the course of time not satisfy entirely by itself, but a
number of studies, however different they may be, will complement one
395   another."* And again he wrote from Nuenen: *"... though my studies are
worth nothing now, this may change later, not so much one by itself as in
conjunction with others."* He later reiterated these thoughts about the whole
of his work which would not be understood by single paintings.

It was not his object to create a few static pieces of art, even if they were
masterpieces, but his entire work was to be the medium for portraying his
life as a whole. His art was not the result of traditional training for a devised
218   purpose; its end was identical with its origin, it was *the essence of life*, as
423   he had said. We remember his avowal in Holland that *he would seek to get
into his work what he wanted even if he would perish by it.* Until he closed
his eyes he did not waver in living up to this pledge. In the unfinished letter
652   found after his death, he said to Theo: *"I risked my life in my work and my
reason has half foundered in it."* It is this uncompromising struggle for
ultimate truth, for integrity and love which he got into his work, that appeals
so strongly to generations after him — as frustration, inability to love and
loneliness are the prevailing symptoms of disintegration of the human personality.

185   As Vincent himself had been an intermediary of *a great hidden force,*
so has his work remained a powerful medium, which he had prophesied
R 57   *would not be outdone.* Indeed, it revives the earliest tradition of the symbolon,

294

the urge for brotherhood and friendship. *"More soul, more love, more heart"* 252
he wanted in the artist's work and he saw a *similarity between art and love.* 259
One will recall his affirmation: *"As my work is, so am I myself"* (page 60). 312
His relations with Theo and others — Christine, Madame Roulin, the postman, Milliet, Gauguin, Gachet — were projected in his work — symbolically
and realistically. As *a link in the chain of artists,* he always dreamed of his 489
idea, the working community of painters, and never did he cease to aver that
his work was done by Theo and him together. Thus it was a means of union
with his friends and brother, a bond of friendship as told by the early legend
of the symbolon. *"To live, to work, to love are really one,"* he had written to 159
Theo at the time he was in love with Kornelia, and later: *"You are good* 538
to the painters, and you should know, the more I think about it the more
I feel that there is nothing more really artistic than to love the people."

Even in his two last letters he dealt with the situation of the artists and 652
their relations with art dealers, but *as far as he knew Theo was not among*
the dealers in man and could really act with humaneness. Here the letter
breaks off. There is something unusual in these last two letters. As plates 114
and 115 show, they begin with practically the same sentence in form and
content. It seems obvious that the undated, unfinished letter (No. 652) was
written first. However as Vincent went deeper into his relationship with Theo,
he discontinued and wrote the other letter, which bears the date 23 July 1890
(inserted by Theo's wife). It starts like the first but then goes over to various
other matters evidently dealt with in Theo's letter to which this one is the
reply. Vincent completed it with some less important items, added a few
sketches of works on which he was engaged, and sent it to Theo. The unfinished letter he kept on himself for four days — until the day he shot
himself. The *relative crisis* he mentioned does not seem to have meant another 652
attack of his illness. But during those four days and nights he must have
struggled with his intention of suicide at which he hints by *"disaster ... that* 652
is where we are" and by an underlined sentence: *"Before there will be a*
chance of talking over matters with a quieter head, it will probably take a
long time." And yet, he called the crisis only relative, because *dying was* 358
perhaps less difficult than living as he had repeatedly asserted.

The gravity of the letter shows his deep concern with his brother, and
in fact, Vincent's death had a fatal effect on Theo. He could not get over
the loss of Vincent and his mind became clouded. It was as if he could not
allow himself to continue *the ideal life with a wife and child* for which his 600

295

Auvers 23 Jul. 1890   13

651

Mon cher frère, Merci de ta lettre d'aujourd'hui et
du billet de 50 fr. qu'elle contenait
Je voudrais peut-être t'écrire sur bien des choses
mais d'abord d'abord l'envie m'en a tellement passé
puis j'en sens l'inutilité
J'espère que tu auras retrouvé ces messieurs
dans de bonnes dispositions à ton égard
Pour ce qu'est de l'état de paix dans
ton ménage, je suis autant convaincu
de la possibilité de la conserver que des
orages qui te menacent
Je préfère ne pas oublier le peu de français
que je sais et certes ne saurais voir
l'utilité d'approfondir le tort ou la raison dans
des discussions éventuelles de part ou autre
Seulement cela m'intéresserait pas
Ici les choses vont vite — Dis tu.
et moi n'en sommes nous pas un
peu plus convaincus le sentons nous
pas un peu davantage que ces dames
Tant mieux pour elles — mais enfin
causer à tête reposée nous n'y
comptons même pas —
En ce qui me regarde je m'applique
sur mes toiles avec toute mon attention
je cherche à faire aussi bien que
de certains peintres que j'ai beaucoup
aimé et admiré —

LAST TWO LETTERS:
114. FIRST PAGE OF LETTER No. 651

296

lettre qu'il portait sur lu. le 23 juillet

Mon cher frère, merci de ta bonne lettre
et du billet de 50 fr. qu'elle contenait
Je voudrais bien t'écrire sur bien des
chôses mais j'en sens l'inutilité
J'espère que tu auras retrouvé ces
messieurs en de bonnes dispositions
à ton égard—

Que tu me rassures sur l'état de paix
de ton ménage— c'était pas la peine
Je crois avoir vu le bien autant que
l'autre côté — Et suis tellement—
D'ailleurs d'accord qu'élever un
gosse dans un quatrième étage est
une lourde corvée tant pour toi
que pour Jo — Puisque cela va bien
ce qui est le principal insisterais je
sur des chôses de moindre importance
ma foi avant qu'il y ait chance de
causer affaires à têtes plus reposées
il y a probablement loin. Voilà la
seule chose qu'à présent je puisse dire
et que cela pour ma part je l'ai constaté
avec un certain effroi je ne l'ai pas caché
déjà mais c'est bien là tout —

brother had yearned in vain. Vincent seemed to have had a presentiment of this when he wrote of *the danger that threatened them all* (pages 173, 275). Suffering from sudden derangement, Theo literally acted as Vincent had so often suggested, *leaving the art dealers* and joining Gauguin as *director of a painters' society* [46]. Only six months after Vincent's suicide, Theo died in a mental hospital at the age of thirty-three.

337, 493

Had the brothers *ruined each other* after all? Had the *extreme solitude* of Vincent's wheatfields, *the image of humanity* and *of death* extended to Theo, and were they finally *lost in each other?* Theo's following Vincent so soon into the grave seems to have been the unavoidable consequence of their unbreakable tie, their mutual dependence. Neither Vincent's compelling intermediation nor Theo's unfailing support of his brother — which was something he had to do, as he had written to their sister — had been for them a matter of choice. It was their fate, the effect of forces beyond reasoning, forces we painfully attempt to grasp, which were even beyond the great affection Theo had for his wife and child. The same forces which drew Vincent into suicide also took away Theo.

648, 649
604
619

The fact that he called his son Vincent, identifying him with his brother, instead of naming him Theo after their father, as was customary in Holland, shows the reciprocal extent of their symbiosis. The day the child was born, Theo had written to Vincent: "As we have told you: we shall name him after you, and I express the wish that he may be as persevering and as courageous as you." On Theo's last birthday, May 1, 1890, he told Jo that a letter from Vincent would be the only thing he would lack to be happy. We remember how, on the other hand, Vincent had been dependent on the letter from Theo as portrayed in the symbolic "Still Life on a Drawing Board."

It may safely be said that without Theo, Vincent's work could not have been achieved. His persistent claim that it had been done by both of them together was not only based on Theo's material support, indispensable as that had been, but no less on Theo's commitment to the same cause — his following the unknown force which led his brother into his consuming creativeness. *Nobody fell before his time* Vincent had once told him and when his unique work was ended, Theo's task also was fulfilled. Their exertion had been too absorbing to allow either of them to enjoy what is called a normal life. This sacrifice had been imposed on them by the magnitude of their mission: to open our eyes to "*... the need of love and religiousness which must manifest itself in the people*" when they will "*...have enough of cynicism, of scepti-*

342

543
542

298

cism, of humbug," as Vincent had written to Theo when reading about Tolstoi (pages 249, 210).

At the beginning of his painting in Holland, Vincent *wanted one of those days to write Theo a letter in which he would tell him all that was necessary.* 316
Theo should then *keep this letter and in case someone might be induced to* 316
take some of his studies, he could tell that man exactly his thoughts and intentions. Theo complied with Vincent's wish but he did more, he kept all, every single one, of his letters. Years had passed since Vincent had made that request. Now, at the end of his life, he writes to Theo: *"I would have* 651/2
liked perhaps to write to you about many things, but first the desire has so much left me and then I feel the uselessness." His work finished, the intermediary could say no more. But more than words, more direct and immediate, is the symbolic language of his art, the portrayal of his life, the life of two brothers—of all brothers—of man. To this art he refers us in the unfinished letter found on his death: *"And truly, we can only make our* 652
paintings speak."

BIOGRAPHICAL DATES

VINCENT WILLEM VAN GOGH

1853 March 30   Born at Zundert, South-Holland

1857 May 1   Brother Theo born

1869 July - 1873 May   Employee at Goupil & Cie., art dealers, The Hague

1873 May - 1876 April   Employee in the firm's branches at London and Paris

1876 April - December   School teacher and lay preacher in England

1877 January - April   Employee in bookshop, Dordrecht, Holland

1877 May - 1878 July   Preparatory study for Theological Seminary, Amsterdam

1878 August - November   Trainee for missionary work in Brussels

1878 November - 1879 July   Evangelist in the Borinage, Belgium

1879 July - 1880 October   Private missionary in the Borinage

1880 July   Started drawing

1880 October - 1881 April   Continued drawing in Brussels

1881 April - December   In parents' home at Etten, Holland

1881 December - 1883 September   In the Hague, with Christine

1882 July   Started painting

1883 September - December   Stay at Drente, North-Holland

1883 December - 1885 November   In parents' home at Nuenen, Holland

1885 November - 1886 February   Stay in Antwerp, Belgium

1886 February - 1888 February   With his brother Theo in Paris

1888 February - 1889 May   Stay at Arles (Bouches-du-Rhône), Southern France

1888 December 23   Catastrophe with Gauguin

1889 May - 1890 May   Voluntary inmate in mental hospital at Saint-Rémy, Provence (Southern France)

1890 May - July   Stay in Auvers-sur-Oise, near Paris

1890 July 27/29   Suicide

NOTES AND REFERENCES

PART I : THE DARK BEGINNING

1 Goupil et Cie., Paris, London, The Hague, Berlin, New York. The firm had originally been founded by an uncle of the painter, also called Vincent Van Gogh, whose successors were Goupil et Cie. See introduction to *The Complete Letters of Vincent Van Gogh* by Johanna Van Gogh, Theo's widow. (Amsterdam: Wereldbibliotheek, 1953-54 and Greenwich, Conn.: The New York Graphic Society, 1958).

2 Auvers, a little town on the river Oise, about 25 kilometers north of Paris, was frequented by painters, particularly by the Impressionists. When the term "impressionism" is used in this book, it includes "post- and neo-impressionism."

3 Renamed by the Rijksmuseum Kröller-Müller, Otterlo, Holland, which acquired the painting some years ago. Van Gogh himself had not given a name to most of his works.

4 For over seventy years the painting had been thought to be unsigned, and only a few years ago the dark signature was discovered by Mrs. Nel Van Gogh, the wife of Theo's son.

PART II : LIGHT BREAKS THROUGH

5 The term "symbiosis," a Greek compound for "living together," has spread from biological applications to the field of psychology. It is used to define a close association which may be advantageous and necessary, but at the same time harmful, parasitic and destructive for both partners. Dr. Charles Mauron of St. Rémy, deals with this aspect of the relationship between the brothers in *Vincent et Théo Van Gogh: Une Symbiose* (Amsterdam: Instituut voor Moderne Kunst, Stedelijk Museum, 1953). The same is done by Professor G. Kraus of Groningen, in *The Relationship Between Theo and Vincent Van Gogh* (Amsterdam: Kröller-Müller Foundation and J. M. Meulenhoff, 1954).

6 "A simultaneous attraction towards and repulsion from an object, person or action" (*Webster's New Collegiate Dictionary*).

7 The French colloquial term *copain* is not easy to translate with exactness. In Van Gogh's time it was used mainly by laborers and by others, such as students, who adopted laborers' talk. Its spirit of fellowship would be comparable to the American expression "pal" or the English "mate."

8 This correspondence between Theo Van Gogh and his youngest sister Wilhelmina is quoted in the introduction to *The Complete Letters of Vincent Van Gogh.*

9 Place and date of origin of this painting is given by the owners, the Rijksmuseum Kröller Müller, as Paris, 1887. Dr. Tralbaut places it in the Arles period.

PART III: THE SUN SHINES AND BURNS

10 Female symbols: Johann Jakob Bachofen, *Gesammelte Werke,* Vols. II, IV (herausgegeben von Karl Meuli, Benno Schwabe & Co., Basel, 1948-54; originally published 1859-61); S. Freud, *Collected Works,* Vol. XI (London: Imago Publishing Co.); E. Neumann, *Die Grosse Mutter* (Zurich: Rhein Verlag, 1956).

11 Lao-Tse, *Tao Te King:* "Always flowing, by which I mean: in farthest distances, by which I mean: returning into itself."

12 These stumps are reminiscent of a marred or reduced form of the phallic symbol, an image of the male organ of sex, symbolizing the generative power in nature; in ancient Greece it was carried in procession in the Dionysian festivals. Cf. S. Freud, *op. cit.,* Vol. XI; C. G. Jung, *Wandlungen und Symbole der Libido* (Franz Deuticke, Leipzig and Wien, 1912, 1938).

13 A person living on income without working.

14 S. Freud, *op. cit.,* Vols. II, III, XV; S. Ferenczi, *Bausteine zur Psycho-Analyse,* Vol. II (Internationaler Psychoanalytischer Verlag, 1927); Otto Rank, *Das Trauma der Geburt* (Internationaler Psychoanalytischer Verlag, 1924); Paul Friedmann, *The Bridge: A Study in Symbolism,* The Psychoanalytical Quarterly, Vol. XXI, 1952).

15 Sizes of canvases:

No.	Portraits	Landscapes
15	65 × 54 cm	65 × 50 cm
20	73 × 60 cm	73 × 54 cm
25	81 × 65 cm	81 × 60 cm
30	92 × 73 cm	92 × 65 cm

16 Dr. Charles Mauron, *op. cit.,* p. 11, states: "One often misappreciates the importance of the allowance regularly given to Vincent by Theo. The 150 francs per month at that time would represent today at least 30,000 francs [in 1953, the equivalent of about 90 dollars, and in the 1880s proportionally higher]. Before the war of 1914 a teacher had a beginning salary of 75 francs. I am not certain that Mallarmé, then professor of English, had more than Van Gogh's income, and yet he had lived in middle class style with a wife and two children to maintain."

17 Written on the back of the sketch "House in Arles," plate 53.

18 It is noteworthy that in psychoanalysis, departure by a train is sometimes interpreted as a symbol of death. S. Freud, *op. cit.,* Vol. XI.

PART IV: CRISIS AND ANTIDOTE

19 *Avant et Après:* Reminiscences by Paul Gauguin, published in 1903, include an account of his stay with Van Gogh in Arles.

20 Reported in *Avant et Après.* There is some disagreement on the date of the accident. Tralbaut reproduces in *Van Gogh: Les Peintres par l'Image* (Paris: Hachette, 1960), an extract from the Arles *Forum Républicain* of December 30, 1888, according to which the accident occurred on Sunday night, a week earlier, i.e., December 23. In *Post Impressionism: From Van Gogh to Gauguin* (New York: Museum of Modern Art, 1956), J. Rewald states that it happened on Saturday, Christmas Eve. That day, December 24, however, was a Monday.

304

21 Of the numerous medical opinions expressed on Van Gogh's illness, the principal conflicting diagnoses are based on the assumption of epilepsy or schizophrenia.

22 Published in *The Complete Letters of Vincent Van Gogh.*

23 F.V. Raspail, *Manual: Annuaire de la Santé,* Paris, 1845-1935.

24 Quoted in the introduction to *The Complete Letters of Vincent Van Gogh.*

25 Dr. Charles Mauron comments in detail on these influences in *Structure de l'Inconscient chez Vincent Van Gogh* (Psyché Nos. 75-78, Imago, 1953); see also references to Mauron and Kraus in note 5.

26 Reported by Dr. Mendes Da Costa, Van Gogh's teacher of ancient languages in Amsterdam. See *The Complete Letters of Vincent Van Gogh.*

27 Recorded in the introduction to *The Complete Letters of Vincent Van Gogh.*

PART V : *...CONSOLING PAINTING*

28 The "non-being" should be understood as a different kind of "being". Lao-Tse *Tao Te King:* "The nothing, the emptiness, gives the vessel its usefulness."

29 *The Secret of the Golden Flower - A Chinese Book of Life,* translated and explained by Richard Wilhelm with a commentary by C.G. Jung, p. 19 (London: Routledge and Kegan Paul, 1931).

30 *I Ching: The Book of the Changes,* oldest Chinese book of wisdom, said to have originated about 4,000 B.C.

31 The choice was made for the exhibition "Masterpieces of Religious Art," held in connection with the second assembly of the World Council of Churches at the Art Institute of Chicago, July 15 to August 15, 1954.

32 Contrary to Van Gogh's statements, Mendes Da Costa (see note 26) writes that he was incapable of concluding his studies.

33 Quoted from D.T. Suzuki, in a preface to *Zen in the Art of Archery,* by Eugen Herrigel (New York: Pantheon, 1959).

34 "Higher Self: Compare with Super Ego," S. Freud, *op. cit.,* Vol. XIII, XV. C.G. Jung, *Symbolik des Geistes; Die Wurzeln des Bewusstseins* (Zurich: Rascher Verlag, 1948, 1958). One of Jung's principal theories, the "Collective Unconscious" and the "Self" found in many of his works, e.g., *Die Beziehungen zwischen dem Ich und dem Unbewussten,* 1935, and *Psychologie und Alchemie,* 1944 (Zurich: Rascher Verlag). Without implying an identity or even a similarity of views, the affinity of the terms used by Van Gogh with the above is remarkable.

35 Quoted from Paul Tillich and Theodore M. Green: *Religious Art,* preface to the catalog of the exhibition in Chicago (see note 31).

36 Quoted from E. Neumann, *Ursprungsgeschichte des Bewusstseins* (Zurich, Rascher, 1950, pp. 64, 244).

37 Quoted from *Zen in the Art of Archery,* p. 91 (see note 33).

PART VI : ENDING THE JOURNEY

38 J. J. Bachofen, *op. cit.,* Vol. IV, pp. 210, 212.

39 Dr. Gachet, a physician who lived in Auvers, with whom Theo had arranged that he should look after Vincent.

40 Instinct for incest with the mother and ensuing hate of father: the Oedipus complex, one of the principal theories of S. Freud.

41 E. Neumann, *op. cit.,* pp. 201/2, 233/4 (see note 36); English edition published by Bollingen Foundation, New York (Pantheon Books, 1954).

42 Guillaume Regamey, an English painter (1837-1875), whom Van Gogh mentioned repeatedly.

43 This is once more comparable to the conception of death in Zen Buddhism (see note 37).

44 Reported in the introduction to *The Complete Letters of Vincent Van Gogh.*

PART VII : AN INTERMEDIARY

45 J. J. Bachofen, *op. cit.,* Vol. IV, pp. 62ff.

46 Reported by J. Rewald, *op. cit.* (see note 20).

ACKNOWLEDGEMENTS

I am under a deep obligation to a number of people; in the first place to Mr. Vincent W. van Gogh of Laren, Holland, who has greatly encouraged me to write this book. He has for a long time helped me in many respects with most valuable information and material, including that required for the reproduction of the many works owned by him. He also permitted for the first time reproduction in colour of the "Almond Branches in Blossom", which the artist had painted for him when hearing of his birth and which is particularly close to his heart.

For a number of years, I had the rare privilege of professional advice from Dr. Gustav Bally, Professor at the University of Zurich and at that time President of the Psychiatric Society of Switzerland, who was immensely helpful in connection with the intricate psychological problems which arose and preoccupied me during my studies. My deepest thanks go to him for the invaluable cooperation he has extended to me in this field. I am also happy to acknowledge here the constructive criticism of Dr. Ilse Graetz-Teitelman, of Haifa, who read the manuscript. I am further greatly indebted to Mr. Robert Sinclair of Amersham, England, for his devoted editorial work.

Particular thanks are also due to Professor A.M. Hammacher, Director, and Miss Ellen Joosten, Curator, of the Rijksmuseum Kröller-Müller of Otterlo, Holland, to Mr. W.A. Sandberg, former Director of the Municipal Museum of Amsterdam, and to Mr. H.J. Siliakus, Manager of its Reproduction Department. They all went out of their way to assist in the material for the illustration of the book, and as the reproduction of large paintings in a small size suitable for book use presents many difficulties, their help was all the more valuable.

Finally, I am most grateful to the many persons who have enabled me to see original works by Van Gogh in their collections and who have given permission to reproduce them. I also wish to thank the publishing houses mentioned in the "Notes and References" from whose publications I have quoted.

H. R. G.

307

LIST OF ILLUSTRATIONS

Numbers printed in **bold** face refer to color plates.

Numbers within brackets, following an F, correspond to the numbers given in the "Catalogue Raisonné" by B.J. De La Faille, 1928.

23. Fishing in Spring. (F 354). Oil. Paris, 1887. Mc Cormick Collection, Courtesy of the Art Institute of Chicago.

24. Wheatfield. (F 310). Oil. Paris, 1887. Collection V.W. van Gogh, Laren.

25. Self-Portrait with Easel. (F 522). Oil. Paris, 1888. Collection V.W. van Gogh, Laren.

26. Cut Sunflowers. (F 452). Oil. Paris, 1887. Rijksmuseum Kröller-Müller, Otterlo. (See "Notes and References", No. 9.)

27. Two Sunflowers. (F 375). Oil. Paris, 1888. Metropolitan Museum of Art, New York.

28. Blossoming Almond Twig. (F 392). Oil. Arles, 1888. Collection V.W. van Gogh, Laren.

29. Orchard in Blossom (Souvenir de Mauve). (F 394). Oil. Arles, 1888. Rijksmuseum Kröller-Müller, Otterlo.

30. Blossoming Pear Tree. (F 405). Oil. Arles, 1888. Collection V.W. van Gogh, Laren.

31. Blossoming Pear Tree. Sketch. Arles, 1888. Collection V.W. van Gogh, Laren.

32. The Drawbridge. (F 397). Oil. Arles, 1888. Rijksmuseum Kröller-Müller, Otterlo.

33. The Drawbridge. (F 400). Oil. Arles, 1888. Collection V.W. van Gogh, Laren.

34. The Breakfast Table. (F 410). Oil. Arles, 1888. Owner unknown.

35. The Breakfast Table. Sketch. Arles, 1888. Collection V.W. van Gogh, Laren.

36. Harvest. (F 412). Oil. Arles, 1888. Collection V.W. van Gogh, Laren.

37. Haystacks. (F 425). Oil. Arles, 1888. Rijksmuseum Kröller-Müller, Otterlo.

38. Fishing Boats at Saintes-Maries. (F 413). Oil. Arles, 1888. Collection V.W. van Gogh, Laren.

39. The Sower (June 1888). (F 422). Oil. Arles. Rijksmuseum Kröller-Müller, Otterlo.

40. Sower. Sketch. Arles, 1888. Collection V.W. van Gogh, Laren.

41. Sower. Sketch. Arles, 1888. Collection V.W. van Gogh, Laren.

42. On the Road to Tarascon. (F 448). Oil. Arles, 1888. Owner unknown.

43. Sunflowers. (F 458). Oil. Arles, 1888. Collection V.W. van Gogh, Laren.

44. Sunflowers. (F 454). Oil. Arles, 1888. Tate Gallery, London.

45. Sunflowers. (F 457). Oil. Arles, 1888. Owner unknown.

46. Eugène Delacroix. Portrait of Mr. Bruyas. Musée Fabre, Montpellier.

47. Sub-Lieutenant Milliet. (F 473). Oil. Arles, 1888. Rijksmuseum Kröller-Müller, Otterlo.

48. Poet's Garden. Sketch. Arles, 1888. Collection V.W. van Gogh, Laren.

49. Evening Walk. (F 704). Oil. St. Rémy, 1889. Museum, São Paulo.

50. Starry Sky. (F 474). Oil. Arles, 1888. Private Collection, Paris.

51. House in Arles. (F 464). Oil. Arles, 1888. Collection V.W. van Gogh, Laren.

52. House in Arles. (F 1413). Water color. Arles, 1888. Collection V.W. van Gogh, Laren.

53. House in Arles. (F 1453). Sketch. Arles, 1888. Owner unknown.

54. The Bedroom. (F 484). Oil. Arles, 1888. Courtesy of the Art Institute of Chicago, Helen Birch Bartlett Memorial Collection.

55. The Sower (October 1888). (F 451). Oil. Arles. Collection V.W. van Gogh, Laren.

56. La Liseuse (Woman Reading Novels). (F 497). Oil. Arles, 1888. Private collection, Switzerland.

57. La Liseuse. Sketch. Arles, 1888. Collection V.W. van Gogh, Laren.

58. Souvenir of the Garden in Etten. Sketch. Arles, 1888. Collection V.W. van Gogh, Laren.

59. Vincent's Chair (The Day). (F 498). Oil. Arles, 1888/9. Tate Gallery, London.

60. Gauguin's Chair (Effect of Night). (F 499). Oil. Arles, 1888/9. Collection V.W. van Gogh, Laren.

61. Self-Portrait with the Bandaged Ear. (F 529). Oil. Arles, 1889. Collection Mr. and Mrs. Leigh Block, Chicago.

62. Still Life on a Drawing Board. (F 604). Oil. Arles, 1889. Rijksmuseum Kröller-Müller, Otterlo.

63. Portrait of Dr. Rey. (F 500). Oil. Arles, 1889. Museum of Modern Art, Moscow.

64. La Berceuse. (F 504). Oil. Arles, 1889. Rijksmuseum Kröller-Müller, Otterlo.

64a. La Berceuse. Detail. Rijksmuseum Kröller-Müller, Otterlo.

65. The Great Lady. Drawing. The Hague, 1882. Collection V.W. van Gogh, Laren.

66. Berceuse with Sunflowers. Sketch. St. Rémy, 1889. Collection V.W. van Gogh, Laren.

67. Fruit Basket with Gloves. (F 502). Oil. Arles, 1889. Owner unknown.

68. The Postman. (F 432). Oil. Arles, 1888. Collection Robert Treat Paine, Boston, Mass. Courtesy, Museum of Fine Arts, Boston.

69. The Postman. (F 436). Oil. Arles, 1889. Rijksmuseum Kröller-Müller, Otterlo.

70. Wheatfield after Storm. (F 611). Oil. St. Rémy, 1889. Carlsberg Glyptotek, Copenhagen.

71. Olive Trees with White Cloud. (F 712). Oil. St. Rémy, 1889. Collection J.H. Whitney, New York. Photograph courtesy of M. Knoedler & Co., Inc., New York.

72. The Cypresses. (F 613). Oil. St. Rémy, 1889. Metropolitan Museum of Art, New York.

73. The Cypresses. (F 1525). Drawing. St. Rémy, 1889. Brooklyn Museum Collection, Brooklyn, N.Y.

74. Cypresses. (F 620). Oil. St. Rémy, 1889. Rijksmuseum Kröller-Müller, Otterlo.

75. Cypresses. (F 1524). Drawing. St. Rémy, 1889. Owner unknown.

76. Road with Cypress. (F 683). Oil. St. Rémy, 1889. Rijksmuseum Kröller-Müller, Otterlo.

77. Road with Cypress. Sketch. Auvers, 1890. Collection V.W. van Gogh, Laren.

78. Cypresses. (F 621). Oil. St. Rémy, 1889. Collection V.W. van Gogh, Laren.

79. The Starry Night. (F 612). Oil. St. Rémy, 1889. Museum of Modern Art, New York. Acquired through the Lillie P. Bliss Bequest.

80. Yin and Yang.

81. Starry Night. (F 1540). Drawing. St. Rémy, 1889. Kunsthalle, Bremen. Photograph Stickelmann, Bremen.

82. The Reaper. (F 618). Oil. St. Rémy, 1889. Collection V.W. van Gogh, Laren.

83. Reaper. (F 1635). Drawing. Arles, 1889. Collection V.W. van Gogh, Laren.

84. Egyptian Woman. (F 1521). Drawing. Arles, 1889. Collection V.W. van Gogh, Laren.

85. Olive Trees. (F 707). Oil. St. Rémy, 1889. Collection V.W. van Gogh, Laren.

86. Olive Picking. (F 655). Oil. St. Rémy, 1889. Courtesy Mr. and Mrs. Ira Haupt, New York.

87. St. Paul's Park. (F 660). Oil. St. Rémy, 1889. Folkwang Museum, Essen.

88. Watch at the Bedside. (F 647). Oil. St. Rémy, 1889. Collection V.W. van Gogh, Laren.

89. First Steps. (F 668). Oil. St. Rémy, 1889. Collection George N. Richard, New York. Photograph courtesy of Dalzell Hatfield Galleries.

90. Almond Branches in Blossom. (F 671). Oil. St. Rémy, 1890. Collection V.W. van Gogh, Laren.

91. The Resurrection of Lazarus. (F 677). Oil. St. Rémy, 1890. Collection V.W. van Gogh, Laren.

92. Rembrandt. The Resurrection of Lazarus. Etching.

93. Self-Portrait. (F 626). Oil. St. Rémy, 1889. Collection J.H. Whitney, New York.

94. Reminiscences of the North. (F 674). Oil. St. Rémy, 1889. Collection of the Barnes Foundation, Merion, Pa.

95. Peasant Going Home. (F 170). Oil, Nuenen, 1885. Collection W.C.A. Huinck, Amsterdam.

96. The Arlésienne. (F 541). Oil. St. Rémy, 1890. Rijksmuseum Kröller-Müller, Otterlo.

97. Paul Gauguin. An Arlésienne. Drawing. St. Rémy, 1890. Collection T. Edward Hanley, Badford, Pa.

98. Egyptian Woman. (F 1520). Drawing. Arles, 1889. Collection V.W. van Gogh, Laren.

99. Egyptian Woman. (F 1520 verso). Drawing. Arles, 1889. Collection V.W. van Gogh, Laren.

100. Old Man. (F 702). Oil. St. Rémy, 1890. Rijksmuseum Kröller-Müller, Otterlo.

101. Worn out. (F 863/4). Drawing. Etten, 1881.

102. Irises. (F 678). Oil. St. Rémy, 1890. Collection V.W. van Gogh, Laren.

103. Portrait of Dr. Gachet. (F 753). Oil. Auvers, 1890. Collection Mrs. S. Skramarsky, New York.

104. Part of Letter No. 638 with sketch of the Portrait of Dr. Gachet. Auvers, 1890. Collection V.W. van Gogh, Laren.

105. Last Self-Portrait. Detail. (F 627). Oil. St. Rémy, 1890. Musée du Louvre, Paris.

106. Church at Auvers. (F 789). Oil. Auvers, 1890. Musée du Louvre, Paris. Photograph Giraudon, Paris.

107. Old Tower. (F 88). Oil. Nuenen, 1884. Collection E.G. Bührle, Zürich.

108. Cottage at Auvers. (F 792). Oil. Auvers, 1890. Musée du Louvre, Paris. Photograph Giraudon, Paris.

109. Landscape at Auvers. (F 781). Oil. Auvers, 1890. Collection Mrs. Marshall Field, Chicago.

110. Townhall in Auvers on July 14. (F 790). Oil. Auvers, 1890. Collection Mr. and Mrs. Leigh Block, Chicago.

111. Wheatfield with Crows. (F 779). Oil. Auvers, 1890. Collection V.W. van Gogh, Laren.

112. Part of Letter N° 649. Auvers, 1890. Collection V.W. van Gogh, Laren.

113. Worshipper of the Eternal Buddha (Self-Portrait). (F 476). Oil. Arles, 1888. Courtesy of the Fogg Art Museum, Harvard University, Maurice Wertheim Collection.

114. First page of letter N° 651. Collection V.W. van Gogh, Laren.

115. First page of letter N° 652. Collection V.W. van Gogh, Laren.

INDEX OF NAMES

315